TRACKS & TRAILS

AN INSIDER'S GUIDE TO THE BEST CROSS COUNTRY SKIING IN THE NORTHEAST

By Christopher Leggett & Woden Teachout

Dawbert Press, Inc.
P.O. Box 2758
Duxbury, Massachusetts 02331

First Edition
Leggett, Christopher
Tracks and Trails by Christopher Leggett and Woden Teachout
Index
1. Cross-country skiing — New England — Guidebooks
2. New England — Guidebooks

ISBN: 0-933603-41-X

Editor: Barbara M. Hayes
Illustrations: Glynn Brannan
Maps: Robert and Dawn Habgood

Manufactured in the United States of America
10 9 8 7 6 5 4 3 2 1

To the Harvard Ski Team

Contents

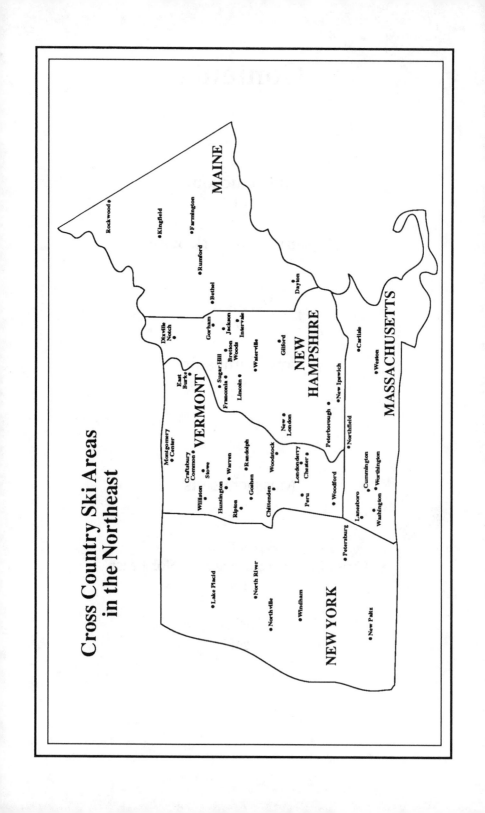

Cross Country Ski Areas
in the Northeast

Introduction

This book was written for cross-country skiers with curious minds and wandering souls — skiers itching to adventure beyond the boundaries of their own backyards. The Northeast is teeming with spectacular touring centers, each different, and each boasting its own point of pride. Every ski area has a story to tell, whether it be a ski-through outhouse, an old potato farm, or a homesick Scandinavian host. Every trail system has a unique feel and its own nooks and crannies to explore. You can rest easy — we've done the exploration for you. We looked and skied and peeked and pried until we knew all there was to know about our favorite places to ski.

Whoever you are and whatever type of skiing you enjoy, we're confident that you'll find plenty here to please you. Our only assumption is that cross country skiing is for everyone. It is for the wooden-skis-and-knickers crowd that still thinks skating happens on frozen ponds. It is for the toned, athletic, spandex types that thrive on grueling climbs and precipitous plunges. It is also for the closet nature-lovers cinched into cities by looping belts of highway. Whether your a pro or a plodder, this sport is for you.

Use this book as a leaping off point. You need not lug it around and freeze your fingers flipping through the pages at every trail junction. Once you arrive at a ski area, follow your own nose. We have designed this guide to be more of an inspirational armchair browser than a step-by-step how-to book. Study it at home and let the feeling of the trails and touring centers seep into your bones. Then get out of your dreams and into your car!

We're a couple of stubborn, opinionated Yankees, and we certainly don't hesitate to voice our opinions. When the grooming, trails, or scenery are less than perfect, we let you know. Fortunately, this was a rare occurrence and, on the whole, we've probably erred on the side of positive enthusiasm. It's terribly difficult to be critical when snow is rushing beneath your skis!

How We Picked Them

Our choice of ski areas was based on a systematic and thoroughly scientific rating system which took into account the following factors: length of trail system, scenic beauty, annual snowfall, geographic location, our opinions, our friends' opinions, our families' opinions, and chance. All of these factors were given raw scores, then normalized with respect to our gut feelings. Your favorite ski areas may differ from ours. In reality, any list purporting to select the best must be based upon subjective and personal choices.

Backcountry skiers must look elsewhere for guidance; we limited our research to groomed trails. Plenty of space has been set aside in the appendix for a complete list of ski areas without grooming, those with modest trail networks, or without a cozy place to sit inside and warm your toes. We admit it: we're not averse to a little pampering. Our final product is an opinionated encyclopedia of the biggest, best, and brightest in groomed Nordic ski areas throughout the Northeast.

We apologize if we overlooked your favorite ski area. But if it really is your favorite, reading about it wouldn't have done you any good anyway. We simply hope our guide will inspire you to ski off your favorite trail and try something new. Although we have both toured, raced, coached, and taught throughout the Northeast for many years, we were still amazed by the quality of some of the touring centers we'd never even heard of. We think that you will be too.

Technique

There are two ways to cross-country ski. You can use the traditional, extended-walk technique, where both skis stay in tracks and you use either a little sticky stuff or scales on your ski bottoms to push yourself forward with the help of the action-reaction principle. If you've never skied before, this is almost certainly the technique you have in mind when you try to imagine what cross country skiing is like. Almost all beginners start with the traditional technique. This isn't to say it's a beginners' technique, per se. It takes many years, substantial strength, and superb balance to perfect the traditional technique. Fortunately, an abbreviated, shuffle version of traditional is extremely easy to learn. Traditional is also referred to as "classical."

Another approach is called "skating," which is just what it sounds like. This is skating with skis instead of skates and with the aid of a pair of poles for an extra push. Most skiers don't try skating until they've had a little experience with classical skiing. Although skating is harder at first, many skiers find it easier to become a master of skating than a master of the traditional technique. Skating is slightly faster, and it's made easier by wider trails, longer poles, and shorter skis. It's a terrific technique for snowmobile trails and skiing on top of crusty snow or frozen lakes.

Although we each have our own favorite technique (and they happen to differ), we try not to gear our writing toward one or the other. You'll find that some of the ski areas have absolutely no trails that are groomed for skating. It's simply too expensive and time-consuming for some of the smaller ski areas to widen their paths. On the other hand, traditional skiers need not worry: all of the ski areas will welcome you.

"Telemarking" is just a fancy way to carve downhill turns when your heels are not attached to your skis. It is a little hard to learn and a bit demanding on the knees, but damned fun once you get the hang of it. Many of the cross country areas in this book offer telemark lessons. Try your luck. Some skis are built especially for telemarking — extra wide and with metal edges — but you'll do fine trying it out on your own "skinny" skis.

Waxing

Wouldn't it be nice to reduce all the wizardry of waxing to a few concise paragraphs? Unfortunately, it can't be done. Our advice is to learn to ski wax-free — start with fishscales or skating skis. Waxing is a hassle you don't need to deal with when you're still getting a feel for the sport. After a few years, once you start to get annoyed by the loud hum or the drag of the scales against the snow, move on to waxable skis.

Waxable skis are faster. They're faster because they don't have the dragging fishscales slowing down your glide, not because of any magical mixture of waxes applied to the bottom. What the waxes do is provide "kick." They give you something sticky to push off when you want to propel yourself down the track. They help you go up hills, not down. When you push the "wax pocket" (the center part of the ski) into the snow, some of the snow crystals need to become embedded in the wax to provide the friction, or "kick." The trick to waxing is to match the hardness of the wax with the sharpness of the snow crystals. New, cold, sharp crystals need a firm, hard wax, so that the crystals don't penetrate too far and slow you down. Older, warmer, more rounded crystals need a softer wax if they are to penetrate at all; harder waxes will slip. Waxes therefore range from hard to soft to match various snow conditions.

That's an overview. To delve further into the mystery, find a shoulder to look over or buy a few waxes to play with. Don't overdo it though. While it's possible to spend hundreds of dollars on a rainbow of wax, you can get by just fine with the primary colors.

What Not to Wear and What to Wear

If you feel like becoming a part of the natural freeze-thaw cycle, bundle up as if you were about to go Alpine skiing. While you're in motion, you'll be swimming uncomfortably in sweat. Short breaks will give you the chills, and long breaks will turn you into an icicle. Spare yourself the trouble and dress down. Usually, one or two thin layers on the bottom and a turtleneck and windbreaker on top will suffice. You may be chilly for a few hundred yards, but you'll be perfectly comfortable the rest of the day. If you plan on taking long breaks, just throw a few extra layers in your backpack, or tie them around your waist.

We highly recommend polypropylene and wool as the materials of choice. They efficiently wick moisture away from your skin, keeping you relatively dry and warm. Don't make the mistake of wearing a cotton T-shirt beneath a wool or polypropylene top! Wool socks are especially effective at keeping toes warm.

Wind can be a major factor. Many trails cut across golf courses or pastures, and a strong, cold wind can quickly blow all of the fun out of the sport. Wear a windbreaker and an extra layer on windy days when you're skiing out in the open. Don't forget a hat. Men may want to invest in a pair of nylon shorts for windy days.

It's very important that your gloves not be bulky. In cross country skiing, unlike Alpine, you really use your poles, and your hands must retain some freedom of movement. If you don't own a thin pair of gloves, buy a cheap pair of work gloves at a hardware store — we find that the white cotton gardening gloves work fairly well. On cold days, wear mittens.

Etiquette

In addition to the "take nothing but pictures, leave nothing but footprints" maxim espoused by hikers, skiers should observe a few additional common courtesies:

- Pay your trail fee. Touring center managers lose blood, sweat and tears on your behalf. In summer they struggle with brambles and wrestle with chainsaws for months to clear the trails. In winter they risk frostbite and sleep deprivation to have their trails groomed before you arrive. The least you can do is pay the trail fee.
- No dogs, unless otherwise indicated. Ski trails are groomed for skiing, and pawprints destroy the smooth surface. Dogs also tend to leave unwelcome reminders of their passing.
- No yellow snow on the trails. If Nature calls, ski off into the woods to find her.

- Downhill skiers have the right of way.
- If you fall, fill in your sitzmark. (A sitzmark is what happens when you 'sitz' down quickly.)
- Some old racers seem to think that when they catch up to a slower skier, they can shout "Track!" and the unfortunate tourist will leap deferentially to the side to let them pass. A better alternative would be to say something like "Great day, isn't it?" to let them know you're there. They'll move out of the way in plenty of time.
- Don't stay on the trails past closing time. If your car is sitting out in the parking lot when dusk begins to fall, touring center managers will assume the worst. They'll send out a snowmobile to comb the trails for your broken body. This is a big hassle for them and will make you feel foolish.
- Don't skate across classical tracks. Skating pushes snow into the tracks and disrupts someone's smooth stride.

A Few Tips

The following cross country skiing tips were collected from friends of ours — veteran skiers eager to share their knowledge:

- Bring a highlighter to the ski area. When you pick up a trail map, you can highlight whichever trails are open that day.
- Wear contacts, not glasses. Glasses fog up very easily during the winter.
- When you put your skis on, after walking around in the snow, be sure to tap the bottom of your boot sharply with your pole before stepping into the binding. This will knock the snow out of the grooves and allow the boot to fit well into the binding.
- Negotiating a downhill corner on cross country skis is easiest with a step turn. Pick up one ski at a time and step 20 or 30 degrees in the direction you want to turn. Don't try to dig your edges in; your skis have no metal edges!
- Snowmobile trails are a great, cheap alternative to cross country centers, especially for skating.
- Road crossings are quicker if you remove only one ski and hop across on the other leg. Look both ways before you try this!
- When you approach steep, abrupt ditches in the trail, try to ski across them diagonally. Skiing straight over them could turn your skis into a temporary bridge, with your own weight in the center. They may break under the pressure.

Ski Phones

All five states have ski phones which tell you the snow conditions at Nordic areas.

Vermont	(802) 828-3239
New Hampshire	(800) 262-6660
Maine	(800) 533-9595
Massachusetts	(800) 632-8038
New York	(800) 225-5697

The Touring Centers

For every touring center, we've listed basic information at the beginning. These sections are snapshots of the facts we found and the opinions we formed at each area. Here's what to expect:

The Trail System

The total number of groomed kilometers of ski trails, followed by a breakdown by type of skiing: classical, skating, or backcountry. Generally managers are honest in reporting these numbers, but their enthusiasm occasionally clouds their good sense, and they double- or triple-count a loop or two. We've tried to indicate in the narrative sections where we think they've stretched the truth.

Our Personal Estimate

A one-line assessment of the trail system; a very abbreviated and unquestionably biased account.

Grooming

We've based this judgement on our own experience on the trails, the equipment belonging to a touring center, the area's reputation, and a third degree inquisition of the groomers. Some areas are purposefully "casual;" others groom the heck out of their snow every day. Hoofprints, footprints, pine needles and other minor annoyances all interfere with the quality of skiing — we've tried to let you know if they are a factor.

Scenic Beauty

A purely subjective rating combining trailside beauty and scenic overlooks. Our scale ranges from 1 to 5. Always keep in mind though, beauty is in the eye of the beholder.

Touring Center

Some areas resemble a small city; others have only a wood stove and a few pairs of skis. All of them are open daily, unless noted otherwise, and offer lessons and rentals. As a general rule they stay open from 9 a.m. to sundown. The price of a trail ticket ranges from $8 to $13; $10 dollars is about average. Most areas knock a couple dollars off their fee for passes sold after 2 p.m.

Favorite Trail

Again, purely subjective.

Lodging

For every area we've listed both budget and more expensive lodging alternatives. Budget establishments tend to run from $25-50/night ($-$$), and the more expensive range from $50 to $200/night ($$$-$$$$). We have not necessarily visited these establishments, but most come well recommended and are viable options to help in planning your trip.

Local's Tip

Every area has some special deal or point of interest that only the locals know about. It might be a restaurant in town, a unique feature on the ski trails, or a police officer who likes to write tickets. We forced them to cough up their secrets.

Maps

These maps are certainly not designed to be used on the trails. They are simply a tool to use while reading the trail descriptions. We hope they will help you develop a coherent image of the ski areas.

Disclaimer

The material contained within *Tracks and Trails* is for descriptive purposes only; you must be the judge of your skill level and act responsibly. The trail conditions and weather are always fluctuating — ski safely. Cross country skiers ski at their own risk. Dawbert Press, Inc. assumes no liability for accidents sustained by readers using this book.

Eastern
New York
State

Mount Van Hoevenberg
Cross Country Ski Center

Cascade Road
Lake Placid, New York 12946
(800) 462-6236, (518) 523-2811

Trail System: *50 km (50 km classical, 50 km skate, 200 km backcountry in adjacent Adirondacks)*
Our Estimate: *A skater's heaven with plenty of difficult loops but with few beginner options.*
Grooming: *Excellent for skating, good for classical*
Scenic Beauty: *3*
Touring Center: *A mid-sized lodge with rentals, lessons, burger-type foods, a plethora of wax rooms, and full retail.*
Favorite Trail: *Ladies five km, a challenging, mountainous loop.*
Payment: *All major credit cards accepted.*
Lodging: *Barkeater Inn-Keene (518-576-2221, $$$, has its own small trail system); White Sled Motel-Lake Placid (518-523-9314, $$)*
Local's Tip: *Try sliding down the Olympic Bobsled Run at Mount Van Hoevenberg. Although it isn't cheap, you only live once! Alternatively, ride the elevator to the top of the Olympic ski jump tower for amazing views of the valley.*

Only three winter Olympics have ever been held in the United States, and two of the three were in Lake Placid. World class racers from Sweden to Russia can rattle off their favorite trails in this tiny Adirondack town, yet surprisingly few New Englanders have ventured across Lake Champlain to try their skis on what may be the most exciting trail system in North America. The trip is worth the trouble. The appeal of Lake Placid extends far beyond skiing; it is a center for *all* winter sports — from ice skating to biathlon to ski jumping to luge. You'd best stay for at least a weekend, because a day trip to Lake Placid would be akin to a ten minute tour of Disney World.

In 1932, the town hosted its first Winter Olympic Games. At the time, the cross country events didn't require a great deal of preparation. The courses weren't packed, and grooming consisted of a few skiers sent out the night before to set the tracks. The distinct advantage of skiing last — in the faster, skied-in tracks — was reserved for the favorites. To prevent the "cross country ski runners" from practicing on the race course, the layout of the course was kept under wraps until the evening before the race.

Preparation for the 1980 Olympics was far more intense. The incipient trail network at Mount Van Hoevenberg needed to be length-

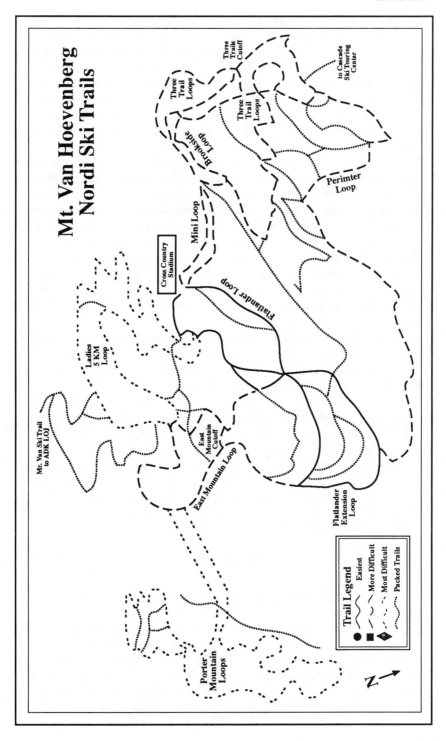

ened and widened substantially, in order to accommodate the sport's revolution from backwoods wandering to fast, groomed, track-set racing. The "Forever Wild" status attached to the area by the state was modified to "Wild *Nearly* All The Time," as trail crews were permitted to hack ski highways out of the forest. (But the best preparation didn't prevent a snow drought, and the weeks before the opening ceremonies found organizers frantically making alternative arrangements: man-made snow, dump trucks, and manure spreaders managed to lay a white carpet through the brown forest, and the show went on.)

The Mount Van Hoevenberg trail system hasn't changed a great deal since 1980, and vicarious Olympians will delight in beginning their tour in the same glorious, flag-lined stadium used by world-class athletes. The trails are a guided celebration of racing, taking you around Olympian loops of all dimensions. Although there *are* a few beginner loops, most of these 50 kilometers were built to test, not to introduce. The loops have the grueling climbs and startling descents needed to challenge the best skiers in the world. Experienced skiers will delight in Lake Placid's terrain. Beginners may be turned off by the limited options, ultra-wide trails, the lack of field loops, and an obvious skating bias.

Unfortunately, the touring center hasn't changed much since 1980 either. While other touring centers bend over backwards to create a feeling of cozy warmth, this state-run venue provides a lodge dominated by waxing rooms and picnic tables.

Those searching for less difficult terrain can experiment with several other cross country ski centers in the Lake Placid area. The adjacent Cascade Ski Touring Center offers narrow, woodsy, classically-oriented trails with golf course skiing across the street. Cunningham's Ski Barn starts close to the center of town and provides a good variety of open and wooded loops. Whiteface Inn, a bit farther out of town in the other direction, is primarily a groomed golf course. Finally, the Barkeater Inn in Keene is a homey, stay-and-ski destination with a modest trail network and an Olympian host.

The Trails

Beginners can whet their appetites on **Flatlander**, a wide, 1 1/2 kilometer loop which snakes luxuriously through spruce and fir with almost no elevation change. The **Extension** to **Flatlander** will add a little more length and get you farther away from the stadium crowds. After these options are exhausted, there is little for a beginner to do but swallow hard and head for intermediate or expert trails. The **Perimeter Loop** provides the only intermediate terrain which might be somewhat palatable to the timid novice. It crosses a bridge, skirts the edge of the biathlon stadium area, then winds alongside a stream through fairly easy wooded terrain.

The **3-Trails Loop** begins with a deceptively easy glide out of the stadium, through a skier culvert, and onto the biathlon side of the trail system. One very steep hill is followed by a brief stream-side segment, then a difficult climb through mixed forest. Next, a prolonged spasm of short hills makes it difficult to develop a steady stride. The trail ends by rolling through tall, awe-inspiring hardwoods, rocketing down a steep hill, then climbing back toward the level of the biathlon stadium.

The **Ladies Five Km Loop** (used for the women's five kilometer race during the 1980 Olympics) and **Porter Mountain Loop** offer intense challenges for more experienced skiers. The **Ladies Five Km** begins by teasing you with a kilometer of gradual uphill. It then slams you with an intense climb, leaving you breathless on a high, forested slope of Mount Van Hoevenberg. The fast downhill drop to the stadium has turns that gather spectators on race days — spectators eager to witness "yard sale" wipe-outs.

Those eager to get away from the crowd—far away—may try their endurance on **Porter Mountain**. This 15 kilometer backbreaker is one of the longest loops in the East built specifically for cross country skiing. Start out early in the day and bring a backpack full of food and water! As **Porter** hurls hill after hill in your direction, you'll start to get the feeling that you're wrestling with an indefatigable monster! Luckily, numerous escape routes allow you to spar briefly with the beast, then turn tail and head back to the stadium. Toward the end of **Porter** (and about 2/3 through **East Mountain Loop**) is what has become known as "**Russian Hill**." The take-off-your-skis-and-walk-up steepness of the climb caused the Russian Women's coach to complain at the 1980 Olympics. In deference to FIS regulations regarding hill difficulty, organizers shaved about 15 meters from the top. Don't take this hill lightly!

For views of the High Peaks, try **Hi-Notch**, an often forgotten and very difficult extension of the **Ladies Five Km.**

Finding your way: Take I-87 north to Exit 30. Follow Route 9 north for two miles, then follow Route 73 west toward Lake Placid. Twenty four miles from the exit, after passing through the town of Keene and climbing over a pass, you'll see a set of roadside flags. Turn left into this "Olympic Sports Complex." The ski center will be one mile down the road on your left.

Minnewaska State Park

Route 44/55
New Paltz, New York   12561
Trail conditions: (914) 255-0752, Rentals and lessons: (914) 255-7059

Trail System: *62 km groomed (62 km classical, 12 km skate and 3 km backcountry)*
Our Personal Estimate: *Mild grades and scenic views make this a good beginner area, although most of the trails are very long.*
Grooming: *Good. However, unless there is a good deal of snow, the gravel from the carriage roads and bike paths gets pulled up onto the ski trails.*
Scenic Beauty: *4 — the forest is unremarkable, but the views from the Castle Point Trail are stunning.*
Touring Center: *Weekends: Small rental/lessons shop, cafeteria, outhouses. Weekdays: Outhouses*
Favorite Trail: *Castle Point Trail, which has spectacular views and feels like the top of the world.*
Payment: *No credit cards*
Lodging: *Mountain Meadows-New Paltz (914-255-6144, $$$); The Chelsea-New Paltz (914-626-3551, $$)*
Local's Tip: *There are no locals.*

Minnewaska State Park is not your usual touring center. The fortress-like cliffs and the scrubby pines give it a western feel — a little bit of misplaced Utah butte. The exposed ridge on the top of the trail system has some spectacular views that highlight the area's particular geology. Bring a windbreaker and a camera. During the week you can have the park all to yourself, but on sunny weekends urban escapees crowd onto the small network of trails near the parking lot. Most of the skiing at Minnewaska has a backcountry flavor. It is not exciting, but it is rife with the pleasures of long, wilderness-style treks.

Minnewaska is a state park. There is no touring center, but there is a privately owned rental hut and a trailer/warming hut serving hot food on weekends. If you're feeling chatty you can go talk to the park rangers at the ranger station. The rates are about half what you would pay at a traditional touring center, but you may miss the benefits that the other half brings. Old carriage roads afford picturesque views, but they don't generate much adrenaline. They were built to take gentry on scenic tours of the property, not to entertain skiers. The utter disregard for imagination in trail naming — Lower Awosting, Upper Awosting, Lake Awosting, to name a few — could only have been achieved by a government agency. It makes it difficult to remember what trail you're on.

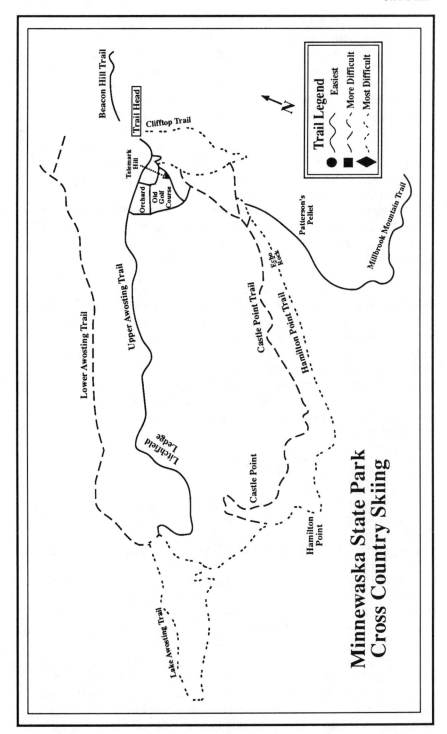

**Minnewaska State Park
Cross Country Skiing**

The area's geology is striking, and it has greatly influenced the ecology. The Shawangunk Ridge was formed when two geologic plates collided; one plate fell down and one stuck up at a diagonal. This explains the vaguely disorienting slant of the land. Throughout the Preserve, you will see quartzite conglomerates (also known as Shawangunk grit) which were formed 400 million years ago from quartz pebbles and sand. This conglomerate cap is stubbornly resistant to weathering, so only a poor, thin veneer of soil covers the bedrock. Few species of vegetation can survive. The pitch pines that grow rampant throughout the park manage well in poor, sandy soil; they are very unusual in this part of the country, and make the park feel vaguely like an oversized Japanese garden.

Minnewaska's history is bound up with the Mohonk House, just a few miles away as the crow flies. The Smiley brothers started Mohonk House as a grand hotel in the late 1800s. The story runs that after a family feud, one brother moved over to Minnewaska in a huff, to start a rival resort. It was very successful. Two hotels — Cliff House and Wildmere Hotel — went up, and carriageways and walking trails were built to entertain the gentry. But the resort's fortunes faded in the middle of this century, as Minnewaska fell prey to financial troubles and fire. Marriott hotels made a bid to purchase the property and continue the hotel tradition, but they were beaten back by local opposition in a bitter fight. Finally, the state purchased the property along with the Nature Conservancy in 1987, and it is now a popular state park. The legacy of the resort is mostly in the carriage roads, but you can easily see the former site of Wildmere House, a broad flat area just above the parking lot.

The Trails

The **Upper Awosting Trail** is a long, straight, wide trail traversing the Park's central ridge. The trail is so flat and the rise so subtle that it should inspire a new difficulty designation: Ultra-Easy. A lower layer of leafy mountain laurel and an upper layer of bare-limbed hardwoods give it a strange, foreign feel. Several miles out, the trail passes under Litchfield Ledge with its startling multi-colored icicles that drip perilously from the rock. They could easily kill a Grendel. The **Millbrook Mountain Trail** is a more isolated beginner trail. It ventures out to the scenic vista on Millbrook Mountain, where you can see opposing ridges. You're likely to run across deer tracks here.

Any but the most determined misanthrope would be crazy to miss the popular **Castle Point Trail**. This windy, scenic trail traces the top of the central ridge, and climbs to the area's highest point, at around 2000 feet. From a string of lookouts on this trail, you can gaze down to where fields and farmland flatten like melted butter below. The stunted trees testify to the fact that there is no neighboring mountain range to curb the wind. Take your windbreaker.

The **Lake Awosting Trail** is rated most difficult only because it is ungroomed and far from the parking area. It circles the long, pretty Lake Awosting with only a mere hint of a hill. Because of the wind and melting patterns, the snow can be thin on the southern side of the lake. Rocks rise to the surface. This is not a good trail for a new pair of skis.

The **Hamilton Point Trail** is probably the most technically challenging at Minnewaska. The far end runs along an exposed ridge, with some steep slopes and turns. The near end slides under a canopy of hemlocks and passes intricate, layered rock outcroppings that a master stonemason would be glad to imitate. The beautiful **Clifftop Trail** rises and falls with the cliffs around Lake Minnewaska. Despite its most difficult rating, this trail attracts a lot of first-time skiers. The curvy downhills take their toll, and skiing the **Clifftop Trail** on a weekend is like making your way through a battlefield after the guns have finished.

Finding your way: Take I-87 to Exit 18 at New Paltz. Drive straight through town on Route 60 west for several miles. When you come to the intersection, take Route 44/55 west. After five miles, you'll see Minnewaska State Park on your left.

Mohonk Mountain House
Ski Touring
Lake Mohonk
New Paltz, New York   12561
(914) 255-1000

Trail System: 50 km groomed (40 km classical, 32 km skate)
Our Personal Estimate: A great area for skiing and sightseeing; not the place for athletic training.
Grooming: Good. Unfortunately, walkers and sightseers leave footprints on the trails.
Scenic Beauty: 5
Touring Center: Rentals, lessons, fireplace, food
Favorite Trail: Humpty Dumpty, a scenic up-and-down ride on the side of a cliff.
Payment: All major credit cards
Lodging: Mohonk Mountain House-New Paltz (800-772-6646, $$$$); The Chelsea-New Paltz (914-626-3551, $$)
Local's Tip: Take one car instead of two. Mohonk charges a trail fee per carload during the middle of the week.

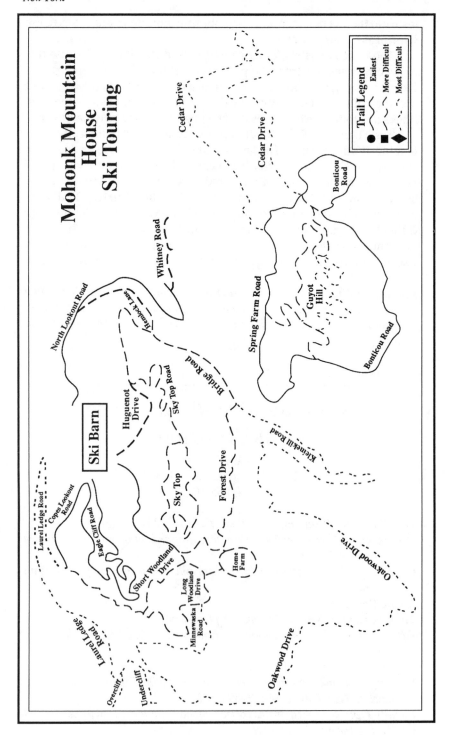

Mohonk Mountain House Ski Touring

Mohonk means 'Skywater Lake', and Mohonk Mountain House is aptly named. The estate straddles the Shawangunk Mountain Range, and the fortress-like Mountain House is built into the cliffs beside a hidden mountain lake. An assortment of architectural styles live in Gothic harmony. Cliffs and crags contribute a sense of untamed wilderness. From Sky Top Hill you see the broad spread of flat farmland far below, and the rearing hills of the Catskill Mountain Range beyond. The Mountain House is exquisite, the panoramic views are stunning, and 50 kilometers of skiing trails ramble about the old estate.

Gatekeepers politely sift day skiers from hotel guests and direct you to separate-but-equal parking lots. Overnight guests are waved up the mile-long access road to the Mountain House, while day skiers park at the gate. The White Cedars Lodge serves as a makeshift touring center — the fireplace, food, and rental equipment should satisfy most of your needs. As a skier you have free range of the grounds, but may enter the hotel only to have a meal.

The trails follow former carriage roads on the estate, and have the graded, predictable, and scenic quality of their predecessors. Skiing at Mohonk is hampered mainly by the large quantity of walkers who use the trails as winter paths. The trails are pockmarked with footprints, especially on busy weekends. The hotel is understandably unwilling to ask a $350/night guest to forego pedestrian sightseeing for the benefit of an $8/day skier. Come here to gape, not to train.

From Skytop Tower you can look down at the lake and the house and get an overview of the history of the place. The dark wooden portion of the house was a roaring mid-nineteenth century tavern belonging to a man named Stokes; when people got too drunk, he'd take them outside and tie them to the trees that stand on the putting green of the golf course. The brothers, Alfred and Albert Smiley, came to Mohonk Lake for a picnic in 1869. The natural beauty touched their Quaker faith, and they bought the place. They established the Mountain House as a place for people not to recreate, but to re-create their inner life. (After a bitter, un-Quakerlike family feud, Alfred went over to the opposing mountain and created a rival hotel at what is now Minnewaska State Park.) While spiritual renewal is hardly the goal of most of today's guests, the Quaker philosophy still maintains a foothold: the hotel has no bar, and there are no televisions, radios, or clocks in the rooms.

The Trails

There are two trail systems: the network of former carriage roads that splay out around the Mountain House, and a smaller cluster of trails across the road. These have been cut more recently, with skating in mind; they lead around and over the knob of Guyot Hill. While less crowded, they have neither the views nor the charm of the Mountain House system.

Mohonk has some magnificently scenic beginner trails. The **North Lookout Road** is a long, steady, mild climb along a panoramic vista. The former carriage road traces the verge of the cliff, with nothing but a cedar fence separating you from a sheer drop-off. The fields and forest of the Rondout Valley spreads out below you, and the Catskills rise up fewer than ten miles away. Just beyond the mountain range lies the forever-famous town of Woodstock.

The easy and popular **Eagle Cliff Road** is a wide carriage road leading onto a rock promontory over the lake. The trail climbs gently, doubles back on itself around the cliffs, and loops down to the Mountain House. The cliff trail tenders views of the Catskills, Lake Mohonk, and Skytop Tower. On the smaller system, **Bonticou Road** is a level, wooded circuit of Guyot Hill. Less populated and almost perfectly flat, it is a great place to practice skating. Cliffs drop off to your right, and an opening in the trees offers a vista of Bonticou Crag, a massive outcrop of Shawangunk conglomerate.

Intermediate trails offer more of the same, with a greater variety of terrain. **Sky Top Road** rises to the very height of the land, where a fire watch tower casts proud glances across the magnificent panorama. The winding road doubles back on itself. At the top, the wind can be fierce. The playful **Humpty Dumpty** clings to the side of the cliff like a fly on the wall. Don't ski this trail if you're afraid of heights. Fear-inspiring boulders threaten to shear off the rock wall and ravage the Lilliputian forests and fields far below. The area's geology is laid bare before you: you can almost see the rocky Shawangunk ridge straining out of its earthly bed.

Guyot Hill Road pirouettes over the twin tops of Guyot Mountain. Beautiful hardwoods part at the summit, offering a suburban vista of New Paltz. With its curvy downhills, **Guyot Hill Road** is the most difficult trail on the system, but it is much less challenging than many New England trails. Yellow exclamation signs look like hyperbole. The old road's width and grade were enough to carry farm vehicles, and expert skiers should manage with ease.

Finding your way: Take I-87 to Exit 18 at New Paltz. Drive straight through town on Route 60 west; just after the bridge leading out of town, turn right and follow the signs for Mohonk Mountain House. The touring center will be on your left in 4 miles.

Garnet Hill Cross Country Ski Center

Thirteenth Lake Road
North River, New York   12856
(518) 251-2444

Trail System: 54 km groomed (54 km classical, 54 km skate, and 30 km backcountry)
Our Personal Estimate: Thanks to the shuttle bus, this system can be as easy or as difficult as you like.
Grooming: Excellent
Scenic Beauty: 4
Touring Center: Rentals, lessons, snacks and drinks, full retail, not as many bathrooms as there should be. A full lunch is available at the nearby Lodge.
Favorite Trail: Joe Pete's Run, a rollicking succession of downhill curves.
Payment: MC and VISA
Lodging: Garnet Hill Lodge-Trailside (518-251-2444, $$); Mountainaire Adventures-Hostel and B&B-North River (800-950-2194, $-$$)
Local's Tip: Bring your backcountry skis. The Siamese Pond Wilderness which begins at the edge of the Garnet Hill Lodge is the largest wilderness area east of the Mississippi without roads. It has remote ponds, high mountains, and such tantalizingly named features as Botheration Brook and Balm of Gilead Mountain. Go on your own, or call one of the outdoor adventure companies for a tour: Mountainaire Adventures (800) 950-2194 or Free Spirit Adventures (518) 924-9275.

Garnet Hill Lodge doesn't look like the site of one of the most astounding advances of the twentieth century. It looks like an imposing Adirondack Great House on a beautiful mountain lake. You wouldn't suspect anything unusual about the superb 54 kilometer trail network. But the whirling brains of Garnet Hill have come up with an invention rivaling the computer, the atom bomb, and the breadmaker: cross country skiing without uphills.

Skiing at Garnet Hill has the easy flow of moving water. Smooth, wide trails slope outward and downward from the lodge, following the path of least resistance. You can float downriver for miles without even a hint of fatigue. This once posed a problem for Garnet Hill's largely beginner and intermediate clientele, who would ski further afield than they realized. At the end of the day they faced a long, painful climb back to the center; by the time they returned, they were frozen, disgruntled, and ready to swear off the sport entirely.

Shuttle buses saved the day. Now you can ski happily to the far reaches of the trail system, secure in the knowledge that you won't have to struggle back up. Shuttle buses sweep the designated pick-up spots

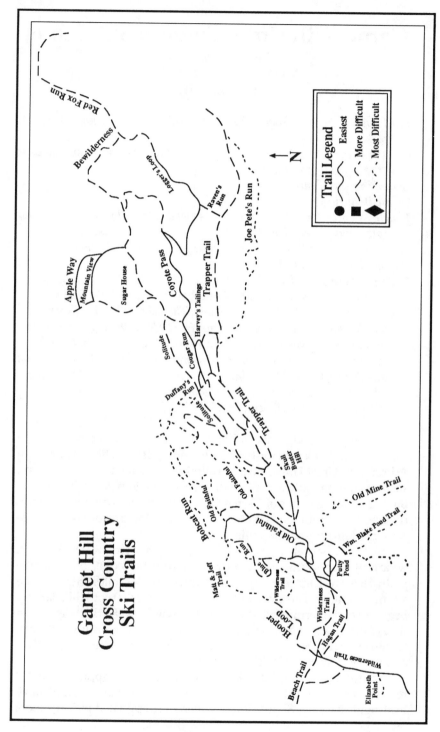

Garnet Hill
Cross Country
Ski Trails

every 45 minutes. Sign up in advance: these are incredibly popular. On busy weekends, the phone starts ringing at 8 a.m. with callers from Albany who want to reserve a slot. Purists can muscle their way back up to the lodge.

Garnet Hill is named for the garnet mines that pockmark this region of the Adirondacks. Many of them are still in use. In the 1890s, local legend Old Frank Hooper discovered the first garnets and the area quickly became a mining camp. Dozens of miners' cottages sprang up overnight in the area where the touring center stands now. (Some of them have been revamped into guest cabins.) You can still see the red one-room schoolhouse where the miners' children were taught. The fireplace in the big Log House is built of stone with garnets embedded in it: look for the tiny, red, rounded minerals. And ski trails run through massive, open "tailings" — pits of the broken, crumbled stone that remains after the garnet had been extracted.

The Trails

There is plenty of easy terrain at Garnet Hill. The popular **Old Faithful** is a two mile loop patched out of old logging roads. Its broad, mellifluous curves meander over infinitely gradual grades and through beautiful hardwoods. **Apple Way** offers one of the best views on the trail system — a vista over fields and trees into the High Peaks of the Adirondacks. The trail itself takes a pretty, pastoral route past old farmhouses and barns and through a narrow alleyway of trees.

The gently flowing **Trapper Trail** is one of the most popular routes down to the shuttle bus pickup area. **Sugarhouse** is a more difficult version, cascading down three hills into an evergreen forest to the bus stop. **Red Fox Path** has the shape of an overturned V. It climbs straight and steady through pines, peaks into the hardwoods, then rides pleasantly downhill with a couple cunning turns. The trail may be icy at a few of the wetland crossings.

The short-and-sweet **Skullbuster** takes the high road through the tailings nearest the touring center. A little plateau at the top shows you the same view as you get from **Apple Way**. The trail then flings itself off the height of the tailings, down and around a birchy corner. It can be exciting even in the best of conditions, since snowplowers regularly push the softer snow to the side. The trail was named in honor of a hard-headed individual who insisted on skiing on glare ice, and who spent the rest of his holiday with his head wrapped in a turban.

Solitude is a thrilling, expert trail carving broad curving swaths across the hillside. The slightly rolling terrain gathers speed and difficulty; it first throws you an easy corner, then a hairpin turn, and finally an unexpected tilted curve at the bottom of the hill. Watch out at the intersection with **Duffney's,** since advanced skiers are likely to be careening down both trails at high speeds. **Joe Pete's Run** is named for the exuberant Joe Pete Wilson, who runs the Barkeater touring center outside of Lake Placid. The trail has plenty of character. It starts with a steady climb through maple and beech trees along the side of Harvey Mountain, then suddenly turns mischievous. The trail carves a series of downward turns designed to sweep you off your feet. Then it drops in and out of a ravine before snaking down the mountain. The corners get looser and looser as you pick up speed. Try frozen waterfalls after you've conquered this beast.

Finding your way: Take I-87 to Exit 25 at Chestertown. Follow Route 8 west to Wevertown. Take a right on Route 28 west to the barely-there town of North River. Where the houses end, take a left on Thirteenth Lake Road, and drive up the hill for 4.5 miles. The center is well-marked.

Lapland Lake
Cross Country Ski Center
252 N. Main Street
Northville, New York   12134
(800) 453-SNOW (for ski conditions), (518) 863-4974

Trail System: 37 km groomed (37 km classical, 37 km skate, 10 km backcountry),
   3 km night skiing on weekends
Our Estimate: Wonderfully long loops for beginners and intermediates.
Grooming: Excellent
Scenic Beauty: 4
Touring Center: A very comfortable lodge with rentals, lessons, wood stove,
   snack bar (and restaurant on weekends), waxing room, some retail,
   changing rooms, and a massage table!
Favorite Trail: Era Polku, a fantastic slow dance through rich evergreens,
   and light hardwoods.
Payment: DSC, MC, and VISA
Lodging: Lapland Lake's Cottages-Trailside (518-863-4974, $)
Local's Tip: Call ahead and set up an appointment for an apres-ski massage!

Some immigrants quickly melt into the American populace. Some band together with fellow foreigners and form their own ethnic enclaves. Olavi Hirvonen chose a different approach: he bought a small, woodsy piece of America and dressed it in Finnish clothing. From the wood-burning sauna to the Finnish trail names to the folk music in the lodge,

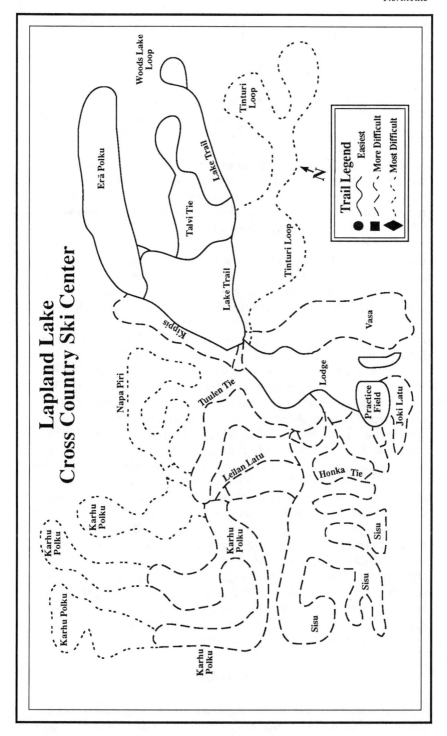

Lapland Lake Cross Country Ski Center

Lapland Lake has undergone a complete conversion into a tiny wedge of Olavi's homeland. As you glide through the evergreens, rolling the sing-songy Finnish trail names back and forth across your tongue, you'll half expect to see a *vasa* (baby reindeer) struggling through the snow beside you.

Olavi discovered his calling late in life. After emigrating from Finland in 1949, he suffered through a few years in New York City, then was drafted by the army to be an instructor at the Arctic Indoctrination School — somewhat more pleasant than New York. He proved to the Army that it really did need a little advice in Nordic matters by winning the armed forces cross country ski championships — despite never having had a formal lesson in his life! After his discharge, he continued to compete, and in 1960, he joined the U.S. squad at the 1960 Winter Olympics in Squaw Valley, California.

After spending several years in the construction industry, Olavi decided it was time to construct a little something for himself. He scoured the backroads of upstate New York in late spring of 1978 for a suitable location for a cross country ski area. The only trace of snow so late in the season were the remnants of a snowbank in Northville. It was there that he planted the blue and white Finnish flag and purchased 300 acres. From the beginning, Lapland Lake has been blessed with unbelievably dependable snowfall. It seems to pile up faster here than anywhere else outside of Finland. (A chart in the lodge boasts snow totals the way one might expect Ford to boast about its revenues.)

Gradually, Lapland Lake matured from a small touring center into a backwoods resort. At first, the changes emerged out of necessity. There wasn't much but endless miles of Adirondack wilderness in his backyard, and Olavi needed to provide skiers with a place to eat and stay overnight. He now has a restaurant and ten rustic cottages on the premises. The lodge boasts four bathrooms, changing rooms, a childcare center, and an on-call massage therapist. Hey, you just might decide to spend the whole winter here!

It's a tribute to the quality of the trail system that one of Olavi's regulars drives 3 1/2 hours — all the way from Connecticut — just to ski for the day at Lapland Lake. Because all of the trails were cut from scratch (and not converted from logging and carriage roads) the terrain has great variety, and simple loops replace what at other areas often becomes a messy tangle of trails. The grooming is superb and it can only improve, now that Olavi's newest grooming toy comes equipped with an enclosed cab and an AM/FM stereo!

The Trails

A 10.5 km loop is available for strong skiers: stay left around the perimeter of the trail system on **Sisu, Karhu Polku,** and **Napa Piiri. Sisu** begins by weaving through red and white pine. With the tall, spindly pines above, you'll feel like a flea zig-zagging your way through the bristles of a toothbrush. After a brief flirtation with the frozen waters of West Stoney Creek, the trail climbs toward an abandoned cellar hole and overgrown orchard. This was once the center of a large family farm. (If you can't find the cellar hole, look for the tall, symmetrical blue spruce growing right out of the middle of it.) While the main trail sticks to the evergreens in the low area of the forest, **Karhu** makes three quick sprints up and down a hillside of hardwoods. Short-circuit a few of the climbs to avoid the extra distance and more difficult terrain. Finally, **Napa Piira** baits you with easy, rolling terrain, then suddenly hurls you into "**The Wall**," a short, but exasperating climb straight over a rocky ledge.

For shorter tours, try **Leilan Latu** or **Tuulen Tie**. Both trails climb through the center of an odd, red pine plantation over quite manageable terrain, before dropping back toward the lodge.

On the other side of the road, **Era Polku** is a fantastic trail for beginners *and* experts. It steers its way through a spectacularly rich, thick, and protected spruce-fir forest for about a kilometer. The wind whistling through the tops of the trees comes nowhere near the forest floor. After winding through the dark conifers, the trail breaks out into a hardwood area dominated by yellow birches and maples. Suddenly among the sunny hardwoods, you'll feel like you just stepped out of an afternoon matinee. **Era Polku** comes with just enough tiny twitches and bumps to excite without fright. **Talvi Tie** is a copy-cat little extension with similar terrain through a mixed forest. From **Talvi Tie**, you can glide over a snow-covered road toward a small lake.

If Olavi had only purchased a little more land! With so many trails packed into such a small area, the trail map begins to look like condensed spaghetti artwork: most of the longer trails loop back on themselves in several spots. All in all, however, Lapland Lake makes for a splendid Finnish ambassador. *Kiitos Kaynnista* (Thanks for Coming)!

Finding your way: New York Thruway west from Albany to Exit 27. Follow Route 30 north 27. 2 miles, then turn left onto Benson Road (a.k.a. Route 6). After 5.2 miles on Benson Road, turn right onto Stover Road. After 3/4 mile, Lapland Lake will be on your right.

Pineridge Cross Country Ski Area

R.D. 1 Box 118
Petersburg, New York 12138
(518) 283-5509

Trail System: 30 km groomed (30 km classical, 12 km skate and 5 km backcountry) 4 km night skiing
Our Personal Estimate: Pineridge has some nice easy terrain, but in general these trails are more difficult than at other areas.
Grooming: Good
Scenic Beauty: 3 — no scenic vistas, but the forest is pretty.
Touring Center: Rentals, lessons, wood stove, snacks and hot drinks, some retail
Favorite Trail: Escape, a solitary run that curls downward underneath a ceiling of hemlocks
Payment: AE
Lodging: The Sedgwick Inn-Berlin (518-658-2334, $$); Inn at Shaker Mill Farm, Canaan (518-794-9345, $$)
Locals' Tip: Go check out the Barberville Falls on the way to the touring center. Barberville is the small settlement at the junction of county roads 40 and 79. (You can tell you're in the right place by all the "No Parking" signs.) The short path is across the bridge headed toward Pineridge; it leads you out to a rock ledge above the magnificent falls. In the winter, the ice comes in twenty different shades of white, looking like mineral deposits from an exotic spring. The upper layer of water turned to ice in mid-cascade, while underneath quick water rushes downward.

One ridge over from the Taconic mountain range in eastern New York, the Pineridge Cross Country Ski Area offers excellent, old-fashioned skiing. Most of the trails are single tracks through the woods. With its narrow trails, tall hemlocks edging out the sky, and few people, Pineridge can feel like a garden maze at an English country manor. Although, any attempt to lose yourself in this forest primeval will be thwarted. Directional signs keep you skiing in the prescribed direction: "One Way", "Do Not Enter", "Ski This Trail First." (One sequence doesn't quibble: "Stop 100 feet;" then, "Stop Auto Road;" then "STOP!") Because trails are one-way, you rarely see other skiers, even on busy weekends. Night skiing seems funnily at odds with the area's isolated, old-fashioned ambiance, but Pineridge has four kilometers of lit trails.

Pineridge offers an extensive and varied network of easy skiing along the level areas of Poestenkill Creek. The intermediate and expert trails climb up, down, and over a good-sized mountain. These trails are difficult because they are so narrow. It can be a thrill to stepturn a corner

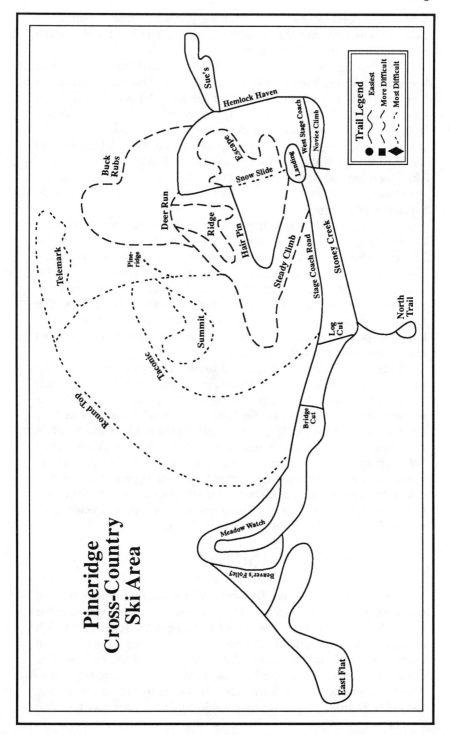

Pineridge
Cross-Country
Ski Area

Trail Legend

● Easiest
■ More Difficult
◆ Most Difficult

Sue's

Hemlock Haven

West Stage Coach

Novice Climb

Buck Rubs

Escade

Snow Slide

Landing

Deer Run

Ridge

Hair Pin

Telemark

Pineridge

Steady Climb

Stage Coach Road

Stoney Creek

North Trail

Summit

Taconic

Log Cut

Round Top

Bridge Cut

Meadow Watch

Beaver's Folley

East Flat

when centripetal force threatens to mate you with a tree! If you're not in an adventurous mood, ask in the touring center to find out which downhill trails are wider-groomed.

The touring center is unpretentious and old fashioned. It feels like a small, revamped barn with its cement floor and wooden rafters, but it was actually the shooting range for the local Albia Fish and Game Club. The Kersch family sheep farm is warmly in evidence. Woolly hides hang from the rafters (you can buy them), and multi-colored yarn sits next to the wax, gloves, and Maxiglide for sale. Picnic tables provide a nice roosting point next to the wood stove. Sign up for lessons here. The Pineridge staff loves to teach. Walter Kersch is a former principal who has enlisted a small army of teachers eager to induct you into the mysteries of skiing.

Pineridge's history is written into its trail system — unfortunately, the winter snow obfuscates many of the more fascinating landmarks. The area's forests were once a major source of charcoal for industrial steel mills in Troy. Locals made charcoal by piling wood into troughs, covering it with dirt, and letting it smoulder underground. The trails run over three old charcoal pits, but you won't know it in the snow. The most recognizable is at the junction of Snowslide, Hairpin, and Escape. Charcoal production also explains why there are more signs of past civilization than present in the area.

Digging through old maps and town annals reveals how transportation shaped the area that is now Pineridge. Two of the major trails — Stagecoach and Roundtop — were once important thoroughfares east and west. If you ski out to the furthest reach of Telemark, you'll see a big rockpile known as Stone Pile Knob. It may not look like much in the winter, but this was the foundation for the tollkeeper's house when Telemark and Roundtop formed part of a private toll road. A roadside spring for watering thirsty horses burbles to your right just as you start down Roundtop. You can also see some startling stonework as you ski down Stoney Creek: the bridge abutment crossing the creek was laid by a skilled mason. It is still in spectacular shape.

The Trails

Easier trails hug the river. **Stoney Creek** is a winding, double-tracked trail that moves with Poestenkill Creek. It serves as an avenue to the longer loops, but it feels like a secret promenade: ducking through balsams, cautiously skirting the marsh, and wobbling over a series of bumps like potato mounds. **East Flat** is a favorite trail among Pineridge devotees. The 3.5 kilometer loop is a lowland tour linking snow-covered meadows and marshlands. The fun is in the up-and-down, variable terrain — you feel the earth shifting under your skis. **East Flat** would probably be an intermediate trail at other areas. After the narrower trails, **Stage Coach West** looks and feels like the racetrack for the Indy 500. The oval trail is cut thirty feet across, groomed for skating, and lit for night skiing. Embrace it or flee.

If you don't know what deer prints look like, you will by the end of skiing **Buck Rubs**. The trail is crisscrossed everywhere by deer tracks, which lead hither and yon through the hardwood forest. The intermediate trail molds itself to the underside of a hill and then shoots downward through some tight corners, ending in a downhill T-intersection with **Hemlock Haven**. **Steady Climb** clambers up the mountain in a herringbone S-curve, suddenly drops (losing most of the elevation you just gained), and climbs determinedly again, first gently and then with a steeper grade. Just before the intersection with **Deer Run** you can see a deer stand at second-story level in the trees. The tightly winding beginning of **Escape** is perhaps the narrowest trail you'll ever ski. The trail curls back and forth through the low growth of young hemlocks whose lacy green boughs form effervescent curtains; you will feel suddenly transported into a northern rainforest. As the trail drops down the hill, the hemlocks grow more mature and the corners widen.

Expert skiers can try Summit, which leads you on a merry dance around the topmost knoll. The **Summit Chute** has a good runout; in other places you'll want to watch out for tight corners. The thinly-forested top has some nice pastoral views of the adjoining hills. If you've been yearning to practice your herringbone, **Taconic** is your chance. The trail climbs inflexibly for the better part of a kilometer before reaching the plateau at the top. From the climb, you can look out over the Taconic Range and Mount Greylock in Massachusetts. **Telemark** is wide enough for telemark turns. It sends you whizzing over a series of rat-a-tat bumps that will make your teeth chatter; the loop back uphill is much more sedate.

Finding your way: The center is actually located in the town of East Poestenkill. Take I-90 to Exit 7. Turn left on Washington Avenue and follow Route 43 through West Sand Lake. Follow Route 351 north to Poestenkill. Take a right on County Route 40 (Plank Road), and follow signs to Pineridge. The center is six miles out of town.

White Birch's Ski Touring Center

Box 35
Windham, New York 12496
(518) 734-3266

Trail System: *17 km groomed (17 km classical, no backcountry)*
Our Estimate: *Scenic, but somewhat difficult skiing for beginners.*
Grooming: *Casual*
Scenic Beauty: *4*
Touring Center: *A large camping lodge with rentals, lessons, wood stove, cafeteria, some retail, and game room.*
Favorite Trail: *"R" — a terrific spin around the rim of the valley*
Payment: *DSC, MC, and VISA*
Lodging: *Thompson House-Windham (518-734-4510, $$$); Point Lookout Mountain Inn-East Windham (518-734-3381, $$-$$$)*
Local's Tip: *Don't miss the "X" trail, even if you have to walk the hills!*

From the narrow, single-tracked classical trails to the tin-can-top trail signs to the juke box in the main lodge, a visit to White Birches feels like a trip back in time. The small lake and large, wooden lodge are wedged into a narrow valley at the far end of a mountain road — a beautiful, isolated little niche for dozens of winter camping sites and 17 kilometers of cross country ski trails. With the Hunter and Windham Alpine areas close by, many of the skiers here are downhill spinoffs, and there is no dearth of flashy neon parkas. But the beauty and character of this tiny resort deserve a separate visit, especially by those yearning for old-style cross country skiing — skiing unpolluted by spandex, skating, commercialism, and health nuts.

Although few skiers at White Birches have cross country skied more than once or twice in their entire lives, the trails are often quite difficult. What would otherwise be easy terrain is sometimes complicated by narrow, two-way skiing on one set of tracks. Only the frozen lake and a few short loops offer completely worry-free striding for beginners. Experts, however, will be glad to find that many of the longer, out-of-the-way trails are wonderfully difficult to tame!

Imaginative trail names add character at most ski areas, but the White Birches trail system is a jumbled alphabet soup. Instead of choosing between Birch Loop, David's Drop, and Screamer, you'll be debating the virtues of "A," "H," or "R." The trail map itself looks like a child's heartless attempt at connecting-the-dots, and the representation of trailside buildings rivals M.C. Escher drawings in its twisted perspective.

Cross country skiing plays second fiddle to camping at White Birches. While cross country trail fees provide a healthy income supple-

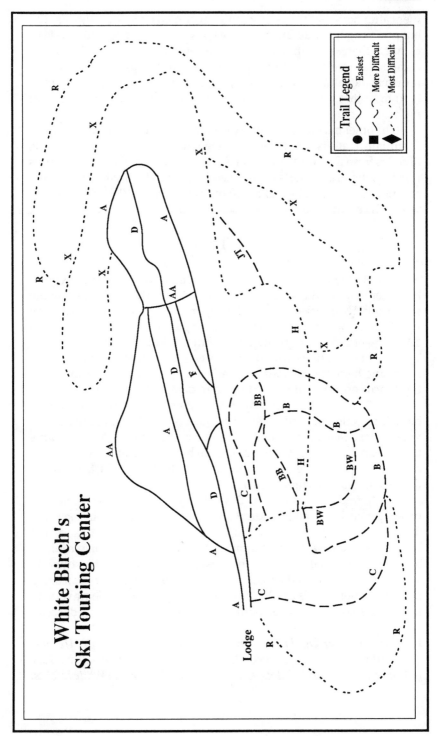

White Birch's
Ski Touring Center

ment after heavy storms, snow can't be counted on in the Catskills. The enormous lodge was built more as a social center for Ted Davis's campers than as a resting place for worn-out cross country skiers. The campers are a close-knit group; most are good friends with Ted and return to the same sites year after year. In fact, the camping community is so tight that it isn't unusual for 20 or 30 campers to get together at night and deluge a local Windham restaurant for dinner.

The other major cross country center in the area is Mountain Trails. Mountain Trails is conveniently located in Tannersville, only a couple of miles from the popular Hunter Alpine slopes, but the area suffers as much as it gains from its centralized location. The hectic atmosphere and not-so-scenic-trails make a 20-minute drive to White Birches well worth the effort.

The Trails

Most of the well-traveled loops begin in the camping area. A good beginner loop would be "A" to "AA" or "A" to "D." "A" begins in the shade of tall hemlocks among the campers, then steadily works its way uphill, crossing small streams and passing a shale pit. A left turn onto "AA" lowers you gently down to Grandpa Lake and back to the lodge. The return to the lodge on "D" begins with a gradual descent through a twisting hemlock corridor and ends with a short, easy climb. A few tight turns on "D" call for slender shoulders and quick feet.

"C" is a terrific little loop that begins by wending through a beautiful section of hardwoods. The track is so subtle and the trees so wide-spaced that the trail nearly blends in with the forest. "C" then turns its head and hops over the top of the hill before cruising down an easy slope back to the lodge. Don't be confused by the "Yell Clear" signs; they are for summertime archers.

You'll find excellent views down into the valley on "B." The trail passes by a caboose and windmill, then peers through the living room window of Ted's hilltop home. Superb views also lurk on "X" and "R," both expert trails which spin around the rim of the valley like roulette balls. These two trails are by far the most beautiful in the entire network, and it would be worth the trouble for an intermediate skier to struggle up the beginning hills of "X," enjoy the valley views while traversing the hillside, and then take off both skis and walk down the final descent.

Finding your way: Off of Exit 21 on I-87, take a left toward 23. After 1/2 mile, get onto Route 23 west. Continue on 23 west 21.7 miles toward Windham. Take right onto Nauvoo Road. Follow road 1 1/2 miles until it ends at White Birches.

Vermont

Tater Hill Cross Country Skiing
RFD #1
Chester, Vermont 05143
(802) 875-2518

Trail System: *25 km (25 km classical, 5 km skate, backcountry on snowmobile trails)*
Our Estimate: *Enough to satisfy a beginner for a day. The more experienced will find plenty of trails but may wish for a longer, out-of-the-way loop.*
Grooming: *Fair*
Scenic Beauty: *4*
Touring Center: *A golfing clubhouse with rentals, lessons, fireplace, soup and hot drinks, some retail, and miscellaneous magazines.*
Favorite Trail: *Spud Run, which cruises through the woods on the quiet side of the hill.*
Payment: *All major credit cards accepted.*
Lodging: *Inn at High View-Andover (802-875-2724, $$$); Stone Hearth Inn-Chester (802-875-2525); Ski dorm between Jamaica and Stratton on Route 30 ($)*
Local's Tip: *Get touchy-feely in the Hugging Bear Inn and Shop in Chester, the largest teddy bear store in New England.*

Despite tremendous potential, Tater Hill languishes as a backwater small potato in the cross country skiing world. Straddling a high, scenic hilltop in southern Vermont, this hibernating golf course has the potential to attract hordes of skiers from throughout southern New England. Thankfully, it doesn't. Instead, it provides early snow, a spacious clubhouse, and spectacular views of the surrounding mountains to a devoted clientele of skiers who aren't particularly fussy about grooming and who have chosen to ignore the skating revolution.

Swedish born Carl-Erik Westberg does his best with the grooming, but there's only so much you can accomplish by dragging an implement that resembles a nineteenth century farming tool behind a snow machine. The funny-looking device was fabricated in a high school metal shop by a local ski coach. The grooming aside, Tater Hill is an outstanding place to classical ski on a sunny day. You'll fall in love with the soft views of the Green Mountains, Carl-Erik's charm, and the warmth and spaciousness of the clubhouse.

The trail map at Tater Hill is pure potato propaganda: Russet Run, Yam's Way, Spud Run, and Sweet Potato. The names reflect the former incarnation of the hilltop as an enormous potato farm, which had been in continuous operation since the late 1700s. It wasn't until 1961 that the owners of the 600-acre farm realized that wealthy humans appreciated

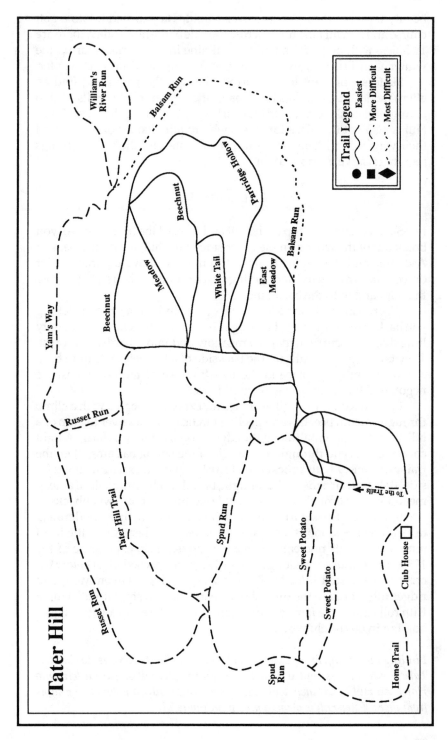

beauty far more than potatoes ever would. They turned it into a golf course and spread nine holes across the side of the hill. Today, there are 18 holes, with plans for an additional nine in the works. During the winter, Carl-Erik borrows the fairways for his cross country ski center.

Skaters will want to flip further through the pages and find an alternate destination. This is too bad, since widening the trails a bit to accommodate skaters would be a fairly easy task on a golf course. Tater Hill is also not the place for skiers who require hand-holding to find their way around. The map is impressionistic and the trail markings require creative interpretation.

The Trails

Ski out across the top of the hill and toward the back nine. As you break out of the woods on the other side of the hill, the pointy peak of Ascutney and the Alpine trails at Okemo rise above the trees. After descending an easy hill and gliding past a crumbing house, hop across the road and onto the back nine.

White Tail and **East Meadow** loop around the meadows, letting you bask in the warm sun. **Partridge Hollow** and **Beechnut** are a pretty little duo that scurry across the meadow and into a hardwood forest. They take separate paths up the backside of a hill before drifting back down to a meeting place in the meadow. All of these trails can be negotiated by a beginner with confidence.

Balsam Run is the trail of choice for experts. It begins with a climb through smooth beeches and peeling birches, bobbles over the top of a hill, then runs downhill along the edge of a Christmas tree farm. A tight corner shoots you through the middle of the young balsams; then the trail turns feisty with a rocketing downhill and hairpin turn on the far side. Balsam Run ends with a straight, brutal climb up the side of a steep meadow — a climb that deserves at least three or four switchbacks.

Spud Run, Russet Run, and the **Tater Hill Trail,** three moderately difficult, wooded loops, lie waiting just on the other side of the front nine. These trails re-create the narrow, classical ski experience of the 1970s. **Spud Run** soars along through bright hardwoods, just below the crest of a forested hillside. Terrific views of high, Green Mountain ridges filter through the trees. After clearing a final short uphill, **Home Run** rolls down the fairways of the front nine like a run away golf cart homing in on the clubhouse.

Finding your way: From Exit 6 off of I-91, follow Route 103 west to Chester. Take Route 11 west out of Chester for about nine miles. Take a left onto Horsenail Hill Road (there will be a sign for Tater Hill), and follow the signs from there. Tater Hill is about a mile from Route 11.

Mountain Top
Cross Country Ski Resort

Mountain Top Road
Chittenden, Vermont 05737
(802) 483-6089

Trail System: *75 km (75 km classical, 75 km skate, 35 km backcountry),*
2 1/2 km of snowmaking
Our Estimate: *A full day of skiing for beginners, a full weekend for experts!*
Grooming: *Excellent*
Scenic Beauty: *5*
Touring Center: *A very comfortable lodge with rentals, lessons, wood stove,*
snacks and hot drinks (restaurant in the inn), waxing bench, full retail.
Fantastic lounging areas upstairs and on porches!
Favorite Trail: *Meadow Trail, an easy meander across the beautiful meadows*
of the Mountain Top Farm
Payment: *AE, MC, and VISA.*
Lodging: *Mountain Top Inn-Trailside (800-445-2100, $$$-$$$$); Tulip Tree*
Inn-Chittenden (802-483-6213, $$$-$$$$); Comfort Inn-Rutland
(802-775-2694, $$)
Local's Tip: *The remnants of New Boston, a failed farming community, can*
be seen (with keen eyes) from the Lost Horizon and New Boston trails. Look
for old apple orchards, cellar holes, and scattered gravestones.

Mountain Top is the sleeping giant of the cross country ski world. Hidden at the high end of a mountain road in the tiny town of Chittenden, several hundred feet above a frozen reservoir, Mountain Top's views rival those from nearby Cloud Nine. Trails gallop across the steep meadows of a mountain farm, wrap themselves around three modest peaks, and glide down toward the reservoir through the overgrown remains of a nineteenth century farming community. Throw in a few trailside cabins, fabulous grooming, snowmaking, and a cadre of ex-Olympians, and you've got what should be one of the most popular cross country ski spots in northern New England. Shhhhhh!

Chittenden is what Bennington and Wilmington and Stowe were like 100 years ago and want to be like today: it's a *real* small town. It hasn't been admired and designated and bronze plaqued until property values soared and locals moved out. Driving through Chittenden and up the winding Mountain Top Road, you may feel like you've landed in some forgotten, rugged corner of Appalachia.

Despite what appears now to be pristine wilderness, the land around the ski area has been recycled several times. At first, loggers had

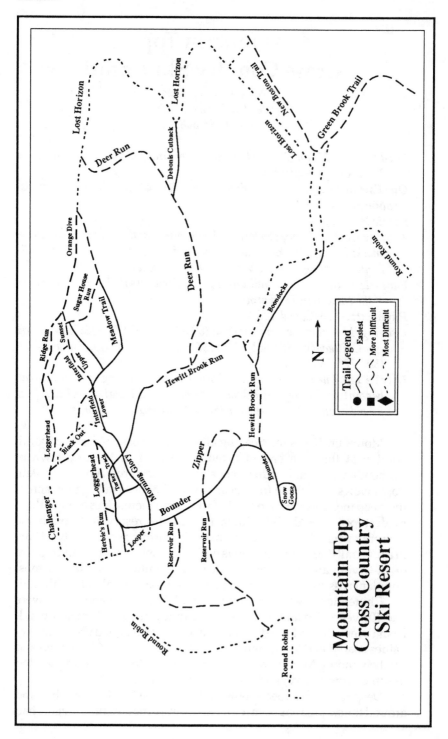

**Mountain Top
Cross Country
Ski Resort**

free reign. They felled every tree in sight to feed the 14 ravenous saw mills that used to dominate the town. An early settlement in Chittenden was named "Slab City" after the slabs of wood produced by the mills. After the forests were cleared, sheep farms spread through the valley and over the hills. One particularly hardy group of farmers climbed high above the town to form a small community called "New Boston" and eke a living out of the thin, mountain soils. After a prolonged series of long winters and short summers, New Boston collapsed and then decayed into the hillside.

For the past several decades, the former New Boston area has catered to skiers and vacationers. In 1964, when nearly all cross country skiing was still informal and off-trail, the Mountain Top Inn began to develop a trail network and convert one of its smaller horse barns into a ski center. With spectacular views and a luxurious inn, success was unavoidable. Snowmaking, which today is still a novelty for Nordic centers, was installed in 1983, providing the area with steady snowfall regardless of Mother Nature's whims.

Today, Mountain Top draws skiers by the hundreds. Visitors from the inn pack cheese and crackers and trek to the hilltop cabin or the nearby sugar house. Young racers train under the watchful eye of three-time Olympian Mike Gallagher. Tourists marvel at the views while the Alpine-oriented members of their families go broke at Killington.

The Trails

The variety of the trails at Mountain Top is astounding. Short loops near the lodge get right to the point: they carry you just high enough to gaze down into the valley. A long, 20 km loop around the **Chittenden Reservoir** tests the staying power of experienced skiers, while several five to ten kilometer loops provide plenty of varied terrain for anyone in-between.

The most difficult climbing is done in your car on the way up the hill from the center of Chittenden. Uphill junkies should make plans for some additional vertical with an excursion to the cabin at the top of **Loggerhead**. Start with a relaxed ski toward a tiny pond on **Interfield**, then head straight up the merciless monster of a hill. Luckily, the cabin teases you from just a kilometer or two away, and its views of the reservoir and sunny front porch are just rewards for the uphill struggle. If you prefer something a bit gentler, ski to the cabin on **Interfield Upper** and the backside of **Loggerhead**. This route doles out views *during* the climb rather than saving the excitement for the end.

Believe it or not, there are two additional warming huts on the trail system! **Sugar House** is probably the easiest of the three to reach. Only a small hill and the meadows of **Mountain Top Farm** separate it from the lodge. Although lacking the high vantage point of the cabin, the trip to the Sugar House provides plenty of scenery, and it offers a warm place to sit down, dry out, and chew a candy bar. The warming hut on the reservoir can be reached in less than five minutes on **Bounder**, a straight, fast downhill behind the inn, but the snow is less consistent and the return trip can be arduous.

Experienced skiers, anxious for an out-of-the-way tour, should begin by climbing past Mountain Top Farm on **Interfield** or **Meadow**. (At the top of the field is "**Mikes' Chair**," a wooden lookout designed and built by three different Mikes.) Head into the evergreens and turn right onto **Sugarhouse Run**. The top section tunnels through thick, green firs, then zips over a knoll as if it were about to hang glide to the reservoir. After a feisty little corner, it scoots downhill through sugar maples and a web of sap lines. From there, head out on **Lost Horizon**, an expert loop with an S-turn descent that starts you on a long tour of the valley. **Deer Run** provides a shortcut to the lodge, but a few of its downhill corners could be labeled "expert" on an icy day. The latter section of **Deer Run** has terrific flat sections for developing a smooth glide. Keep an eye out for deer tracks!

Challenger curls through hardwoods on the back side of the mountain, providing fabulous views to the west. The wide, relatively straight downhills are easily tamed in powder and slush, but they can be life-threatening on fast snow.

Overall, the trails above the inn are far superior to those down near the reservoir. Save yourself the long trip back up to the inn and lodge by staying on the higher side. Be sure to bring a little extra cash; trail fees are a bit higher here than they are elsewhere.

Finding your way: From Route 4 west: take a right onto Meadow Lake. Drive five miles from Pico Mountain. After 1.7 miles, take a right at the stop sign onto Chittenden Road. Continue 2.7 miles, then take a left across the bridge (onto Holden Road). Immediately after the bridge, Holden Road curves to the left; continue straight onto Mountain Top Road. The inn and ski center are about 1 1/2 miles up the hill. From Rutland, take Route 4 east and turn left onto Meadow Lake Drive 3.7 miles from Route 7.

Craftsbury Nordic Center
Box 31-W
Craftsbury Common, Vermont 05827
(800) 729-7751

Trail System: *110 km groomed (110 km classical, 110 km skate, and 50 km backcountry), soccer field lit for night skiing*
Our Personal Estimate: *More trails than the average skier can ski in a week.*
Grooming: *Good. Excellent near the center, less consistent on outlying trails.*
Scenic Beauty: *4*
Touring Center: *Rentals, lessons, wood stove, soup and bread, wax benches, some retail*
Favorite Trail: *Sam's Run, a long scenic trek that rises out of a forested valley into high meadows.*
Payment: *MC and VISA*
Lodging: *Inn on the Common-Craftsbury Common (802-586-9619, $$$-$$$$); The Village Motel-Hardwick (802-472-5211, $$); Dorm rooms-Craftsbury (800-729-7751, $/meals included)*
Local's Tip: *Free skiing until December 15.*

Craftsbury Nordic Center lies between two lakes in a snow pocket in the midst of Vermont's rugged Northeast Kingdom. Highland scenery, exciting terrain, and many kilometers of well-groomed trails combine for some of the best skiing in the East. This is where snow-hungry skiers head at the first scent of winter, and where they eke out the last of the corn snow in spring. Craftsbury is a mecca for serious athletes, but you don't have to own a lycra suit and four pairs of skis to enjoy it: the atmosphere is friendly and relaxed. The vast trail system swallows you up, and on weekdays you can ski for hours without a glimpse of another soul.

The long low buildings that make up the Nordic center were originally intended to be an Andover-in-the-woods — a wilderness prep school to turn boys into men. It soon failed, and the buildings were bought in the mid-1970s by Russell and Janet Spring. The Springs emigrated from Wall Street to Craftsbury in search of the simple life, and in setting up the Nordic Center they certainly found it. During the first years nobody came. It was then that Russell, in the absence of human company, developed his appreciation for nature. He is always willing to discuss moose tracks and bird sightings and other natural wonders.

Now two generations of Springs manage the center, which sponsors year-round programs dedicated to physical exhaustion: ski touring, rowing and running camps, mountain bike touring, Elderhostel, and walking tours. The Nordic Center offers other amenities for over-

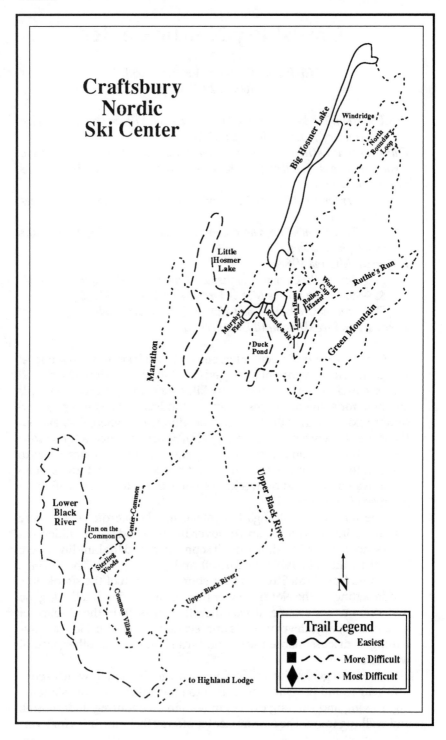

Craftsbury
Nordic
Ski Center

Big Hosmer Lake

Windridge

North Boundary Loop

Little Hosmer Lake

Ruthie's Run

Marathon

Murphy's Field

Round-a-bit

Lemon's Haunt

Bailey's Hazard

World Cup

Green Mountain

Duck Pond

Upper Black River

Lower Black River

Inn on the Common

Center-Common

Sterling Woods

Common Village

Upper Black River

to Highland Lodge

N

Trail Legend

● 〜〜 Easiest

■ ⌐ ⌐ More Difficult

◆ ⋯⋯ Most Difficult

night guests, including a modest weight room with a rowing machine, a sauna, and one VCR. The small, spare beds and shared bathrooms will make you feel like a twentieth century Puritan, but the incomparable country kitchen compensates for the lack of creature comforts and has spawned its own mini-industry: the sale of *The Craftsbury Center Cookbook*.

The Trails

Beginners or the timid-at-heart may want to restrict themselves to the track around the soccer field (lighted at night), a good place to regain your ski legs or practice a wobbly glide. **Murphy's Fields** offers a one kilometer track which loops around a rolling hay field and provides a gentle introduction to hills. **Duck Pond** tosses and turns through an evergreen forest, offering greater variety and solid intermediate skiing during the week. On weekends, ski elsewhere: the **Duck Pond** probably has the highest population density in the entire Northeast Kingdom.

The seven kilometer perimeter of **Big Hosmer Lake** (pronounced 'Osmer) is a long, level track, good for an easy day tour or a moonlit night. The shoreline is your best bet for tracks, scat, and other evidence of wildlife. On almost any given day, ice fishermen will be tending their holes, shaking their heads, and wondering about all the crazy skiers. The lake is unprotected, and can be bitterly cold on windy days.

Craftsbury's core trails — **Wally's Lament, Dennis' Demise**, and the **Race Loop** — lie scattered across a long forested hillside, providing some challenging terrain. The five kilometer **Race Loop** begins with a smooth series of downhill curves; the trail's second half is a long, steady, wooded climb to the touring center. On weekends, spectators and coaches gather along the trail to cheer competitors as they churn their way up the final ascents.

Elinor's Hill, a spectacular S-turn on a wide sloping field, affords an equally spectacular view of northern Vermont. **Ruthie's Run** and the less-traveled **Sam's Run** (both named for Spring family dogs) swoop down into the Black River Valley and more-or-less gradually ascend into open farm fields. They meet in time to plunge back into the woods for a curving, controlled downhill that you can take as fast or as slow as you want.

Further afield, trails crisscross over lakes, through fields, and past farmhouses, offering panoramic views of the Lowell Mountains. The **Common Trail** stretches to the hilltop settlement of Craftsbury Common, a town well known for its old New England charm. A custom dictating that all houses be painted white keeps the town looking quaint and old-fashioned.

The ten kilometer **Black River Trail** gently descends through snow-laden forests, along the edge of farm fields, and over snowmobile tracks to dip into Craftsbury Village, where thirsty skiers can stop to tipple at the Craftsbury Inn. For a small fee, the touring center staff will come pick you up. For the hardy or persistent, the mostly flat **Lower Black River Trail** wends its way homewards through snow-covered cattails, with a herringbone climb up to Craftsbury Common. Formerly groomed, it has reverted to a wilderness trail and to the upkeep of local snowmobilers. This trail is particularly lovely in the slanting sun of late afternoon but can be a blustery slog on a windy day.

Craftsbury has added a new property in the last couple of years: Eden Mountain, with about 20 kilometers of groomed trails. Skiers venturing to Eden Mountain are relatively rare, and those who do, benefit from its backcountry flavor. Here snow falls even earlier and melts later than in Craftsbury, and your chances of seeing wildlife are excellent. The **Beaver Pond Loop** boasts a fine dam, and hare prints race across the tracks. The Eden Mountain area is about a 20-minute drive from Craftsbury Common.

Finding your way: Take I-91 to Exit 21 in St. Johnsbury. Follow Route 2 west to West Danville, then take a right onto Route 15 west and follow it until you come to Hardwick. Turn right onto Route 14 north for eight or nine miles. You'll see signs to your right for Craftsbury Common; follow them. One mile beyond the Common, bear right onto the dirt road and follow the signs to the Craftsbury Nordic Center.

Burke Mountain Cross Country
RR 1 Box 62A
East Burke, Vermont 05832
(800) 786-8338

Trail System: *63 km groomed (55 km classical, 53 km skate)*
Our Personal Estimate: *Hilly trails with significant changes in elevation. If you see a "Caution!" sign, you know they mean it.*
Grooming: *Excellent*
Scenic Beauty: *4*
Touring Center: *Rentals, lessons, wood stove, food, wax benches, some retail*
Payment: *MC and VISA*
Lodging: *Old Cutter Inn, East Burke (802-626-5152, $$);*
Days Inn-Lyndonville (802-626-9316, $)
Favorite Trail: *Four Hills, a mercurial climb into the beautiful hardwoods of Burke Mountain*
Local's Tip: *The Old Cutter Inn welcomes skiers to its excellent Sunday brunch; ski trails lead directly to their door. Reservations are a good idea.*

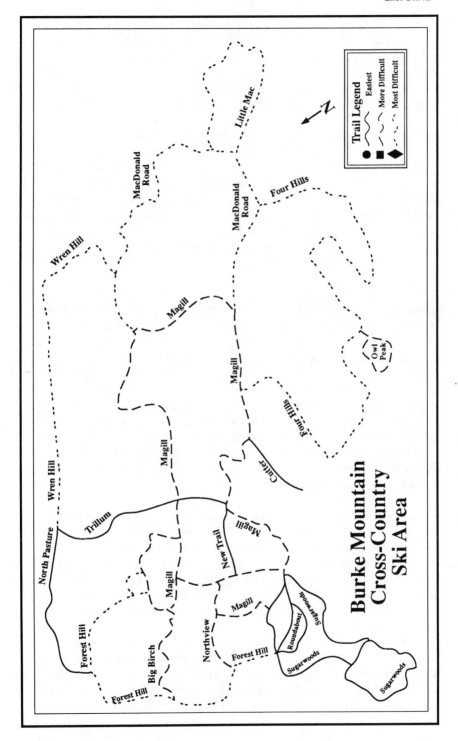

**Burke Mountain
Cross-Country
Ski Area**

Several years ago, the *Caledonian Record* ran a front-page article with the headline: "SKIER COLLIDES WITH DEER." A local elementary school student had been innocently skiing with her classmates at Burke Mountain Cross Country Ski Area. She rounded a corner, moving pretty quickly, and startled a deer standing in the ski trail. Both of them saw it coming. She moved left, the deer moved right, and they met with a crash that knocked both of them out. Most ski centers offer to bring you in close contact with nature. At Burke, they deliver.

High in the Northeast Kingdom, bounded by high fields and snowy hills, this modest ski touring center runs one of the best operations around. The trail network is a work of art, dreamed up and sweated over by a longtime skier. You will never find a race here; you probably won't even find many people. You will find animal tracks, highland views, and challenging, hilly trails that are a delight to ski. Burke Mountain doesn't spend their time or money angling for customers. They put their energy into the trails and hold to the maxim, "If we build it, they will come."

Although Burke Mountain is owned by the Alpine area, you'd never know it. You can ski all day and catch only vague reminders of the Alpine area's existence: a scenic vista of the mountain, a far-off "Yah hoo!" from the slopes. Burke Mountain Cross Country maintains a rare independence from its flashier sibling. It wasn't always that way. Until 1982, the cross country area was a sham operation run as a satellite for the downhill area. The management used to send a boy over in the morning with 25 single dollars to lie in wait for customers. Grooming consisted of dragging a bedspring behind a snowmobile, and the guy who taught lessons didn't know how to ski himself.

These days, they know how to ski at Burke Mountain. They also know a lot of other things. Manager Stanley Swaim and his assistant aim to foster curiosity and appreciation. They pride themselves on being able to tell you about the area's natural and human history, from the life cycles of snowfleas to tales of bootleg rumrunners during Prohibition. If you know what to look for, you'll see signs of fishercat, snowshoe hare, and deer; you can see where bears have left clawmarks on beech trees, climbing up for the nuts; if you're lucky you may hear a great horned owl up on Owl's Peak. The center posts a list of skiers who have seen a moose. The trails wind through the world's southernmost extent of boreal forest: a forest of pointy-topped trees like spruce and fir which shed the snow.

Inside the touring center, the atmosphere is homey and eclectic. A fire burns heartily in the wood stove, the edifying tones of National Public Radio float over the airwaves, and a rainbow of rug samples nailed to old wooden benches softens the seating. Mrs. Swaim's menu makes daily variations on the theme of muffins, chili, cookies, and hot drinks.

The Trails

The intermediate **Magill** loop forms the centerpiece of the Burke system. The western end links a gradually ascending series of fields, where you can see the distinctive U-shaped Willoughby Gap and, on a clear day, to Jay Peak and Smugglers Notch. The trail bows low into a swamp of cedar trees, where hairy bark and feathery boughs give the trail the character of a strange, snow-covered bayou. The eastern end commandeers an old logging road, climbing and then contouring the hillside; it passes through houses and meadows under the shadow of Burke Mountain. The trail descends back to the center through evergreen shrouded wetlands, passing over beaver ponds and, incredible as it may seem, a troll crossing. Ski it to believe it.

The sheltered, secret **Trillium** is the easiest trail on the property and a good trek for windy days. Tall trees crowd the path. It makes gentle curves through a spruce forest, climbing imperceptibly in elevation; at the furthermost tip, it abandons its easy status and shoots down to a T-intersection.

Sugarwoods is a loop whose high ends tie together at the touring center. Its first half is the picture of loveliness, dropping down across fields and through evergreens which tower over the trail; its second half climbs steadily back through mixed forest. A shortcut eliminates the larger hills. The full trail would be considered intermediate at most areas; to ski it you should have a confident snowplow.

The intermediate **Candy Bar Hill** got its name from the kids' ski program. The first one to make it down the hill without falling could lay claim to a candy bar. The straight balsam tunnel slopes sharply upward behind the touring center. Skiing up it will get your heart pumping on a cold morning; skiing down it is a zippy pleasure.

Burke's expert trails are unquestionably difficult. **MacDonald** is a pastiche of old logging roads, named for the man who logged the area. It is the Mount Everest of Burke. The trail climbs for nearly two miles. Switchbacks make the climb easier. You can take **Little Mac** to cut it short, or push up the less-traveled final section to the evergreen pass. At the pinnacle, you'll see the trunk of a maple tree crooked into an S-curve. Native Americans used to mark forest paths by bending young saplings so that they grew in this way. (This tree may be naturally bent; it is not more than 70 years old.) The descent to **Little Mac** is a real challenge, narrow and curvy, with no terrain to check the flow of gravity; after that, the trail widens out.

Good luck trying to find the four hills that constitute **Four Hills**. There are hundreds. While **MacDonald** is a simple ascent and descent, **Four Hills** playfully bounces all over the mountain. Although its basic trajectory is up, it goes through a hundred different moods: steep

41

ascents of fields and forest; a ruler-straight herringbone through spruce and balsam trees; the traverse of a maple mountainside; and the bumpy, curvy crossing of hillside ravines. Ski this trail in the early morning when horizontal shafts of sunlight slide onto the slopes; by late afternoon the sun drops behind Burke Mountain, leaving **Four Hills** to cool in shadow.

Finding your way: Take I-91 to Exit 23 at Lyndonville. Turn right off the ramp and follow Route 5 north through the town of Lyndonville until you reach Route 114. Follow Route 114 north to the town of East Burke; at the far end of town take a right, following the signs to Burke Mountain. Continue past the Sherburne Base Lodge for another quarter mile. The entrance to the cross country operation is on the left.

Blueberry Hill Ski Touring Center
Goshen, Vermont 05733
(802) 247-6735

Trail System: *60 km groomed (40 km classical, 20 km skate, and unlimited backcountry)*
Our Personal Estimate: *Long, more difficult treks make Blueberry Hill challenging; it is better suited to intermediates and experts than beginners.*
Grooming: *Good. Some skate trails are shared with snowmobiles.*
Scenic Beauty: *5*
Touring Center: *Rentals, lessons, wood stove, wax bench, self-serve food, some retail*
Favorite Trail: *Halfdan Kuhnle Trail, which herringbones up a mountain and dives down the other side*
Payment: *MC and VISA*
Lodging: *Blueberry Hill Inn-Trailside (800-448-0707, $$$); Brandon Motor Lodge-Brandon (802-247-9594, $)*
Local's Tip: *Help yourself to the soup bubbling on the wood stove: it comes free with your trail fee. The sauna out behind the Inn is also available to skiers.*

Unlike many other inns, skiing at Blueberry Hill Inn is far more than a thinly disguised carrot to lure overnight guests. Sixty kilometers of some of the best skiing in the East spreads in clover-shaped trails into the wilderness. The trails are extensive, isolated, and well-planned. One was voted "most scenic" by *Vermont Life* magazine; another is the highest groomed trail in the state. The only drawback is inconsistent snow. Despite the great views and skiing, Blueberry Hill is notorious for fickle snow. Be sure to call for a ski report.

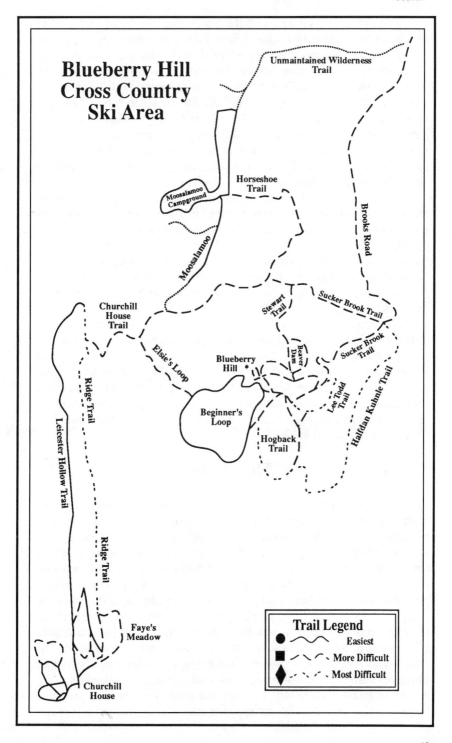

Blueberry Hill
Cross Country
Ski Area

The skiing is wild and remote. You'll find the heart and soul of Blueberry Hill in long treks through the National Forest. Eighty percent of trails are in protected lands, and you'll ski past lots of signs announcing "Entering Green Mountain National Forest." (You are never sure when you leave the National Forest, but you enter it repeatedly.) There are two types of terrain to explore. Trails tackle the steep contour lines of Hogback and Romance mountains, offering rugged climbs and spectacular views. Or, if you don't mind sharing with snowmobilers, follow the long, wide abandoned roads that run north and south through the forest. You can ski to the remote and lovely Silver Lake, which is accessible only to hikers and snow travelers.

Blueberry Hill has been around since the beginning of American cross-country skiing, and has developed its own quirky aesthetic over the years. The touring center, a welcoming blue-painted barn, sits directly across from the blue-painted Blueberry Hill Inn. Inside, the walls are hung with signs and memorabilia from the center's earliest days, old wooden skis have been nailed to the stairs as railings, and the far wall is papered with trail maps from cross country ski centers as far away as Norway.

The area hosts two races annually. The American Ski Marathon is a classic-style race modeled after Scandinavian marathon events. In late January every year, serious skiers converge on the center to exhaust themselves over the 60 kilometer course. The Pig Race is an entirely different affair, held in March as the snow is fading fast. It is a ten kilometer event at which skiers get a little crazy, there are costumes, obstacles, live music, and a feast of roast pig and other culinary delights. General zaniness prevails.

The Trails

Blueberry Hill's mountainous terrain means that easy trails are hard to come by. The **Beginners Loop** was cut specifically to answer this need. It is a mostly flat five km loop through diverse woodlands; you'll ski through a bumpy hemlock tunnel, then move out into an spacious forest dominated by yellow birch, then break out into a meadow. From there you can see the lay of the land, views look up to the pointy prominences of Hogback and Romance Mountains, and down to the dimple where the touring center lies. The flat, straight **Leicester Hollow** (pronounced Holler) trail is a long out-and-back trek which passes Silver Lake and continues southward to the Churchill House Inn. The trail lies in a ravine with steep walls rising on either side. It crosses Leicester Hollow brook several times, and explores marshy areas.

Elsie's Loop is a bridge between the easy and intermediate level trails. It's also your best bet for spotting tracks, scat, and wildlife. Elsie is the Blueberry Hill cook, and she's the one responsible for the delicious lunchtime soup. She used to ski to work on this route long before it became a groomed trail. The trail slides along through a flat forest where beeches still cling to their yellow leaves, passes through a tall stand of black spruce, then runs along a stone wall. Only a couple of hills interrupt the mild terrain.

The bulk of Blueberry Hill's trails are intermediate level. The very popular **Hogback Trail** hugs a mountainside littered with silvery-gray boulders, and climbs to a clearing of old pastureland where the mountainside slopes away. Two mountain ranges, one near and one far, march off into the blue yonder. This hill is blueberry heaven in the summertime. The trail ducks into the valley separating Hogback and Romance Mountains, and slides along the verge of a ravine, where birches occupy the quick-dropping embankment. Don't leave Blueberry Hill without skiing this trail!

The intermediate **Sucker Brook Trail** meanders away from the touring center through hardwood forest. It humps over the lower regions of Romance Mountain, but the ups-and-downs are never very steep. The trail turns to follow the brook itself in the tiny Sucker Brook clearing; from there, it is a series of playful twists on an essentially level run. At the far end you catch a quick glimpse of the reservoir with its eerie Siberian-style landscape.

Halfdan Kuhnle should be attempted only if you have legs of steel and a will of iron. It begins mildly enough, winding up an old road to a trail head for hikers. There the climb begins, and it is up up up for a very long one-mile herringbone trek. Don't get caught up in the dogged pursuit of elevation — you might miss some spectacular glimpses of mother nature. Looking back over the valley you can see the rise of the Brandon Gap, and all around you is the dark golden scruffiness of yellow birches. A spruce pass stands sentinel at the top, and through the trees you can see blue and white patterns of Champlain Valley farmland. The trail heads into a mile-long dipping, curving, downward passageway — hang on! If it is icy you may want to save this trail for another day.

Finding your way: Take I-89 to Exit 3 at Bethel; follow Route 107 west to the intersection with Route 100. Take Route 100 north for eight miles; turn left on Route 73 west. Follow this for 11 miles into Goshen. Blueberry Hill is 2.5 miles north on Forest Road #32.

Camel's Hump Nordic Ski Center
RR 1, Box 422
Huntington, Vermont 05462
(802) 434-2704

Trail System: 35 km groomed (35 km classical, 35 km skate, and 35 km backcountry)

Our Personal Estimate: A well-cut system with scenic views and mostly intermediate trails.

Grooming: Good

Scenic Beauty: 4

Touring Center: The basement of the Brautigams' home. Rentals, lessons, fireplace, food (soup, fruit, cookies), wax bench, some retail, outhouse

Favorite Trail: Owl's Glen, a ledge-lined curving descent with some surprise turns.

Payment: MC and VISA.

Lodging: Millbrook Inn-Waitsfield (802-496-2405, $$$); West Hill House-Warren (802) 496-7162, $$)

Local's Tip: The Catamount Trail runs through the top of the trail system. A popular backcountry trek is to take the Honey Hollow Trail (part of the Catamount Trail north) down 12 km to Route 2. The trail winds down a drainage basin between ridges, and drops 1500 feet to the Winooski River. Honey Hollow is an intermediate-level trail with several steep and challenging chutes at the top.

The Camel's Hump Nordic Ski Center offers glorious skiing in the boondocks. You won't stumble on this place by mistake. The center roosts at the end of a bumpy dirt road in a small town in the scenic shadow of Vermont's favorite mountain, Camel's Hump. Their small, devoted clientele appreciate the views, the Mom 'n Pop feel, and an impressive trail system. Trails spread out across the hillside, through a nice mix of forest and open land. Half of the system is groomed and tracked, while half of it is left untouched for backcountry skiing.

Camel's Hump is a work in progress, and it probably always will be. Dave and Myra Brautigam are constantly plotting out additional terrain and cutting new trails. The two dreamed up the center in the late 1970s as a young couple, looking for a way to make a living on their own terms. The 230 acres of land had been a hillside farm belonging to Myra's family; from their own cross country treks they realized that it would be the perfect spot for a ski center. They spent the months after they got married with a chainsaw in the woods cutting the first trail — appropriately named Honeymooner. Further trails developed as the center grew. These early trails were steep and difficult. As you ski the

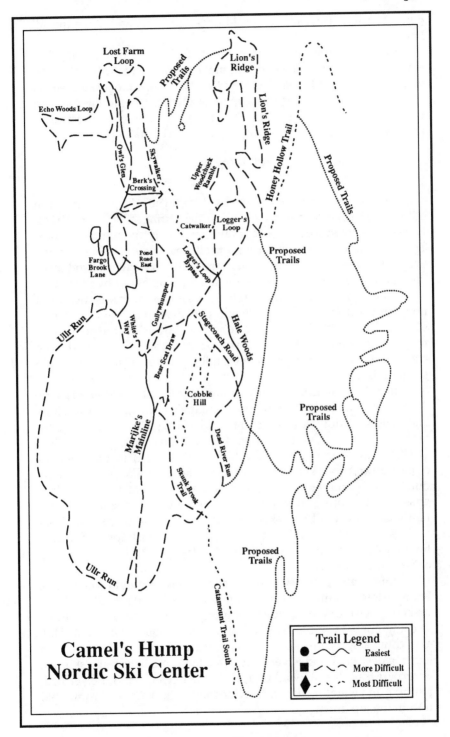

Camel's Hump Nordic Ski Center

47

current system, you can see the old tracks going up and down the fall line.

Camel's Hump has a rustic, family feel. The touring center is a small, cement-paved duo of rooms in the basement of the Brautigams' wooden clapboard home. A central fireplace keeps the place cheerful and warm. Hungry skiers can help themselves to a picnic table spread with soup, fruit, cookies, candy, cider, and hot drinks — afterwards, they can stroll out to the cold outhouse in the barn.

The Trails

There are no flat areas at Camel's Hump. The hills prohibit it. The mildest terrain hovers in the woods above the touring center. **Fargo Brook Lane** glides down the side of the Brautigams' field and into the woods. The trail climbs upwards through pretty hardwoods while a ridge drops off to the right; it changes its name to **Pond Road East** and turns into rolling terrain that traverses the hill and comes out by the pond.

Honeymooner is another pretty across-the-mountainside trail. It floats upward for most of its length and then tails downward in a sloping descent. This hillside was once a sugarbush (a forest of sugar maples), and you can still see the pans from the sugarhouse under the snow. Most of the maples have been logged, but there are a couple grandaddies left.

The **Echo Woods Loop** circles around the top of a hardwood ridge. At the furthermost tip there are spectacular views of the westward hills and hollows; a downhill curve to the ridge's edge brings you face-to-face with a vista of Camel's Hump. The protective evergreens that line **Owl's Glen** are home to hawks and bard owls. Ledges rise on both sides of the trail and you ski down the middle. The trail follows the graceful, quick-flowing curves of a central stream, and a pair of narrow bridges crisscross the brook unexpectedly. **Gullywhumper** sounds like a nonsense word until you ski it. The trail dives into three in-and-out ravines and makes a mild climb through a thick, dark spruce forest. It links the center's concentrated network of trails with a loose federation of far-ranging loops.

Camel's Hump's most difficult trails cluster at the highest elevation. Snow lasts longer up on the mountain, and there can be excellent skiing up here when the field outside the touring center is patchy and melting. The ungroomed **Cobble Hill Trail** traces the silhouette of Cobble Hill. You climb a spruce ridge, then skirt cliffs and cut switchbacks in an exciting descent. **Dead River Run** is rated intermediate, but it skis like an expert trail. It follows the capricious whims of an old river bed, jumping and wiggling through ravines and gullies in a wild romp. Ski it from the top down.

Ullr's Run has another delightful series of difficult downhill corners. The first part meanders around the far side of the hill into an unusual monoculture forest, where only maples grow. That's where gravity takes over and the fun begins: you'll encounter more 'esses' on this trail than in spelling 'Mississippi'. Watch out for the devilish last corner where you'll find yourself struggling to avoid the embrace of an evergreen about your size.

Finding your way: Take I-89 to Exit 11 in Richmond. Follow the signs one mile south on Route 2 into Richmond Four Corners. At the light, take a right and drive a half mile to the Round Church. Follow the road as it bears right, and take it seven miles to Huntington Village. Just past Jaques Store, bear left on the weak arm of the Y onto East Street. Follow the signs 2.8 miles to the ski center.

Viking Ski Touring Centre

RR 1 Box 70
Londonderry, Vermont   05148
(802) 824-3933

Trail System: 40 km groomed (40 km classical, 13 km backcountry, 3 km night skiing)
Our Personal Estimate: Woodsy, classical trails over relatively level terrain.
Grooming: Excellent. Viking regularly teaches other areas how to groom.
Scenic Beauty: 2
Touring Center: Rentals, lessons, soup and sandwiches, full retail
Favorite Trail: Goat's Path, a nimble little trail up and over forbidding terrain.
Payment: MC and VISA
Lodging: The Three Clock Inn-South Londonderry (802-824-6327, $$$); Viking Guest House-Londonderry (802-824-3933, $$)
Local's Tip: For a cheap date, you can't beat their Saturday night special. You get a full dinner (soup to dessert, with a drink) and night skiing for $8.95. Reservations are necessary.

What are the secrets to a long-lasting ski center? A love of skiing and a sense of humor. The small, friendly, and deservedly popular Viking Ski Center in Londonderry has both. Skiing at Viking feels like what it is — skiing at the birthplace of American cross-country skiing. The operation is arguably the oldest ski touring center in the country. Viking's trails retain that old-fashioned feeling — narrow, wooded

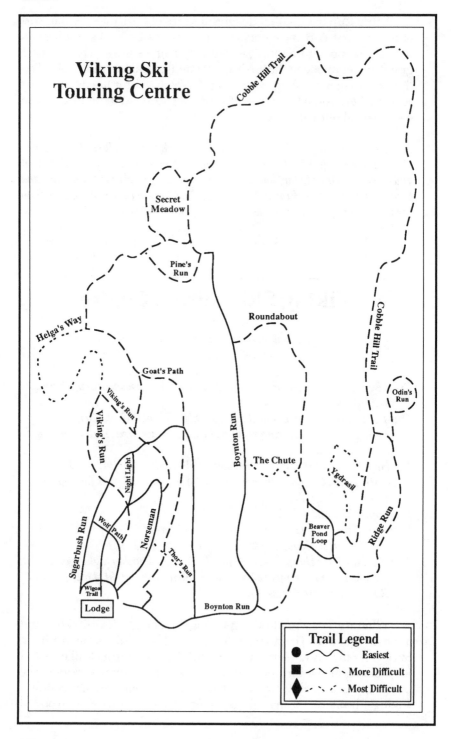

Viking Ski Touring Centre

Cobble Hill Trail

Secret Meadow

Pine's Run

Helga's Way

Roundabout

Cobble Hill Trail

Goat's Path

Viking's Run

Viking's Run

Odin's Run

Boynton Run

The Chute

Ygdrasil

Night Light

Sugarbush Run

Wolf Path

Norseman

Thor's Run

Beaver Pond Loop

Ridge Run

Wigoa Trail

Lodge

Boynton Run

Trail Legend

● ∿∿∿ Easiest

■ ∕∖∕⌢ More Difficult

◆ ∙∙∕∖∙∕ Most Difficult

single tracks wending their way around tight corners. The trails near the center have been graded to accommodate beginners, but there are some wild and delightful bumps on the far runs.

The staff jokes that Viking was started by a bunch of hippies with a dream; they have a photo showing hairy, bearded skiers enthusiastically nailing the first signs to trees. Lee and Stan Allaben were two brothers who loved skiing. They built the touring center on their uncle's property. They cut trails, hung signs, set out a donation bucket, and declared themselves open for business. Because Viking was one of the first places to import Nordic skiing from Norway, they went hog-wild on the Scandinavian theme, and the trail names reek of Nordic mythology: Wigö's Path, Viking Run, Helga's Way, Ygdrasil (pronounce it if you dare), and Odin's Ring. There are more.

There were two problems during those early years. First, the bull at the Riverside Farm developed a yen for skiers. Whenever he heard them coming he would bust out and chase them back down the Cobble Hill Trail. Second, cross country skiing was a novelty in the United States. It wasn't long before the Allabens realized that Americans couldn't get hold of ski touring equipment. They started the first Nordic mail-order business, called Nordic Traders, shipping skis, poles and boots from Norway, and specially crafted woolen knickers from England.

The Trails

There are a number of core trails in the woods which make great beginner skiing. These trails share the same basic character, weaving and interlocking in an evergreen forest. **Wolf Path** is a short, barely breathing trail that makes a nice little loop over gently rolling hills. The popular **Norseman** wends up and over small hills through the evergreens; it can be bumper-to-bumper with skiers on busy weekends. Further afield, the three km **Boynton Run** is a long, level promenade through mixed forest that feels like an old logging road.

Intermediate trails are fun and frequent. The unpredictable **Goat's Path** turns quick corners, leaps over knobs and hillocks, and dives down narrow chutes. Because it is sometimes too narrow to snowplow, you will have to stepturn the corners. **Pine's Run** is a lovely, peaceful old logging road that slides under a cathedral of red pines. **Ridge Run** slides down a knobby ridge onto a real wingdinger of a downhill, where a rapid-fire succession of little bumps make your teeth chatter. The trail has been recently forested, and the spindly trees and little gaps make it feel like skiing down the backbone of a partially plucked chicken.

Most of the expert trails are short downhills cutting down the fall line. **Ygdrasil** is a mountainside pathway to heaven. The trail is notched into the hillside of a beautiful open forest; it leads to the top of a ridge where beech trees congregate, and then turns down for a wide, steep descent. The 12 km **Cobble Hill Trail** is designated expert mostly because of its length. **Cobble Hill** is a constant succession of terrain changes: a curvy section where the trail disappears behind another tree every five feet; a sloping Christmas tree farm; overgrown pastureland and obsolete stone walls; meadows with views of the perfectly parabolic **Cobble Hill** and the Alpine trails of Stratton Mountain; and back through farmland and forest. It is a lovely trek, and offers the only field skiing at Viking.

Finding your way: Take I-91 to Exit 7 at Springfield. Follow Route 11 west almost to Londonderry. About a mile before town, you'll see a sign pointing to Little Pond Road on your right. The ski center is less than a mile.

Hazen's Notch
Cross Country Ski Area

RR1 Box 730
Montgomery Center, Vermont   05471
(802) 326-4708

Trail System: 30 km (30 km classical, no skating, 20 km backcountry)
Our Estimate: A tangled, woodsy web, with several shorter field loops.
Grooming: Casual
Scenic Beauty: 3
Touring Center: Rentals, lessons, wood stove, hot drinks, and wax bench.
   Deutsch wird hier gesprochen!
Favorite Trail: East Meadows, a gentle, 5 km jog through evergreens and old
   cow pastures
Payment: No credit cards accepted.
Lodging: Black Lantern-Montgomery Center (800-255-8661, $$$); Hazen's
   Notch Guesthouse-Montgomery Center (802-326-4708, $)
Local's Tip: Rock-lovers will find it difficult to stick to the packed trails;
   retreating glaciers spilled scores of car-sized, gneissic boulders throughout
   the hills.

In Vermont, a ski area's proximity to the Quebec Frontier can to some degree be gauged by the amount of French you hear on the trails. By this rough measure, Hazen's Notch is only a hop, skip, and a quick skidoo ride from the border. The percentage of Canadian visitors floats somewhere between 25% and 50%, varying with the relative strength of the Canadian dollar. Despite the French Canadian contingent, owner Val Schadinger's subtle Austrian accent, and a series of colorful flags

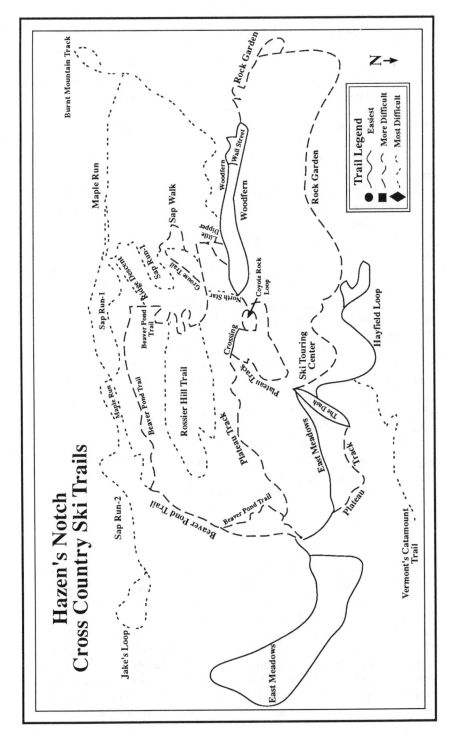

**Hazen's Notch
Cross Country Ski Trails**

N→

Trail Legend
● Easiest
■ More Difficult
◆ Most Difficult

Burnt Mountain Track

Rock Garden

Wall Street

Woodfern

Woodfern

Maple Run

Sap Walk

Little Dipper

Sap Run-1

Grouse Trail

Ridge Descent

Sap Run-1

Beaver Pond Trail

North Star

Coyote Rock Loop

Rock Garden

Maple Run

Beaver Pond Trail

Rossier Hill Trail

Crossing

Ski Touring Center

Hayfield Loop

Plateau Track

The Dash

Sap Run-2

East Meadows

Plateau Track

Jake's Loop

Beaver Pond Trail

Beaver Pond Trail

Plateau

Vermont's Catamount Trail

East Meadows

hanging from the ceiling of the warming hut, skiing at Hazen's Notch is far from a bustling international experience. Hazen's Notch is a quiet place. The little parking lot would choke on 20 cars. Even on busy days, skiers at this one-time dairy farm couldn't come close to replicating the feeling of energy and activity that must have reigned 50 years ago, as hundreds of meandering cows mowed the grass on a bouldery hillside. Today, most of the pastures have ceded to a thick, hardwood forest. Only the skinny tree trunks and the meandering, mid-forest stone walls hint at the former life of the land.

Val Schadinger was not always a lover of cross country skiing. He describes his own introduction to the sport in Austria several decades ago as "utilitarian." When blizzards made the local roads impassable, he would reluctantly adjust his Alpine skis for a cross country trudge to the local store, returning with victuals for his mother. The trip to America initially had no effect on his enthusiasm for the sport: he worked for several years as an Alpine instructor at nearby Jay Peak. One year, when the Austrian Ski Club of Montreal came to visit, they discovered splendid skiing in the pastures above Val's farmhouse. Soon, Val was linking pasture to pasture with ski trails, blazing his way deep into the woods, kilometer by kilometer.

Hazen's Notch still feels more like a friend's farm than an established ski center. If you insist on exquisitely groomed trails, ski elsewhere. Val describes his grooming as "less intense" and you may occasionally find that although the base is well-packed, your own two skis have been enlisted to provide the finishing touches. You won't be the only one setting tracks in the woods: keep an eye out for deer, moose, and other four-legged Vermonters on many of the wooded trails.

Before you recklessly rush off to the far fringes of the forest, grab a topo map, a compass, and a rabbit's foot. You may find interpreting the trail map and signs more taxing than casually chatting in French while struggling up a steep hill. We hope you have more luck than we did!

The Trails

Most of the trails on the upper part of the trail system wrap in and out of former pastures, gliding through thick, young maples and past huge boulders that farmers never bothered to move out of the way. **Beaver Pond Trail** (intermediate) climbs reluctantly away from the farmhouse and fields, then scurries into the woods for a long, steady climb up several switchbacks. After about two kilometers of climbing, the trail passes the shell of a sugar house and a steeply sloping field — offering both fine views of the valley and a great spot to fine-tune your telemark turns. The trail then drops slowly down the other side of the hill, passing through a mature hardwood forest with glimpses of Burnt

Mountain filtering through the trunks. Listen for the distant drone of snowmobiles.

On **Beaver Pond Trail** you'll pass by an abandoned home, an overgrown apple orchard, and the farmhouse of the last of a series of Calvinist ministers that once lived in the area. The trail ends on a long straight downhill. Enjoy the speed and the bumps, but beware of the road crossing at the bottom!

The lower section of the trail system offers skiing of a completely different flavor. Here are the remnants of the open pastures and the spectacular views that stunned members of the Austrian Ski Club many years ago. **East Meadow Loop** offers fabulous beginner skiing. It traverses long, open meadows, follows a stone wall along the edge of a pasture, then swings back through pretty, dense stands of evergreens. On clear days, many of the lower fields offer splendid views of the valley and nearby mountain peaks.

The **Burnt Mountain Trail** and the **Rossier Hill Trail** tempt more accomplished skiers with challenging terrain, but hotshots will have to wait for the forest to recover from a recent spat of logging before they can try these two trails.

Finding your way: I-89 to Waterbury (Exit 10). Follow Route 100 north 21 miles to Eden, then left onto Route 118. After about 14 1/2 miles, you will enter Montgomery Center. In Montgomery Center, take a right on Route 58. 1 1/2 miles up the road on you left is Hazen's Notch. (Warning: you can't cross over from the other side of Route 58 in the winter!)

Wild Wings Ski Touring Center

Peru, Vermont   05152
(802) 824-6793

Trail System: 25 km groomed (25 km classical)
Our Personal Estimate: Great easy skiing; the perfect place to introduce kids
to the sport.
Grooming: Good
Scenic Beauty: 2
Touring Center: Rentals, lessons, wood stove, chili and brownies, some retail,
outhouses
Favorite Trail: Blue Jay, a bumpy climb to the top of the land followed by a
smooth and speedy descent.
Payment: No credit cards
Lodging: Johnny Seesaws-Peru (802-824-5533, $$$); Londonderry Inn-
Londondery (802-824-5226, $$)
Local's Tip: Karl Pfister's horse drawn sleigh rides are the best in the business.
By daylight he will take you on beautiful sleigh rides through the town of
Landgrove. On his moonlit sleigh rides he takes you over roads and trails,
and turns off the lights on the sleigh so all you can hear are the jingling
bells. By appointment only: (802) 824-6320.

Wild Wings Ski Touring Center is a tiny, family-run ski center that
has purposefully stayed small and unpretentious. It has its own style,
and has attracted a dedicated following of skiers. It's a good bet that
Wild Wings has snow. The center stands high in the snowy town of
Peru, on the leeward side of the spine of the Green Mountains. Unnatu-
rally level ground above a filled-in glacial pond has provided Wild
Wings with excellent easy skiing, and plenty of it.

Most touring centers mete out beginner trails in tiny, lollipop-sized
chunks. Easy trails chase their own tails around tiny fields within sight
of the lodge. It's no wonder so many beginners abandon Nordic skiing
after one or two tries, dismissing it as "boring." Wild Wings offers an
alternative introduction to the sport. Beginner loops swing out and
back from the center, making you feel that you've really been somewhere. Gentle downward slopes allow beginners to stride out and glide
effortlessly through the woods. They can enjoy the thrill of skiing,
without having to worry about bumps and changing terrain.

You may wonder about the name. Angus Black is a committed bird
watcher; he has done work for the local Audubon Society, and keeps a
lifelong list of the birds he's seen. All of the trails are named after birds,
and you can follow trails by following the image of the birds encased in
blue diamonds and nailed to the trees. The Blacks started Wild Wings

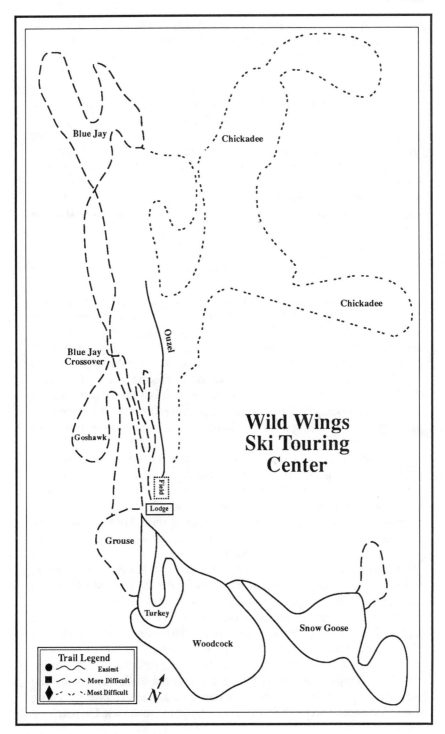

Blue Jay

Chickadee

Chickadee

Ouzel

Blue Jay
Crossover

Goshawk

**Wild Wings
Ski Touring
Center**

Field

Lodge

Grouse

Turkey

Woodcock

Snow Goose

Trail Legend
● ～～～ Easiest
■ ～◡～ More Difficult
◆ ～◞～ Most Difficult

N

in the early 1970s, when they rented out skis and pointed skiers up an unimproved logging road. Skiers would ski two miles up, turn around, and be back in a jiffy. The next year the state improved the road, and the Blacks were forced to cut trails in the woods. Now their son and his family run the center.

There is no room for pretension at Wild Wings. Everything is homemade and cozy. A green, tin-roofed horse barn divided by partitions has been transformed into a touring center. The rental and ticket shop is a 10' x 10' x 10' wooden cubby; skis hang from the rafters and milk crates kick underfoot or double as chairs. The somber, gravel-floored warming room is cavernous by comparison. An idiosyncratic wood stove tinkered together out of two large barrels dominates the end of the room; it could pass for modern art. Skiers sit and eat at the four wooden picnic tables.

The Trails

The beginner trails spread out on the level terrain near the touring center and across the road. The pleasant **Snowgoose** trail ventures on a winding 2.5 kilometers loop that is closed after 3:30 p.m. The flat terrain and wide-spaced trees evoke a bog that has gelled. **Woodcock** passes by a beaver pond, through a hemlock pass, and through a ragged clearing where the Civilian Conservation Corps ran a sawmill during the 1930s. The big mound of snow on your left is a pile of sawdust left over from those days. The trail encompasses more varied terrain than **Snowgoose**, including a couple baby herringbone climbs and some point-and-shoot downhills.

Intermediate trails are a significant step up in difficulty from the easy ones. **Goshawk** is a shorter trail which makes gentle switchbacks while climbing into mixed hardwoods above the touring center. This land was pastureland at one time, and you'll see old stone walls hanging about as evidence. The trail tangles with **Blue Jay** in a complicated intersection, but the one-way directional signs are clear and let you know where you *are* and *aren't* welcome.

Chickadee is the center's longest trail at 6.5 kilometers. It climbs mildly to higher ground and tours a scruffy, desolate forest where you have a good chance of seeing wildlife tracks or scat. Deer and rabbits are common, and signs of bobcat have also been found in the area. The **Chickadee** trail loops back on itself two or three times, which is both a blessing and a curse. You can easily lop distance off, if you're tired or it's late but these intersections can make skiing the full distance feel futile.

Wild Wings' one expert trail is the climb-and-descend **Blue Jay** trail. The trail's first section is a continuous curvy, bumpy climb through a beech and birch forest, very similar to **Goshawk**. On reaching the top, the trail glides down over bumpy terrain, and then curls into a gradual chute. But the last and best part of the trail is a downhill section of old road. Set your feet, get into a tuck, and you'll whoosh down the entire length of the hillside in under two minutes. Pay attention to the "Sharp Curve" sign just before the bottom: the trail suddenly and surprisingly takes an S-turn with corners so sharp that it more closely resembles a Z.

Finding your way: Take I-91 to Exit 7 in Springfield. Follow Route 11 west through Londonderry; take a right into the village of Peru. Turn right at the church onto Hapgood Pond Road and follow this for a mile. Bear left onto North Road. The Ski Touring Center will be on your left in less than a mile.

Green Mountain Ski Touring Center

RD #2, Stock Farm Road
Randolph, Vermont   05060
(800) 424-5575, (802) 728-5575

Trail System: *30 km groomed (30 km classical, 30 km skate, and 20 km backcountry)*
Our Personal Estimate: *Manageable, intermediate trails following old carriage roads.*
Grooming: *Good*
Scenic Beauty: *3*
Touring Center: *Rentals, lessons (by appointment), hot drinks, some retail, comfortable couches. Lunch available in the inn.*
Favorite Trail: *Trail Two; climbs to an open field at the height of the land*
Payment: *MC and VISA*
Lodging: *Three Stallion Inn-Trailside (800-424-5575, $$); Greenhurst Inn-Bethel (802-234-9474, $$-$$$)*
Local's Tip: *The attached Three Stallion Inn has some great midweek ski-and-stay deals.*

Arriving at Green Mountain Stock Farm is like entering a three dimensional Christmas card. The white farmhouse is decked with green shutters and red-ribboned wreaths. A small river wends its way through the enchanting, wide-bottomed valley. Ski trails climb purposefully to the height of the land, where a meadow gazes out at a broad blue and green panorama of high hilltops. Morgan horses pace gracefully around their ancestral home.

Until recently, the Green Mountain Stock Farm was a hillside farm.

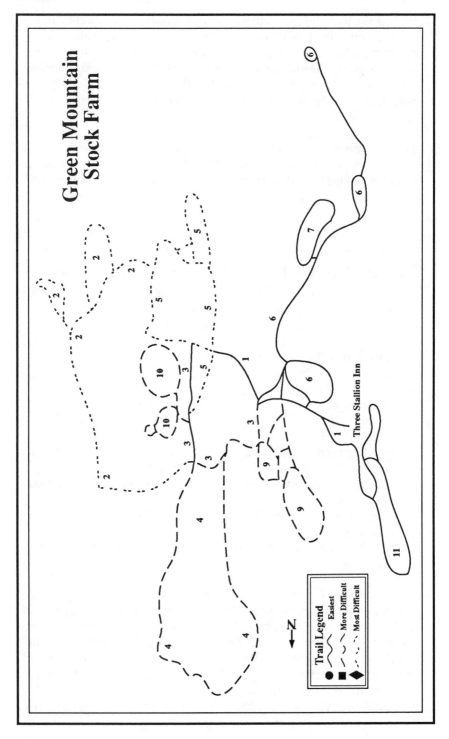

Green Mountain
Stock Farm

Three Stallion Inn

Trail Legend
Easiest
More Difficult
Most Difficult

N

Until recently, the Green Mountain Stock Farm was a hillside farm. Most of the ski trails have the wide, gradual character of old farm roads. Gentle avenues trace the perimeters of fields along tumbling stone walls. It's easy to imagine wagons lumbering along these same byways with loads of hay and apples. Now the farm's 1300 acres are gradually being developed. So far, construction has been confined to the lands off the central road; ski trails climb through a small neighborhood, past gardens and back porches. Although the overall feeling is still old pastureland, this may not hold true forever.

The land has its own niche in equestrian history. In the early 1800s, a local farmer by the name of Justin Morgan developed the horse that bears his name. The chestnut-coated animal was a versatile wonder, pulling buggies and hauling heavy loads around the farm. Morgans were bred larger and bulkier during the Civil War when they were used by Union troops as a military workhorse. Later, a man named Robert Lippitt Knight made it his personal mission to restore the sullied bloodline. He used the Green Mountain Stock Farm to breed the horses back to their original character. There are still Morgan horses at the farm, and you can watch the graceful animals from the picture window in the ski touring center.

The casual elegance of the Three Stallion Inn contributes to the area's aura of civilized country living. Skiers are welcome in the high-ceilinged dining room. You can sip a frothy mug of hot chocolate topped with whipped cream or get an inexpensive lunch of chili, soup, and sandwiches. Their dinner menu is famous for its quality, quantity, and economy. Overnight guests can soak their bones in the hot tub or bake them in the sauna. Insatiable exercise fiends will be thrilled by the weight room; the mirrored, carpeted facility is as well-appointed as any gym.

The Trails

Beginners should walk fifty feet down to the golf course below the Three Stallion Inn. **Trail Eleven** traces various loops through the hummocky golf course, depending on the day and the mood of the groomer. There are long flat sections for learning, but surprise dips and turns will keep experts from getting too cocky. For a real thrill, tuck down the sledding hill across the bridge.

Gentle, pretty **Trail Six** follows the stream's curves through a wooded gully until it crosses the road onto expansive cornfields; from there it traces the wide bows of the river before turning back on itself. A small extension off the tennis courts loops onto a ridge of red pines with a steep overlook; this is a pretty and less-traveled addition. The broad, unpretentious **Trail One** serves as a central artery. It heads straight up the hill behind the touring center, while trails spin off on all sides. Unless you are doing interval hill training you might want to choose a more interesting sidekick.

Trail Four is a great intermediate trail that hikes up a quick, steep hill and through the woods in an entertaining series of bumps and dips. A hulking outcropping of sandstone by the side of the trail looks like a sleeping Stegosaurus. The trail dips into a secret clearing and through an evergreen tunnel out into open territory; the second half climbs to high ground and weaves a scenic path through hills and houses. **Trail Five** feels the most like an old carriage road. From the bottom it is a steady, utilitarian climb; from the top it is a delightful downhill curving its way through a forest of huge tree trunks. There are no turns sudden enough to upset an apple cart.

Trail Two climbs to high ground along the perimeter of fields and past private homes. Crossing the road near mailboxes and playing dogs, you feel like you are skiing through a neighborhood. You are. Above the road you leave the houses behind and ski along a sheep fence and a stone wall — remnants of the farm. You reach the best views and the apex of the trail system at the top of a giant field; from there you can see a panorama of Pico Peak, Killington Ski Area, and the local Cushman range. The field is good practice for baby telemarkers.

Finding your way: Take I-89 to Exit 4 in Randolph, and follow Route 66 west for 2.5 miles. Just before you reach Randolph you'll see signs to the left for the Green Mountain Stock Farm and Three Stallion Inn. The center is less than a mile down Stock Farm Road.

Carroll & Jane Rikert Ski Touring Center

Bread Loaf Campus
Ripton, Vermont 05766
(802) 388-2759

Trail System: 42 km groomed (42 km classical, 13 km skate)
Our Personal Estimate: Playful trails on a wooded hillside; an abundance of squiggly little connector trails mean that you'll have a hard time trying to ski it all.
Grooming: Good
Scenic Beauty: 3
Touring Center: Rentals, lessons, snacks and hot drinks, wax rooms, some retail, comfy chairs
Favorite Trail: Intercollegiate Racing Trail, a rigorous circuit with tight curves and long hills to challenge even top college racers.
Payment: MC and VISA
Lodging: Swift House Inn-Middlebury (802-388-9928, $$$-$$$$); Sugar House Motor Inn-Middlebury (802-388-2770, $$)
Local's Tip: Down the road, the Forest Service has created an interpretive Robert Frost Trail by placing his poems in the landscape. Skiing the one-mile trail is a unique experience: backcountry, quiet, deserted, and lined with poetry. The trail is a mile west of the Rikert Ski Center on Route 125.

You'll find one of the best, least populated ski areas in Vermont tucked behind the unmistakable mustard-colored fleet of buildings that constitute Middlebury's Breadloaf campus. The Carroll and Jane Rikert Ski Touring Center is owned by Middlebury College, and is the official training ground for the college's top flight ski team. They don't advertise. On weekday mornings, you'll find a deserted trail system for your private pleasure; on weekday afternoons, local school kids raise a ruckus and learn how to ski; and on weekends, lycra-clad competitors whiz around the race loop to the delight of cheering throngs.

The Rikert Center lies on the top of the Green Mountains just beneath the sky. Trails tracked for classical skiing spread out over the college land and into National Forests. A relatively level network of beginner and intermediate trails lurks in the spruce forest adjacent to the center; across the road, two big fields serve as practice loops; and the bulk of the system extends up and around the wooded Firetower Hill. The terrain is hilly rather than mountainous; for its location, there are surprisingly few steep grades. But the hills are constant. You are always either going up one, coming down one, or traversing one.

The trail system can be confusing. At some point Middlebury

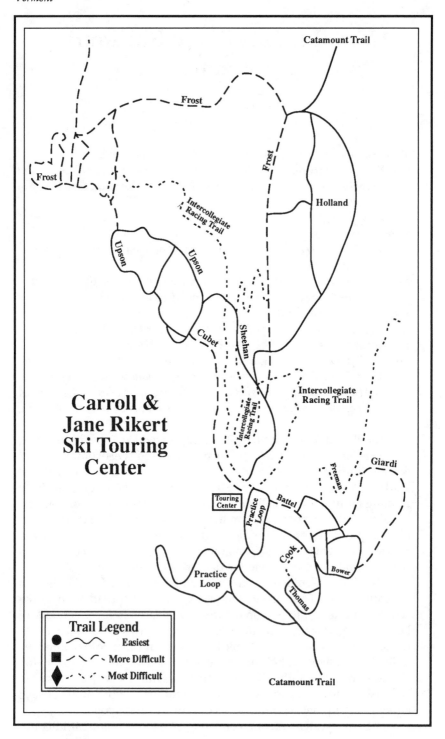

Catamount Trail

Frost

Frost

Frost

Holland

Intercollegiate Racing Trail

Upson

Upson

Cubet

Sheehan

Intercollegiate Racing Trail

Intercollegiate Racing Trail

Carroll & Jane Rikert Ski Touring Center

Giardi

Freeman

Touring Center

Practice Loop

Battel

Cook

Bower

Practice Loop

Thomas

Trail Legend

● 〜〜〜 Easiest

■ 〜 ⌒ More Difficult

◆ ⋯ 〜 Most Difficult

Catamount Trail

College decided that a quick and painless way to honor VIPs was to name ski trails after them. They replaced all the good, memorable names (Snowsnake, The Way Home, Timberline, etc...) with the surnames of deans and benefactors. This may have brought gold and goodwill to the college's coffers, but it makes the trail names hard to remember. There are also a number of nameless flourishes, wiggles, and connector trails. Not every trail is marked. But the staff is very good about posting maps at intersections, especially farther out on the system. It is possible to get lost, but hard to stay lost. If you don't know where you are, don't worry. You're likely within a kilometer of the touring center.

The center itself is a rabbit warren of rooms for warming up, waxing, changing, eating, and even napping. The rag-tag assortment of comfortable chairs and couches have been worn to threadbare comfort. The staff is a band of friendly, knowledgeable professionals with a storehouse of local lore and a good sense of humor. John Rubright, who has run the touring center for over twenty years, is affectionately and mysteriously known as "Hedgepig." His self-guided natural history tour will sharpen your eyes and your understanding, it uses landmarks along the way to provide insight into geology, water conservation, animal and plant interaction, and land use heritage.

The area's history is dominated by the twin themes of preservation and poetry. The land was bought by the eccentric philanthropist Joseph Battel around the turn of the century. He hated the "timber butchers" —as he called the loggers—and bought 35,000 acres of land to preserve woodlands against their blades. This is the land you ski on. Since he didn't want to leave the area he invited his friends to come to him, and built the hotel, cottages, and other clustering buildings for them to stay in. When Battel gave the land to Middlebury, he apparently stipulated that the buildings remain painted his favorite mustard-yellow color.

Middlebury College uses the campus for the famous Breadloaf Writer's Conference, and hundreds of poets and writers have sought inspiration in these very woods. Perhaps best known is Robert Frost. Ski trails lead right out to the green-trimmed log cabin where he lived.

The Trails

Someone did the easy **Practice Loop** a disservice when giving it its name. It is actually a very pretty Figure 8 circuit of two large fields divided by a high central ridge. Fields flow downward on either side, and the trail carves smooth curves around their perimeters. Mountains pop up all around.

The first part of **Bower** (known as Porcupine in the good old days) is probably the easiest trail on the system. The first part of the winding, flat trail buries itself in a thick spruce forest; the second part dives into a series of decidedly un-beginnerish downhills. They aren't steep, but they drop and curve at the same time.

Most of the Rikert trails are intermediate. **Battel** (once Hedgepig) is the heart and soul of the tightly woven trail system. After an initial uphill, it passes through a meadow and into acres and acres of dark spruce. At the far reaches, the land tilts upward and the trail breaks momentarily into hardwoods before reverting to the forest through a downhill tunnel. The hillside **Upson** (Figure Eight) was patched together out of former bridle paths. The upper arm slopes gently down through hardwoods, while the lower arm skirts the upper edge of the conifers and dips into them. **Upson** is predominantly easy skiing, but a duo of quirky downhills toss you a challenge.

For high jinks, try the technically challenging **Intercollegiate Racing Trail**. This lively trail hikes up the hillside and twists downward with curves and whorls more intricate than your fingerprint; the second half climbs an extended hill which slopes upward with increasing severity, makes a zigzag through **Upson**, and drops back downhill on a trail that is only a little too mild to be called a chute.

Ski **Frost** from left to right. The trail makes some fun, meadowy loops below the Frost Cabin and then heads into a long, gradual ascent of Firetower Hill on the path of an old logging road. The top section changes moods more frequently than an adolescent. It charges into an uphill herringbone, bumps and wrinkles along the upper hillside, and meanders aimlessly in the woods. The last kilometer shoots down a wide straight run to the touring center.

The 13 km **Outer Loop** circles the mountain and takes several hours to ski. It starts with a solid climb through hardwood forest, then heads downhill and joins up with Road 59 which it shares with snowmobilers. The trail's farthest reaches are beautiful, rolling curves through a desolate evergreen forest, with mature spruce, young balsams springing up, and acres and acres of evenly-spaced, towering red pines just above the Frost Cabin. If the sight of them doesn't rouse your spirit and inflame your nobler instincts, you are a lost soul indeed.

Finding your way: Take I-89 to Exit 3 in Bethel; follow Route 107 west to the intersection with Route 100. Take Route 100 north for 12 miles; turn left on Route 125 west. Follow this for nine miles until you reach the Breadloaf Campus. The touring center is the farthest building in the rear. Alternatively-take I-87 to Exit 29 at North Hudson. Follow Route 9 north for approximately four miles; turn right, and follow the country road to Port Henry. Turn right onto Route 22 south, and drive three miles to the junction with Route 17. Take Route 17 east into Vermont. After five miles, turn right onto Route 125 east, and follow this road through Middlebury and Ripton. The Breadloaf Campus will be three miles beyond Ripton on your left.

Stowe Mountain Resort
Cross Country Center
(formerly Mount Mansfield)

5781 Mountain Road
Stowe, Vermont 05672
(802) 253-3688

Trail System: 35 km (35 km classical, 35 km skate, 40 km backcountry), plus groomed connections to two other extensive trail systems.
Our Estimate: The perfect complement to the nearby Trapp Family Lodge's Nordic trails, with plenty of beginner terrain and a good mix of narrow, woodsy valley trails.
Grooming: Good
Scenic Beauty: 4
Touring Center: Rentals, lessons, wood stove, hot drinks, and some retail.
Favorite Trail: Old Camp, one of the craziest wild bulls you'll ever try to ride! Triple black diamond.
Payment: All major credit cards
Lodging: Stowe Mountain Resort-Stowe (802-253-3000, $$$-$$$$); Vermont State Ski Dorm-Stowe (802-253-4010, $)
Local's Tip: For budding telemarkers, Stowe Mountain Resort is an ideal place to learn. The cross country ticket buys unlimited chairlift rides: 750 feet up a fairly easy hill.

Wedged into a steep river valley between two skiing titans — the Trapp Family Lodge's Nordic trails and the Mount Mansfield Alpine trails — Stowe Mountain Resort's trail system is easy to overlook. This is unfortunate. While *tourists* are lured by the hundreds to Trapp by a savvy combination of family lore and marketing, *skiers* are left alone to explore Stowe's fantastic terrain in peace. Long, forested loops with feisty, convulsive bumps and twists make this area a favorite destination for racers, locals, and other cross country connoisseurs.

The dramatic valley has been logged on and off for more than a century, but it shows few scars. The dark, steep forest regenerates itself, closing over recent wounds with dense new growth. However, forestry has left its mark in other ways. Skiing has been a weekend pastime for loggers since the early part of the century, and it was the loggers who cut Stowe's first trails. A few extra swaths through the forest was no big deal for men whose job it was to fell trees! Well-liked loggers have been immortalized in trail names at Stowe, and the site of their logging camp is an easy ski up the valley on the Burt Trail.

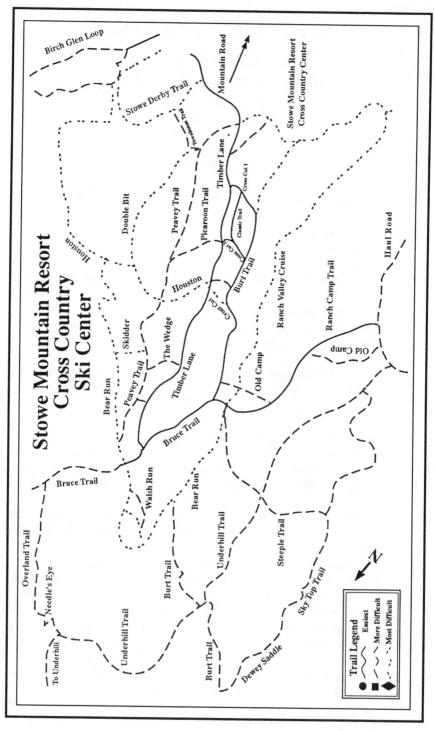

Stowe Mountain Resort
Cross Country
Ski Center

Trails at Stowe trace the valley like contour lines. Since steep hillsides send all unattached objects tumbling toward the river, the trail designers had very little creative leeway. Trails traverse uphill on one side of the valley for as long as possible, then drop across the river and head back down on the other side. The result is a giant series of nested Vs. Choose a V to match your ability level: the easier ones are small and stick close to the river, while the expert trails form big Vs that bully their way farther up the hillsides before reluctantly dropping to the other side of the river and racing back to the touring center.

Your trail pass also provides access to the extensive Topnotch and Trapp trail systems. While you couldn't possibly ski all three in a day, you should certainly take advantage of the warmth, socializing, and hearty food at the trailside Trapp Cabin.

The Trails

Take your pick among the various V's of the valley. Just remember: inner is easier. The most popular beginner loop starts up **Timber Lane** and returns on the **Bruce** and **Burt** trails. **Timber Lane** coaxes you up the valley with a long, gentle climb through second-growth hardwoods. You'll see **Sky Top Ridge** and **Round Top** floating through the trees. By taking one of the "cross cuts," you can avoid the steeper hills toward the end, but you'll also miss a lot of the better scenery. **Timber Lane** finally spins down toward the river and lets **Bruce** carry you across the stream. **Bruce** starts with a straight downhill shot, but eventually settles into an easy glide that follows the snow-choked river down the valley. **Burt** finishes the job by chasing the river the rest of the way to the touring center.

Beginners may also want to try the **Ranch Camp Trail**, which winds slowly uphill toward the **Trapp Cabin** (six km one way). You can experience both trail systems and find hearty soup and a satisfying vista at the top. The descent may be a little fast, but the trails are wide and smooth.

Wild, rollicking, twisty expert terrain awaits on the outer V: **Double Bit** and **Bear Run**. **Double Bit** starts with a brave climb away from the ravine and toward Mount Mansfield. Although foreshadowing things to come, the trail itself is not unmanageably steep. Off of **Double Bit**, follow **Bear Run** along the remainder of the traverse. At first, the steep uncompromising hills of **Bear Run** threaten to scale Mansfield head-on; later, the trail relaxes into a bumpy traverse, following the contour of the hill. Further along the trail, "Carcass Corner" sounds like a place to take off your skis and walk, but don't let the name scare you. This is where trail crews discovered a bobcat gnawing on the remains of a deer. The valley eventually tightens, pinching **Bear Run** across the stream bumps and dips, but softens into a fabulous, long, floating brookside glide toward **Ranch Camp Trail. Peavey Trail,** a "middle V," resembles **Bear Run,** but without some of the more grueling climbs. **Peavey Trail** takes a lower line up the valley — more appropriate for intermediates, but still including a long stretch of bumpy terrain.

Cross country skiers with a penchant for Alpine may enjoy **Houston** and the **Ranch Camp Trail.** The bumps will try to toss you into the air, and the corners do their best to hurl you against strategically placed trees. These downhills are XXX! **Steeple Trail,** a two-kilometer backcountry cliff, won't let you out alive.

Finding your way: From Exit 10 off of I-89, follow Route 100 north. In the center of Stowe, 9 1/2 miles from the exit, turn left onto Route 108 north. The touring center is on the left, about five miles up the road.

Trapp Family Lodge
Stowe, Vermont   05672
(800) 826-7000, (802) 253-8511

Trail System: 50 km (50 km classical, 45 km skate, 30 km backcountry), plus groomed connections to two other extensive trail systems
Our Estimate: An unbelievably extensive network of trails, although beginners may need to search for easy terrain.
Grooming: Flawless
Scenic Beauty: 5
Touring Center: A small lodge with rentals, lessons, fireplace, snacks, and hot drinks wax bench, some retail, and a large, sunny room for relaxing.
Favorite Trail: The long, smooth, picturesque descent on the Haul Road.
Payment: All major credit cards accepted.
Lodging: Trapp Family Lodge-Trailside (802-253-8511, $$$$-call early for reservations); The Vermont State Ski Dorms-Stowe (802-253-4010, $)
Local's Tip: For a more gradual ascent to the Trapp Cabin, try starting at Stowe Mountain Resort.

The Trapp Family Lodge is a world apart. Every winter, a steady stream of pilgrims climbs to the top of a scenic hill in Stowe to visit the Austrian-style lodge and its heavenly ski trails. The stream is fed by two different sources: those who love skiing and those who love *The Sound of Music.* Neither group is disappointed. Your trail fee grants you entrance to a separate, fanciful realm. Smooth, velvety trails and a fairy tale setting make skiing at Trapp feel like a childhood memory of a Christmas morning.

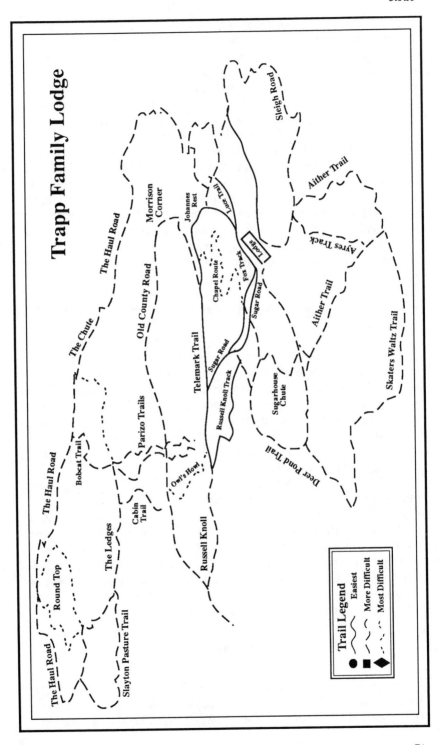

Trapp Family Lodge

Trail Legend
● Easiest
■ More Difficult
◆ Most Difficult

The quality of the skiing at Trapp gives visitors a sense of security. Many other eastern touring centers seem to be either on the brink of financial collapse. Trapp seems to stand apart from all worries. Masterful groomers and meticulous trail crews have removed even the tiniest distractions from the trails. The skiing is luxurious. It's more soothing than guiding a Mercedes on cruise-control over a winding road in the Bavarian Alps. Focus only on the feel of your skis, the serenity of the forest, and the beauty of the nearby Green Mountains.

Some visitors are not at all interested in skiing. They come simply to soak up Trapp family lore: half history and half Hollywood. *The Sound of Music* has stuck to the Trapp family like an obedient shadow. The movie's closing scene shows the family escaping from Hitler's army over the Swiss Alps; afterwards, the Baron and Baroness Von Trapp, along with their nine children and chaplain, found their way to the United States. For nearly twenty years, the family traveled and sang before enraptured audiences throughout the world. When they were ready to settle down, they purchased a hillside farm and built an Austrian-style lodge in the picturesque little town of Stowe. Today, Johannes, one of the original nine children, continues to operate the family business.

The Nordic trails at Trapp were, of course, the brainchild of a Northern European. Norwegian Per Sorlie began leading guests on cross country ski tours along logging roads while working in the lodge at night. Soon, a cross country center sprouted out of an old stable and the Trapps invested in several pairs of wooden skis. In 1971, a log cabin was dragged up the back side of Round Top and set on a small knoll as a destination for skiers. With a comfortable lodge, picturesque trails, and a trail-side cabin, Trapp quickly evolved into one of the premier cross country resorts in the world.

All ski areas want to boast an even distribution of beginner, intermediate, and expert trails. Some design a good mix into their system from the start, while others try to achieve the mix artificially, *ex post facto*, with the help of green, blue, and black pens. Although Trapp seems to indulge in a little of the latter, it does do a good job of massaging its trails for easy use by beginners. There are no flat trails at Trapp, but by using the science of trail maintenance and the magic of grooming, Trapp alchemists have converted a truly challenging hillside into a system accessible to most novices.

The Trails

Beginners can start by wandering comfortably up and down **Sugar Road** and **Russel Knoll**. These wide, easy trails climb gently away from the lodge and up the forested hillside. A return via **Telemark** adds some downhill spice on a trail that should be labeled intermediate. **Sugar Road** passes by the cellar hole of the original farmhouse. Robert Frost's "The Birthplace," a favorite poem of Johannes von Trapp, is inscribed on a small plaque next to the hole. Across the road, the top part of the **Sleigh Road** provides additional easy terrain, although it may be a little too exposed on windy days, and some may balk at skiing through timeshare front yards.

Sooner or later, you'll want to attempt the five kilometer climb to the cabin. Beginner or expert, the warm soups and pretty views will lure you up the mountainside. After resting and soaking in some sun on **Picnic Knoll**, start up the narrow, sinuous **Owl's Howl** toward the **Cabin Trail**. Neither trail is at all shy about climbing! Be prepared for a nasty brew of herring-bones and curses. (If you don't enjoy the thought of climbing steeply for several kilometers, Stowe Mountain Touring Center provides a much easier approach from the opposite side of the mountain.) The reward is a sunny final approach along a stately avenue of white birches, and a warm cabin with plenty to eat. The **Haul Road** provides a much easier and more scenic descent than the **Parizo Trails**. It swings around the back side of **Round Top**, providing views of Smuggler's Notch, Mount Mansfield, and the Alpine trails at Stowe. After a long, fairly gradual descent, the **Lower Haul Road** crosses a few fields and guides you into the woods before returning to the lodge.

Strong skiers should try their luck on the hairpins of **Bobcat** and **Oslo**. Both climb briefly from the top of the **Parizo Trails**, then drop into a high-speed Super GS on the way to the **Haul Road**. The kilometer-hungry can easily access the Topnotch and Stowe Mountain trail systems from the **Haul Road**. Your Trapp trail pass will let you ski (but not drive) to the other cross country centers.

The lower section of the trail system, located across the road from the lodge, provides good intermediate skiing, but it lacks the remote, wilderness feeling of the higher elevations. It also has less consistent snow cover. The **Skater's Waltz** is a popular trail that crosses several meadows before rolling through the forest toward a final, long ascent. **Sleigh Ride** provides freedom from the forest as it scoots across the top of a long, slanting field. After dropping into the woods, it rambles back the way it came, finishing with a steep climb across a meadow.

Finding your way: From Exit 10 on I-89, follow 100 north seven miles. Turn left onto Moscow Road (before the center of Stowe, there will be a sign for Trapp). After 1 1/2 miles, turn right onto Barrows Road. After another 1 1/2 miles, you'll come to a stop sign. Turn left. One mile later, bear left onto Trapp Hill Road. The ski center is just beyond the Trapp Family Lodge, one mile up the road on your right.

Ole's Cross Country Center

Sugarbush Airport
Warren, Vermont 05674
(802) 496-3430

Trail System: 48 km groomed (38 km classical, 10 km skate, and 12 km backcountry)
Our Personal Estimate: A loose network of medium-length trails with several long loops.
Grooming: Good
Scenic Beauty: 5
Touring Center: Rentals, lessons, food, some retail
Favorite Trail: Holly Kings Trail, a graceful meadowy run with beautiful mountain views
Payment: Cash and personal checks
Lodging: The Inn at the Round Barn-Waitsfield (802-496-2276, $$$-$$$$); Mad River Barn-Waitsfield (802-496-3310, $$-$$$)
Local's Tip: To see where gourmet meets hippie, stop in at the Warren Store in the center of town. They boast a renowned deli, the feel of an old-fashioned country store, and exhibits by local artists on the walls.

In most respects, Ole's Cross Country Center is what you imagine when you close your eyes and let a Nordic ski center form in your mind. Nestled in the Green Mountains, it offers astounding views of the surrounding Alpine region. Single-tracked, classical trails pass through gaps in farm fences, linking maple-lined meadows. A friendly and personable Norwegian host greets you at the door. But Ole's Cross Country Center has one odd twist: it's run out of an airport.

The Warren Airport is a tiny summertime operation, home to Sugarbush Soaring and a half a dozen gliders. This is no O'Hare or JFK. There is no radio controller, no flight attendant, and no pavement. The grass on the flat landing field is closely cropped in summer; when covered with snow, this unnaturally flat and white expanse feels like a cake platter in the midst of the mountains. On the periphery, a tall and skinny control tower sticks up like an awkward blue candle. The touring center runs out of this building.

Inside, the place feels like a fairy castle, four stories high. The rental shop lurks in the dark dungeony basement. Ole rents skis in all shapes and sizes, from the newest Salomon bindings to three-pin woodies for nostalgic sentimentalists. The main floor is a sociable receiving room where you can buy your ticket. Up one flight you'll find Café Ole, which is nothing more than a counter well-stocked with soup, bread, fruit, cookies, and twenty kinds of herb tea. The top flight is painted in summertime blue and stocked with garden furniture. Here you can eat,

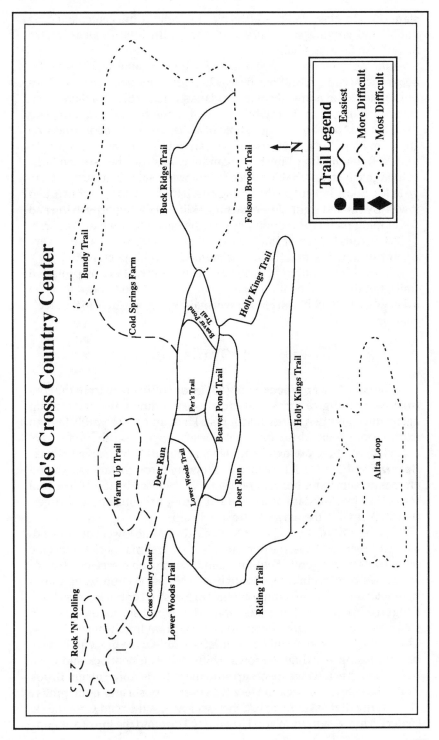

stare out the glass walls, and relax. Throughout the center building you'll find smiling snapshots, captioned with little in-jokes, of the Sugarbush Soaring Club.

Ole Mosesen grew up skiing and salmon fishing in Norway, far above the Arctic Circle. When he was 25 years of age he came to America but left his skis at home since Norwegians scoffed at the idea there could be good skiing here. That winter he sent home a plea, "Send my skis over," and a New York Times photo of a blizzard as proof of American snow. In New York, he worked as a carpenter and started a ski shop with a free-wheeling bunch of Scandinavians; on the weekends he helped coach area club skiers. One fateful weekend he was supposed to go to Mt. Snow but got on the wrong bus. It took him to Sugarbush, and it was love at first sight. After teaching skiing at the Sugarbush Inn and developing their cross country system, he began his own operation in 1977. Ole runs the center as a one-man show — seven days a week, sun-up to sun-down — and the area is imbued with his personality.

A word of warning: Ole's can be fiercely windy. There are protected trails, but the most beautiful skiing is in the open. Don't head there on a day when windchill and bluster will make you insensitive to the area's charms.

The Trails

The easy **Lower Woods Trail** (#2) leads softly away from the control tower through a series of gradually descending trails, and then up again through open hardwood forest. Here and there you'll find an extra loop, groomed for fun, that doesn't appear on the map. Like everywhere, there are excellent views of Sugarbush's Alpine slopes. **Beaver Pond Trail** (#8) takes a little alleyway through dark woods and crosses an enormous beaver pond entirely enclosed by forest. The trail traces the long, low dam, and meanders through the stumps of old trees, that stick up like the masts of drowned ships.

The beautiful, pastoral **Deer Run** (#5) drops into lower pastureland, along a stream and past the pond that feeds it. It climbs back to meet the other trails with a gentle field-long climb which you scarcely notice for the views of surrounding mountains. The last section leads into a kilometer and a half of bumpy evergreen forest. Deer tracks cross **Buck Ridge** (#7) with shocking abandon. This wood-shrouded trail is a sheltered ski along a mounded ridge, while a ravine shears off below. The bumpy trail moves under your feet — unlike the graceful lines of pasture skiing — while the forest shifts between hemlock and open hardwood. **Buck Ridge** meets up with the experts-only **Folsom Brook Trail**; the connector back to **Deer Run** is an easy ski and quite pretty.

Intermediate skiers can test their wax across the road from the ski center on the meadowy **Warm Up Trail** (#1) around the top of a sloping hill. The two kilometer trail loops through and past clumps of sugar maples; the view of mountains and farms is spectacular. The ten kilometer **Holly Kings Trail** (#4) is a scenic tour with some stunning views of Sugarbush and some narrow woodsy interludes. The trail skims down long pastures, always heading towards the lovely northern pathway of the Mad River Valley.

Experts are in luck. Ole has something to test your mettle. The nine kilometer **Alta Loop** (#11) starts with a steep climb up a thin forest road, dips into an exciting downhill, then rises nearly to the summit of Burnt Mountain. At the top you'll ski over **Stengmark's Pass**, whose giant slalom-like curves were inspired by the great Alpine skier. The **Folsom Brook Trail** (#6) is the most difficult trail on the system. There used to be a sign at the beginning saying "No telephone, no services for the next four miles." The trail drops steeply along a giant downhill for two kilometers, then follows the brook to the Bundy Art Gallery, where it turns upward for a kilometer of climb. Both of these trails are groomed less often than the others.

Finding your way: Take I-89 to Exit 9 in Middlesex. Follow Route 100B south to where it joins with Route 100; follow Route 100 south to Warren; turn left off the state highway towards the town of Warren. At the beginning of town, turn left onto Brook Road and follow the signs to Ole's.

Catamount Family Center

421 Governor Chittenden Road
Williston, Vermont 05495
(802) 879-6001

Trail System: *35 km. (30 km. classical, 30 km skate, 5 km backcountry), 4 km night skiing*
Our Personal Estimate: *A relatively easy system with a few good thrillers.*
Grooming: *Very good on weekends; spotty during the week*
Scenic Beauty: *4*
Touring Center: *Rentals, lessons, hot drinks and snacks, wax benches, some retail, change rooms, couches*
Favorite Trail: *Skidway, a rushing descent that tries to sweep you off your feet*
Payment: *DSC, MC, and VISA*
Lodging: *Homeplace-Jericho (802-899-4694, $$); Susse Chalet-Williston (800-858-5008, $$)*
Local's Tip: *The Catamount Family Center hosts Saturday Night Live, a popular on-ice party at their hockey rink. From 7 to 10 p.m. on Saturday nights, you can get skating, music, pizza and hot chocolate for $5.*

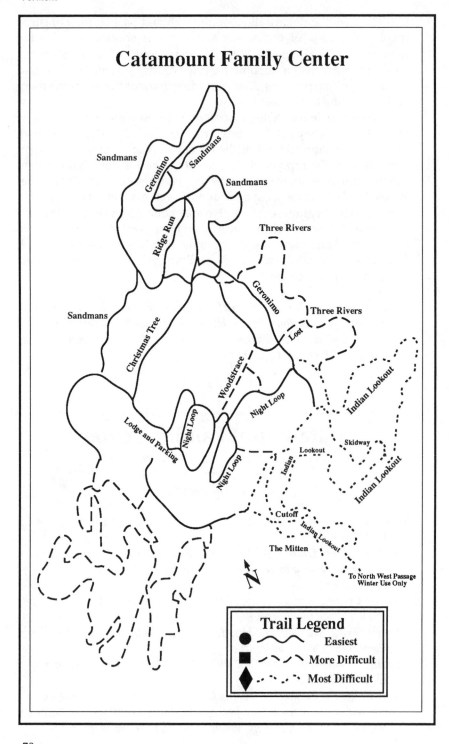

Catamount Family Center

Sandmans

Geronimo

Sandmans

Sandmans

Ridge Run

Three Rivers

Geronimo

Sandmans

Three Rivers

Christmas Tree

Lost

Woodstrace

Indian Lookout

Night Loop

Night Loop

Lodge and Parking

Night Loop

Indian Lookout

Skidway

Indian Lookout

Indian Lookout

Indian Lookout

Cutoff

The Mitten

To North West Passage
Winter Use Only

N

Trail Legend

● ～～～ Easiest

■ ⌒⌒⌒ More Difficult

◆ ⋯⋯⋯ Most Difficult

Just beyond the pale of Williston's condominium outreach, the unpaved Governor Chittenden road rises a half mile over broad farmland to the Catamount Family Center. Here you will find excellent skiing only an easy lope from Burlington. Right on the Catamount trail system the wide flat land of the Champlain Valley meets the foothills of the Green Mountains. The trails take full advantage of this geographical fortuity, and there is something for everyone.

Catamount is driven by a love of sport: skiing, skating, snowshoeing, hiking, mountain biking, you name it. Burlington area racers frequent the trails in snazzy outfits. Dogs and little kids frolic in the snow. An abundance of clinics and special events make for a lively place — a speed skating clinic, a seniors' ski and snowshoe clinic, a kids adventure tour, a women-only clinic, corporate night, and an evening restaurant tour (café discount included). And that's all in one week!

The McCullough family, which has owned the land for six generations, once ran it as a dairy farm; now their farming operations have diversified to include a Christmas tree farm, managed woodlots, a little haying, and an organic garden. Trails traipse through all of these operations. From the top of the property you can see striking views of Mount Mansfield, Camel's Hump, and the Adirondacks. The scenery is more pastoral than dramatic — white fields, yellowed summer grasses, and blue hills recede into the distance. It doesn't require a clear day to find Catamount beautiful.

At the top of the trail system you can look down into the Winooski River valley, which was a critical transportation artery for Native Americans and early settlers of the area. Thomas Chittenden, after whom the Governor Chittenden road is named, brought his family to Williston in 1763 as part of an early wave of settlement. Chittenden was the first governor of Vermont and, momentarily, during the state's brief period as an independent republic, the President. He generously built houses for each of his eight sons, some of which are still standing — the old farmhouse which is now home to the touring center and the family homestead that was built for his son Giles in 1796.

Once inside the touring center, this past is easy to imagine. Resting in a low-ceilinged ell off the main house, the center's exposed beams, creaky old-fashioned benches, and broad floorboards lend the visual flavor of well-worn wood. Tacked to the historic walls, skiing posters jostle layers of modern sporting equipment for elbow room. You can rent skis, skates, or snowshoes.

Upstairs, secondhand couches sprawl in front of the heater, and a table of hot drinks and snacks operates on the honor system. The little W.C. out back is usually cold but clean.

The Trails

Most of Catamount's trails were logging roads at one time, but they have been re-routed to take full advantage of the scenery and geography. This work is ingenious. By making one-way downhills and tracking cleverly with the topography, Catamount has created mountains out of a molehill.

The easier trails lie in evergreen lowlands which slope down from the parking lot. **Sandman's** is a winding, meandering trail through giant hemlocks too big and old to hug. The trail is particularly popular on days when the wind scours the open fields bare of skiers. You can hear the rush of air in the trees above, but the trail is perfectly protected from its gusts. The mild mannered **Night Loop** is "gently rolling" at its most aggressive, but avoids boredom with curious twists and turns. This snow is worked to a drubbing by avid Burlington skiers.

Intermediate trails crisscross the beginner trails in the woods. **Geronimo** has some quick dips and more challenging downhills, and **Three Rivers** is a steady gentle climb to get your rhythms moving. Across the road above the touring center, a host of nameless trails weave through open rolling fields and into the woods. This is where to seek out scenery.

The easternmost section of Catamount's land rises and drops steeply, and that's where advanced skiers should head for thrills. The one-way **Indian Lookout** trail makes screaming use of the side of the mountain. It drops precipitously, then cuts switchbacks up the powerlines to the height of the land, and skis along the ridge through a deciduous forest. The spectacular Indian Lookout vista peers out over the ridged cornfields and the confluence of rivers below. In the early days of Vermont's white settlement, Native Americans came here to monitor the river traffic.

The exciting **Skidway** will have your heart in your throat. The ground drops off and the trees close in to form a natural slalom course as tight and technical as any artificial one. Fast and furious stepturns will get you through. **Northwest Passage** is a wilderness trail as rugged as its name — it drops narrowly through ravines, and in one particularly confidence-shaking section you ski downhill while the ground falls away on both sides. Be sure to let them know in the touring center if you plan to ski this trail.

Finding your way: Take I-89 north to the Williston exit; head north on Route 2A to the second traffic signal. Turn right and drive 3.5 miles. Then follow the signs to the Catamount Family Center.

Prospect Mountain Cross Country Ski Touring Center

Route 9
Woodford, Vermont 05201
(802) 442-2575

Trail System: *30 km (30 km classical, 30 km skate, backcountry tours only)*
Our Estimate: *A small well-groomed network for beginners and intermediates, with two medium-length expert trails that lead away from the commotion.*
Grooming: *Excellent on the main trails, good on others.*
Scenic Beauty: *3*
Touring Center: *An old Alpine lodge with rentals, lessons, fireplace, cafeteria, waxing room, and plenty of black-and-white photos from old times.*
Favorite Trail: *Whistle Pig, which provides a great chance to stretch out the stride and glide along on gradual downhills*
Payment: *All major credit cards accepted.*
Lodging: *Molly Stark Inn-Bennington (802-442-9631, $$-$$$); Darling Kelly's Motel-Bennington (802-442-2322, $$)*
Local's Tip: *Inquire about the moonlight dinner and ski tours: dinner in the base lodge restaurant, then ski out to the pond and rouse the beavers with a bonfire.*

How refreshing it is to watch a cross country ski area thrive after sinking its roots into the decaying remains of an Alpine mountain! Prospect's cross country trails teem with visitors on sunny winter weekends, twirling their tendrils up and around the vacant downhill trails and underneath the quiet cables of the old t-bar. Nordic skiers joyfully overrun the comfortable base lodge, large rental building, restaurant, and other made-for-Alpine amenities. Telemark skiers delight in the wide-open terrain, as do snowboarders and sledders. As manager Steve Whitham says, "People love to play with gravity...they'll climb up and slide down until they're too tired to do it anymore."

Prospect began as a downhill area in the 1940s. Its t-bars and ropetows pulled decades of skiers to the top of the mountain. In 1980, the first cross country trails were cut, and for 12 years Alpine and Nordic skiers coexisted quite comfortably. In 1992, a snow drought and a few bad business decisions convinced Prospect's owner to find the quickest, quietest route away from Woodford and the local banks. After some serious negotiation with the banks, Steve Whitham—who had managed the cross country side of the business for years—succeeded in purchasing the entire ski area. Ever since then, cross country skiing has reigned supreme at Prospect Mountain.

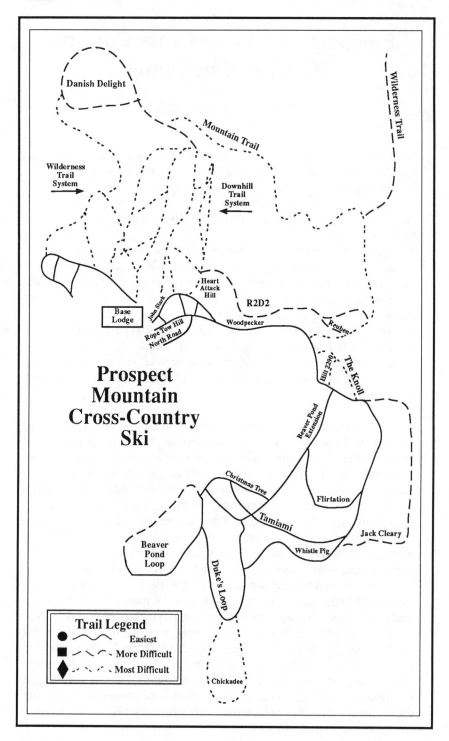

Danish Delight

Mountain Trail

Wilderness Trail

Wilderness Trail System

Downhill Trail System

Heart Attack Hill

R2D2

Base Lodge

John Stark

Rope Tow Hill North Road

Woodpecker

Reuben

Prospect Mountain Cross-Country Ski

Hill 2290'

The Knoll

Beaver Pond Extension

Christmas Tree

Flirtation

Tamiami

Beaver Pond Loop

Jack Cleary

Whistle Pig

Duke's Loop

Trail Legend

● ⌇ Easiest

■ ⌇ More Difficult

◆ ⌇ Most Difficult

Chickadee

Don't think for a moment that the trails simply wind in and out of subtly-disguised Alpine slopes! Prospect's cross country network was developed long before the demise of the downhill area, and the trails were designed to quickly escape the base area melée. When Steve was sculpting the trails, he commanded a well-trained contingent of heavy machinery that succeeded in kneading uneven terrain into wide, smooth trails with good drainage. As a result, the majority of Prospect's trails are friendly beginner/intermediate loops. However, the fact that the highly-regarded Williams College Ski Team trains at Prospect indicates that there is plenty of challenging terrain to choose from as well.

Resting 2250 feet above sea level on a high plateau in southern Vermont, the mountain is a chronic, greedy, insatiable collector of snow. When ski areas farther north can only shrug their shoulders, shovel, and pray, droves of skiers coax their cars up the steep hills of Route 9 toward Prospect Mountain to play in the early snow. Prospect's widespread reputation for snow has created distorted business cycles: when New England suffers through dry spells, Prospect thrives; when snow is plentiful in other areas, Prospect suffers.

Beginners love Prospect for its smooth, wide trails. Skaters love Prospect for the chance to spread their tips without any track-tromping guilt. Athletes love Prospect for its formidable, Alpine climbs and early season skiing. The only complaints about this touring center might come from managers of competing ski areas.

The Trails

The heart of the trail system is about a kilometer away from the lodge via **Woodpecker**, a double-tracked *and* skate-groomed easy rider. For a fun, low-key loop, head out on **Whistle Pig** and **Duke's Loop**, then return via **Christmas Tree** and the **Beaver Pond Extension**. Whistle Pig winds luxuriously through mixed forest, providing gradual downhill stretches for easy cruising: gravity's subtle boost will make you feel like an Olympian! **Duke's Loop** swings past a lookout that juts out over the rest of the high, forested plateau, then **Christmas Tree** takes you on a short, dreamy holiday tour through mid-sized spruces and firs.

Off of **Whistle Pig**, the zesty **Chickadee** climbs a short, steep hill (a favorite vantage point for coaches during college races). A clear-cut area to the left allows the sun to bathe the trail in a soft, warm light. After cresting the hill, **Chickadee** swings around a hardwood hilltop, allowing 360 degrees of low mountains to swing slowly in and out of view. A wide, racy downhill then drops you back onto **Duke's Loop**.

Those willing to suffer through a quick, steep ascent can climb **R2D2** to a hillside terrace with elegant maples, yellow birches, and fine views down the mountainside. A screaming downhill run at the end terrorizes the Alpine slope, scaring away beginners and intermediates.

The longer, more roughly-hewn **Mountain Trail** wrestles with the backside of the Alpine mountain in isolated hardwoods that push up against the George D. Aiken Wilderness Area. It begins with several kilometers of climbing and ends with either a steep Alpine drop (if groomed) or the tricky, winding hill that you just climbed.

Finding your way: Take exit 2 off of I-91 and follow Route 9 west. Continue for 31 miles, and Prospect Mountain will be on your left, 7/10 mile past the Peter Pan Motel. From Bennington, follow Route 9 east several miles uphill. Prospect Mountain will be on your right.

Woodstock Ski Touring Center
Route 106
Woodstock, Vermont   05091
(802) 457-6674

Trail System: 61 km groomed (50 km classical, 20 km skate)
Our Personal Estimate: The two trail systems have totally different terrain: one is mild and scenic, the other excitingly mountainous. Between them you can find whatever you're looking for.
Grooming: Excellent
Scenic Beauty: 4
Touring Center: Rentals, lessons, restaurant, full retail shop, locker rooms
Favorite Trail: Trail of the Fallen Women, a sharply sloping mountainside trail crossing a series of small ravines.
Payment: All major credit cards
Lodging: Kedron Valley Inn-South Woodstock (800-457-1473, $$$-$$$$); Winslow House-Woodstock (802-457-1820, $$-$$$)
Local's Tip: With your day pass for skiing, you get a half-price entry to the sauna, Jacuzzi, swimming pool, and other athletic amenities at the Woodstock Inn's Sports Center.

If none of the towns in Vermont matches up to your idea of what a Vermont town should be, come to Woodstock. With Yankee cunning and an ocean of white paint, Woodstock has made itself the living emblem of the legend. You can buy maple syrup, cheddar cheese, and Ben and Jerry's; you can stay in a fleet of gracious inns; you can snap photos of olde-tyme New England. Best of all, you can gracefully kick and glide over an outstanding cross country trail system.

The town has a claim on skiing. A Woodstock dairy farm was the site of the first rope tow in 1934. You can see the site of that jerry-rigged

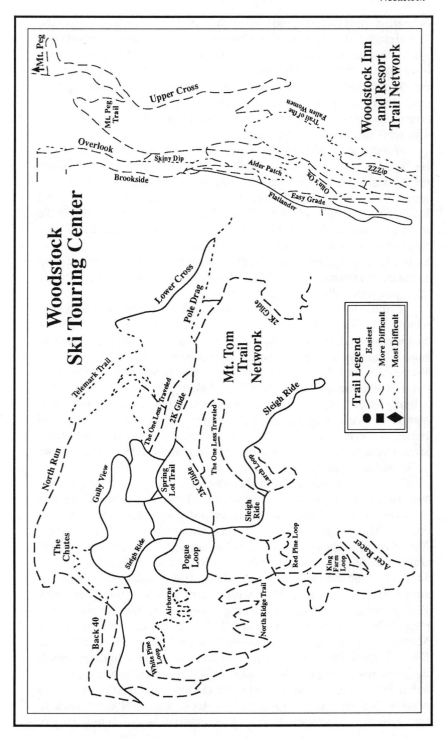

operation from the wide and well-maintained cross country trails of the Woodstock Ski Touring Center. The center is, as you would expect from the town, classy and well-kept. It is not snobby—Nordic skiing doesn't lend itself to that — but it is luxurious. The locker rooms boast carpet, full-length mirrors, and showers. The full-service restaurant caters to your every culinary desire. And the retail shop is nothing if not complete: you could walk in wearing nothing but your birthday suit and walk out in full skiing armor.

Woodstock's two trail systems were unfortunately switched at birth. If Lady Luck were reasonable, she would have put the milder terrain next to the touring center and the golf course, and the expert terrain at the other site. She didn't. The golf course is set in a long and lovely river valley, with terrain as civilized as human hands can make it. But the wooded Mount Peg rises in a steep and rugged wall that defies even the most inventive trail designer to carve easy trails from its slopes. Curvy, squirrelly narrow byways crisscross each other and cling to the side of the mountain. If downhills and challenging terrain titillate you, you'll be rolling in hog heaven.

You'll find easier, more pastoral skiing less than two miles away at Mount Tom. This former estate will someday be Vermont's first national historic park. The lovely old carriage roads were constructed purely to take advantage of scenic touring, and they succeeded. The views of Woodstock and the surrounding hills are vintage Vermont. The trails run through managed woodlands, and skiing them carries you under a bouquet of trees: inconceivably tall red pines; thickly interwoven stands of Norway spruce, so tightly grown that little snow can fall between them; graceful, hillside sugar maples; and purple-barked, straight-backed larch. If you don't know much about trees, Mount Tom will certainly spark your curiosity.

The Marsh-Billings National Historic Park will be dedicated to the historical interpretation of conservation. The land was once the estate of George Perkins Marsh, the man generally regarded as the father of conservation. While wandering about these very woods and fields, Marsh came to the conclusion that human activity has the capacity to transform the environment in which we live. *Man and Nature,* written by Marsh in 1864, advances this hypothesis and is today considered the first environmental text. Meanwhile, there was the young Frederick Billings, who was a pauper boy living in town under the stern rule of the sheriff. One can only imagine how he felt, year after year, walking by the Marsh estate and gazing enviously at it and all that it represented. Billings worked his way through school and went West, finding himself in California during the Gold Rush of 1849; he started the first law firm in San Francisco, and made a fortune in claims litigation off contentious miners. But he did not forget Woodstock, and later came back to purchase the old Marsh property. It is remarkable that in the litany of his successes, Billings considered the design and construction of the Mount Tom carriage roads to be one of his greatest accomplishments.

Mount Peg Trails

The flattest of the beginner trails is **Flatlander**, a pleasant trail that winds along the golf course by the side of the brook. Ten kilometers of tracks crisscross the golf course. **Flatlander** is an unflattering epithet Vermonters use to describe out-of-staters; it is also an unerring description of this trail. You could find more hills on a lake.

The **Mount Peg Trail** is a steady, unremitting climb to an ideal picnic spot. The trail switches back and forth across the mountain through mixed forest for 2.5 kilometers. Just when you think you've reached the top there is a disconcerting drop and the trail runs out onto a spectacular meadow, where the surrounding world opens up into a lovely 180° panorama. **ZZZip** is a zany hillside trail in the dark heart of the woods. It careens over outrageous ups and downs; only its long, manageable runouts keep it from being labeled expert.

Who wouldn't love the **Trail of the Fallen Women** simply because of its name? Lots of people. Irate feminists of both sexes have come in demanding an explanation. The story is that a Woodstock resident used to ski a Trail of the Fallen Women in Canada; she suggested it for an expert route during the touring center's trail-naming days. Despite the ruckus, this trail is great expert skiing. It dips and rises over a hillside of gullies where narrow bridges cross mountain streams; at the farthest extreme, a flying hairpin turn careens downhill.

Mount Tom Trails

Beginners who actually want to feel as though they are going somewhere can ski up the wide, double-tracked **Sleigh Ride**. This former carriage road rises gently up the mountain, passing through old growth forest and over a remarkable stone causeway draped in hemlock, which looks like something out of Celtic mythology. The roundabout at the top of the mountain offers wonderful panoramic views of Woodstock below and the mountain pastures beyond.

Acer Racer is named for the great hulking sugar maples along the trail (Acer is the species' Latin tag). It starts with a quick-moving section of downhill curves, then climbs upward through a solemn stand of red pines. Hundreds of the straight-trunked trees were planted after the hurricane of 1938, and skiing through them is a gloriously aesthetic experience. The trail crosses the base of a mountain meadow, ducks shortly into the woods, and emerges at the top with a lovely view of Woodstock's softly rolling hills.

Telemark slings back and forth across an old Alpine slope, taking hard corners over a lumpy, bumpy meadow. The trail is tracked wide, leaving plenty of room for maneuvering, or you can forgo the tracks altogether and strike out down the hill.

Finding your way: From the junction of I-89 and I-91 in White River Junction, take Route 4 west to Woodstock. In town, follow the signs for Route 106 south. The ski touring center is less than a mile out of town.

New Hampshire

Bretton Woods
Cross Country Ski Area

Mount Washington Resort
Bretton Woods, New Hampshire   03575
(800) 232-2972, (603) 278-5181

Trail System: *88 km groomed (88 km classical, 84 km skate and 2 km backcountry)*
Our Personal Estimate: *Enough trails to get lost.*
Grooming: *Excellent*
Scenic Beauty: *5*
Touring Center: *Rentals, lessons, wax benches, cafeteria, brown bag area, some retail*
Favorite Trail: *Nancy Barton, which jiggles and jogs along the river.*
Payment: *All major credit cards*
Lodging: *Bretton Woods Motor Inn-Bretton Woods (800-258-0330, 603-278-1000, $$-$$$); Above the Notch Motor Inn (603) 846-5156, $-$$)*
Local's Tip: *Skiers can stay for free in the mountain cabin at the top of the Ammonoosuc Spring Trail. The small cabin has two bunks and can fit up to four people who are very good friends. It contains a wood stove, firewood, pots and pans, candles and an oil lamp (bring your own oil). The trail is narrow, steep backcountry skiing and rated most difficult. By reservation only through Bretton Woods Cross Country Ski Area.*

Rising above Crawford Notch in the White Mountains of New Hampshire, Bretton Woods packs potent punches of scenery and skiing. The shining white Mount Washington Hotel appears like a celestial vision, its red-capped roofs standing out against snowy white fields and tongues of green trees. Above and beyond the hotel, and against the backdrop of deep blue skies, rise the imposing white heights of Mount Washington. Gentle, manicured trails crisscross the open fields of the golf course, while more challenging terrain climbs up the wooded sides of the surrounding mountains.

The Mount Washington Hotel is the culmination of a legacy of grand and grander hotels in Crawford Notch. Built in 1902 by a railroad tycoon, it passed to his widow, who turned herself into a princess through an advantageous marriage to French royalty. During the early part of the century, up to 57 trains a day chugged up to Crawford Notch, filled with fashionable representatives from all the best families. In 1944, the hotel hosted the famous Bretton Woods International Monetary Conference, where financiers from 44 countries met to stabilize the world currency rate and prevent international collapse after World

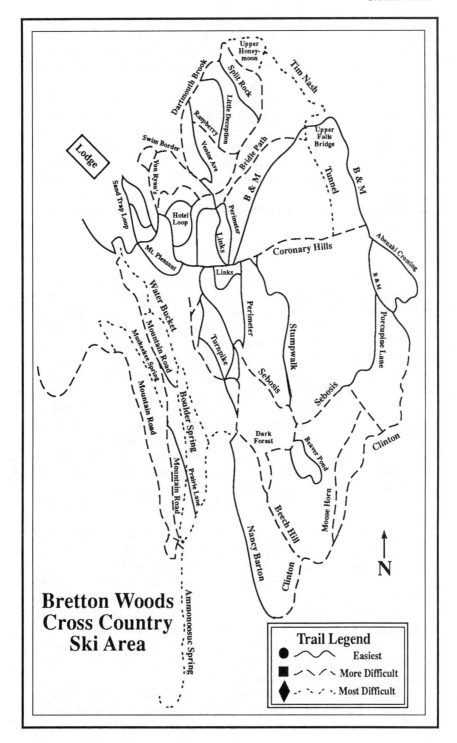

**Bretton Woods
Cross Country
Ski Area**

N

Trail Legend

● 〰 Easiest
■ ⌇⌇ More Difficult
◆ ⋯⋯ Most Difficult

War II. Although the Mount Washington Hotel still opens her doors to summer guests, she stands proud, yet empty, through the winter. Never mind that her historic moment has passed. Never mind that her paint is peeling. The Mount Washington Hotel lives on like a grande dame conscious of her faded glory.

You can deduce the area's geological history from the shape of the Notch and the glacial erratics along the trail system. During the Ice Age, glaciers crawled down from the north, plucking boulders from the sides of the mountains and carrying them along with the ice. The Bretton Woods area was a giant bathtub of ice with Crawford Notch as the plug. As the earth warmed, the force of the meltwater converted the notch into a giant spillway, and the water ran south along the present path of Route 302. Boulders left behind by the melting ice now line the ski trails.

The Trails

Three major trail systems spin out from the well-stocked and fully-staffed touring center and the scenic golf course area. The **Ammoonusuc Trail System** extends into the basin below Mount Washington and makes up just over half of the total kilometers at Bretton Woods. These trails are largely easy and intermediate and meander through wooded hillside territory. Protected by trees, they are a good place to ski on a windy day but offer few glimpses of the hotel and mountains. The smaller and less populated **Deception Trail System** extends over rolling terrain to the nether regions of Deception Mountain, affording good intermediate skiing. Its southern exposure means that its trails open later in the season. This is the best place to find bobcat, deer, coyote, rabbit, and other wildlife tracks. The bulk of the more challenging terrain lies along the **Stickney Trail System**, traversing the side of the Alpine mountain. The topography rises steeply. Here expert trails throw you madcap downhills and occasional scenic vistas through the trees.

If your eyes are bigger than your legs are strong, set off on any one of the open trails near the Mount Washington Hotel. The **Perimeter Trail**, the **Hotel Loop**, and **Mount Pleasant** all meander gently through the knolly, rolling golf course and offer stunning views. There are enough kilometers here to keep you entertained for a while. If the open areas are windy, head for the **B&M trail**, an abandoned railroad bed. The B&M trail is good for Zen meditation or pretending you are on a Nordic Track exercise machine looking at a pretty poster of New Hampshire forests. The evergreens that line the trail bow overhead with heavy snows and turn it into an endless tunnel.

Nancy Barton is a playful trail for advanced beginners which humps and bumps along the low riverbed. The trail is named for an indentured servant girl at Crawford House who was engaged to marry the stable boy. One snowy night she awoke to discover that her fiancé had disappeared with her savings. She charged out into the storm to find him, and followed his trail to where he had camped by the river. She found the ashes of his fire still glowing, but the river had soaked her clothing and the cold air froze it. Nancy Barton died of hypothermia wandering down the Notch following her lover's path.

The intermediate **Mountain Road** is one of the most popular trails at Bretton Woods. A free shuttle takes you to the bottom of the Alpine area, where for $5 you can ride the chairlift to the top. You can see the whole Presidential mountain range and eat in style at the panoramic Top o' Quad restaurant. The trail itself crosses the downhill trails (Watch out!) and enters the White Mountain National Forest for a steady five mile descent. A few hardy souls ski up.

Closer to home, **Sebosis** and **Dark Forest** are white ribbony trails that waft upward through dense evergreen growth. The quick-changing terrain vibrates under your skis for good intermediate skiing. Take a quick detour through the one kilometer **Beaver Pond Bypass** which loops through a series of small ponds. Farther up on Clinton Mountain, **Moosehorn** has recently suffered through an unfortunate bout of intense logging. The high, traversing trail once was a happy hunting ground for evidence of moose; now the animals have fled and the trail plows right through the unsightly roughage of stumps and branches left in the wake of a clearcut. The silver lining: **Moosehorn** strings together a series of open areas, and you can piece together a nearly 360° view. This is unusual for the more difficult trails at Bretton Woods, which tend to be enclosed by trees.

If it is a workout you want, **Tim Nash** provides the steepest uphill. The two feeder trails are skied one-way only, with good reason. Tim Nash also boasts a beautiful view of the Notch and ski area, and a thrilling downhill run through open hardwood forest. The trail is named for the first white man to hike through Crawford Notch; his discovery led to a much faster trade route through the White Mountains in the early days of New Hampshire's settlement.

For advanced skiers, **Waterbucket** is a rollicking traverse of Stickney Mountain, named for its leaky springs. Hundreds of rivulets run down the bouldery hillside, and make it tough going in early winter or late spring. The out-and-back **Ammonoosuc Spring** climbs to 2600 hundred feet on a narrow, backcountry trail. Hardy skiers will find the mountain cabin at the top, as well as excellent glade skiing through the open forest.

Finding your way: Take I-93 north to Exit 35 for Route 3 north. At the town of Twin Mountain, take Route 302 east for six miles to Bretton Woods.

The Balsams Wilderness

The Balsams Grand Resort Hotel
Dixville Notch, New Hampshire   03576
(603) 255-3400 — extension: 2543

Trail System: 60 km groomed (60 km classical, 60 km skate, and
16 km backcountry)
Our Personal Estimate: Largely intermediate trails, although the system is
designed so that beginners can ski out to the most scenic spots.
Grooming: Excellent. Not a snowflake out of place.
Scenic Beauty: 5
Touring Center: In the main lobby of hotel. Rentals, lessons, wax bench, some
retail. Meals elsewhere in hotel.
Favorite Trail: The Canal Trail, which winds along an old canal bed under the
cover of protective evergreens.
Payment: All major credit cards except DC
Lodging: The Balsams-Trailside (800-255-0600 except N.H., 800-255-0800
in N.H., $$$$); Errol Motel-Errol (603-482-3256, $$)
Local's Tip: This resort is *not* for those with a tight budget, but if you call in
March during the middle of the week, they may be willing to fill rooms at
less than the listed price.

Way up north in New Hampshire, further from civilization than it
has any right to be, the Balsams Hotel roosts in the craggy, Gothic
Dixville Notch. There are many excellent reasons to ski the Balsams —
plentiful snow, the dramatic notch, the wide smooth trails — but you
will remember it primarily as an aesthetic experience. The Balsams is
one of the last Grand Old Hotels in New Hampshire, and its glorious
existence will make you mourn the passing of the others.

If you want picturesque skiing, look no farther. The Balsams has a
abundance of woodsy trails and relatively few skiers, so skiing is an
isolated experience. With the secluded setting and beautiful trails,
you'll feel as though you could ski onto the cover of a travel brochure.
Signboards nailed to trees tell natural history tales of local flora and
fauna. Animal tracks skitter obligingly across the trails. But bring a
windbreaker and extra warm clothes, since the Notch collects wind and
snow coming from the Northwest. It can be cold.

The touring center consists of a little rotunda in the main lobby of
the hotel. The staff cannot be too helpful. Sit at one of the little garden
tables with a view of the Notch, and they will wax your skis, make trail
recommendations, and everything but spoon feed you. There is a
workbench and iron, but this is not the place to do a ski tuning overhaul:
that's quality carpet underneath your feet. In addition to skis, the

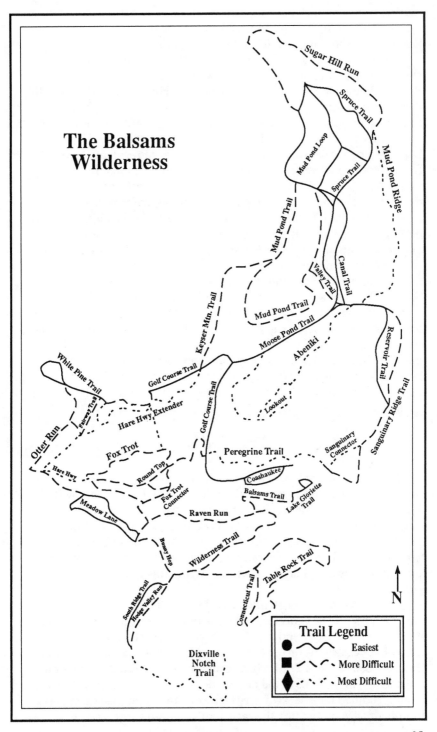

The Balsams Wilderness

touring center rents skates, snowshoes, and a pulk (a device for towing the children along behind you), all of which are gratis to overnight guests. So is the skiing, both Nordic and Alpine.

It is impossible not to be fascinated by the hotel itself. People float about — guests in outdoor gear, bellboys, waiters, the staff naturalist. You might even see the in-house musicians. Housemaids flutter with their dusters through grand old rooms dedicated to every possible activity: ballroom, cabaret room, children's room, arcade, social room, and billiards room. In the ballot room, the 18 registered voters of Dixville Notch cast the nation's first votes every Presidential election. Day skiers are welcome to partake of the luncheon buffet in the dining room. Don't worry if you use the wrong fork. The staff is so well-trained that if you do something wrong *they* will apologize to *you*.

You can read The Balsams' posh history from the clippings and photographs on its walls. Once a small hotel, the resort came into its own as a destination in the 1880s. With the advent of planes in the 1920s, several flights a day would airlift in "the necessities:" fresh lobster, cut flowers, and the latest editions of big-city newspapers. The current owner, Mr. Tillotson, bought the resort after making a fortune in the novelty balloon industry during the Great Depression. At that time, balloons were made by hand, at a rate of only 30 per hour, and the combination of chemicals often caused the balloon makers to catch on fire! Mr. Tillotson developed a machine process which eliminated this health hazard and increased efficiency a hundredfold. His factory for manufacturing surgical gloves is so subtly grafted to the hotel that most guests don't know it's there.

The Trails

Beginning skiers won't find much of a plateau in the Notch, but there are some pleasant, easy options. The sociable **Golf Course Road Trail** is a skier's highway, and the main artery to the trail system. The trailhead can be difficult to find. Walk or ski a quarter mile down Golf Course Road, then slide one ski after another up the long gradual climb to the height of the land. The trail originates at the crest of the Panorama Golf Course, from where you can see mountains in Canada and Vermont.

Farther from the resort, the **Canal Trail** is one of the prettiest trails you'll ever ski. The peaceful, noiseless trail follows an old canal once used for hydroelectric power. Protective evergreens line the narrow track, and skiers glide on top of the mounded burrow of earth dug from the canal bed. **Spruce Trail, Mud Pond Loop**, and **Mud Pond Extender** are narrow, quiet trails at the far northern end of the system. They are left ungroomed for a backcountry feel, and are a good place to surprise moose, or as is more often the case, let the moose surprise you!

Intermediate skiers who prize variety should head up the **Sanguinary Ridge Trail**, named for the deep red color of the north notch in the setting sun. Skied downward, this is a rollercoaster ride; skied upward, it is an ascent to the top of the world, through lovely open hardwood forests. The **Mud Pond Trail** traces old logging roads around a high, wooded 4.5 kilometer loop. Mud Pond itself is a stumpy frozen surface thickly rimmed with evergreens and boasting a scenic vista of nearby Van Dyck Mountain. The adventurous **Table Rock Trail** climbs backcountry to an altitude of 2,500 feet at the top of the Notch, and returns with some nice drops down the mountain to the Alpine trails. **Table Rock** can be skied only by guided tour; all skiers must have safety straps. Call for further information.

Hotshots looking to test themselves should try the **Hare Highway Extender**, which jumps and twists: so will you! Fast corners and a lot of ups and downs make this trail more fun than necessary. The short but not-to-be-sneezed-at **T-Pole** trail double-drops right down the powerlines, and is your best bet for telemarking at the Balsams. Advanced skiers can also access the **Peregrine Trail**, which runs underneath peregrine falcon nesting areas on the cliffs behind the hotel. The touring center has binoculars for the curious.

Finding your way: Take I-93 north to Route 3 north and drive a very long way to Colebrook. Turn onto Route 26 south for 11 miles to the hotel.

Franconia Inn Cross Country Center
Easton Road
Franconia, New Hampshire   03580
(800) 473-5299, (603) 823-5542

Trail System: 65 km (65 km classical, 5 km skate, 20 km backcountry)
Our Estimate: A solid trail system for several long, inn-to-inn tours.
Grooming: Good; after every snowfall.
Scenic Beauty: 3 — great views of surrounding mountains from the fields, but
   the wooded trails are sometimes handicapped by recent logging and
   occasional sand pits.
Touring Center: Half of a barn with rentals, lessons, wood stove, hot drinks
   (and lunch at the inn), and some retail.
Favorite Trail: Flat Track Circle. Although short and flat, it offers terrific
   views of Cannon Mountain and Mount Lafayette.
Payment: All major credit cards.
Lodging: Franconia Inn-Trailside (603-823-5542, $$-$$$); Stonybrook
   Motor Lodge-Franconia (603-823-8196, $-$$)
Local's Tip: Bring your own lunch. The ski center offers no snacks, and the
   inn's lunch, although certainly tasty, may be a little expensive.

Only a fool would rush recklessly to the ski trails at the Franconia
Inn. Resting at the bottom of a wide, picturesque river valley in the
shadows of Cannon Mountain, the turn-of-the-century inn and its
scenic surroundings demand to be savored slowly. The leftover farmlands of the valley — unusual in a state which has steadily abandoned
its rocky pastures — stretch majestically away from the inn in all
directions toward steep, dark mountainsides.

Manager Jeff Morgan describes the skiing at Franconia as "the way
it was in the sixties, only groomed." Lycra stretch suit sightings average
about one per year, and skating lessons are as frequent as presidential
elections. This certainly is no watering hole for the speed crowd. Yet
with 65 kilometers of groomed trails linking four delightful inns,
Franconia would be a superb destination for both classically-inclined
hotshots *and* family oriented, wool-coated baby-boomers.

The cross country center occupies the front half of a horse barn next
to the inn. (The back half is still reserved for horses.) Jeff warms the
room with a large wood stove and with his own free-wheeling, animated
hospitality. While damp boots dry in a metal cage hanging over the
wood stove, the rental skis — hand-me-downs from Loon — wait
patiently in rubber-banded pairs for backwoods excursions.

From year to year, the path for those backwoods excursions could
vary greatly, Franconia's trail system shifts restlessly when land changes

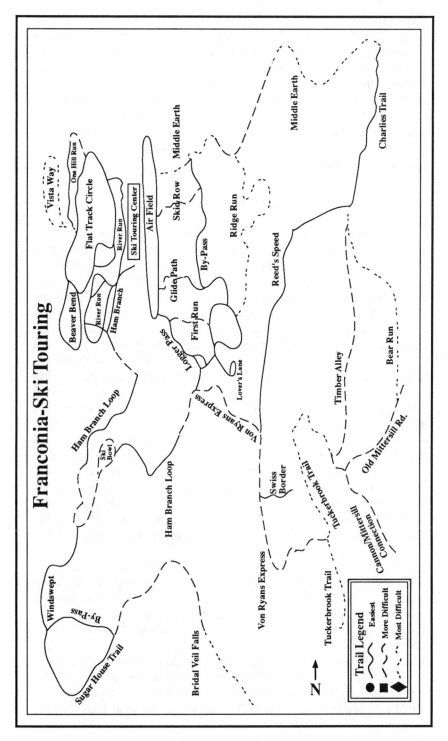

Franconia-Ski Touring

Vista Way

One Hill Run

Beaver Bend

River Run

Ham Branch

Flat Track Circle

River Run

Ski Touring Center

Air Field

Glide Path

Skid Row

Middle Earth

Middle Earth

Charlies Trail

By-Pass

First Run

Ridge Run

Logger Pass

Lover's Lane

Reed's Speed

Von Ryans Express

Ham Branch Loop

Ski Bowl

Ham Branch Loop

Ham Branch Loop

Swiss Border

Tuckerbrook Trail

Timber Alley

Bear Run

Old Mittersill Rd.

Cannon/Mittersill Connection

Windswept

By-Pass

Sugar House Trail

Bridal Veil Falls

Von Ryans Express

Tuckerbrook Trail

Trail Legend

Easiest

More Difficult

Most Difficult

● ■ ◆

N

hands between persons of unequal fondness for ski trails. Although originally settled by just three logging families, Easton Valley is now a mosaic of private parcels. The task of maintaining an integrated network of trails through the valley is comparable to building a highway through the German city-states of the early nineteenth century. Any decision to spend money on the improvement of a section of trail must take into account the risk of losing that trail in the future to an uncooperative landowner. As a result, many of the trails remain narrow and bumpy — perfect for old-style classical skiing, but not as good for skating or for side-by-side striding.

The Trails

Among the cross country ski areas in New England, there seems to be a lot of jostling for position on the history bandwagon. One wants to be the first ski area, another the first to offer lessons, and still another the first to have trails cut exclusively for cross country skiing. Franconia Inn's obscure claim to fame is to have the oldest continually used cross country trail north of Franconia Notch: **The Ham Branch Loop**.

Beginners and experts alike should begin their day on the historic **Ham Branch Loop**. You'll be delighted by the early morning views of Cannon Mountain. If it's not windy, start out with a lap around **Flat Track Circle**, which hugs the edge of the Ham Branch floodplain. Looking across the fields, you'll see Cannon and Lafayette rearing up behind the inn. The short climb up **Vista Way** adds a bit to your elevation, but not quite as much to the view.

Ham Branch quickly finds its way into a fairly level evergreen forest. The few small dips and rises provide variety but nothing to quicken the pulse. Before turning back toward the inn, the trail pays a visit to the "Ski Bowl," a sandpit amphitheater created for two purposes: to obtain sand for the construction of Franconia's section of I-93, and to provide an ideal spot to test two or three telemark turns. After the Ski Bowl, the trail crosses Route 116, then slithers its way back to the inn along narrow evergreen passageways.

If you've brought a water bottle, a lunch, and some endurance, Jeff will surely point you toward what he calls the **Big Loop**. The **Big Loop** carries you out of the valley toward more challenging skiing. Start by climbing away from the airfield on **Middle Earth** through mixed hardwoods. At the top of the climb, the snow-capped Presidentials can be seen far in the distance. After dropping down to the fields near Lovett's Inn (with a view of the northern peaks of Franconia Ridge and the Alpine trails at Cannon), **Charlie's Trail** guides you through a flat section toward the Horse and Hound Inn. From there, choose between **Reed's Speed** (a flat shortcut), **Timber Alley**, and **Bear Run**. Timber

Alley's logging roads provide a challenging climb, but they don't spare you the view of a chainsaw-ravaged forest. **Von Ryan's Express** climbs briefly, then drops back into the valley with spectacular, swooping turns through a sunny grove of white birches — highly recommended.

The more adventurous could make their way up **Bridal Veil Falls**, which Jeff describes as a "healthy" two mile climb to a beautiful set of falls. Alternatively, take a lift to the top of Cannon Mountain and telemark down the **Tucker Brook Trail** — a precipitous, narrow plunge down the mountainside for experts with chutzpah and a few loose screws.

Finding your way: Take I-93 to exit 38. Take left off exit. At stop sign, go straight (onto Route 116 south). After 2.3 miles, Franconia Inn will be on your right. Park on the left side of the road, across the street from the red barn.

Gunstock Cross Country
Route 11A
Gilford, New Hampshire   03246
(800) GUNSTOCK, (603) 293-4341

Trail System: 42 km (25 km classical, 42 km skate, 15 km backcountry)
Our Estimate: A day or two of skiing for all abilities, wrapped around a small mountain.
Grooming: Very Good
Scenic Beauty: 3
Touring Center: A small warming hut with rentals, lessons, wood stove, snacks and hot drinks, some retail, and outhouses.
Favorite Trail: Birch Loop, an out-of-the-way trail through a beautiful hardwood forest
Payment: All major credit cards accepted.
Lodging: Gunstock Inn-Gilford (603-293-2021, $$$$); Misty Harbor Resort-Gilford (603-293-4500, $$-$$$)
Local's Tip: World class ski jumps nearby. Call to check when there's a competition, and watch the skiers soar. If you don't like the skiing after 1/2 hour, they'll give you your money back!

At Gunstock, the emphasis is on family skiing. Hotshots stay on I-93 and head for Waterville or Loon. The family-oriented, casual skiers turn east toward Gunstock. Of course families are made up of many individuals, each of whom is likely to voice an opinion on *the* perfect ski vacation. If your children complain about how boring, difficult, and

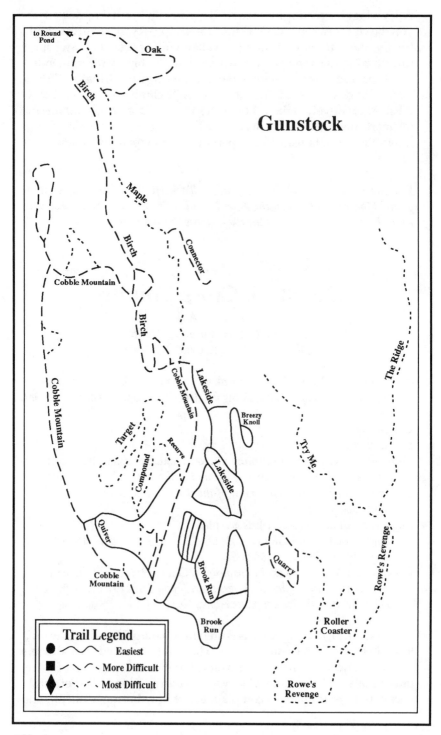

Gunstock

to Round Pond

Oak

Birch

Maple

Birch

Connector

Cobble Mountain

Birch

Cobble Mountain

Lakeside

Breezy Knoll

The Ridge

Cobble Mountain

Target

Cobble Mountain

Recurve

Lakeside

Compound

Try Me

Quiver

Quarry

Rowe's Revenge

Cobble Mountain

Brook Run

Roller Coaster

Brook Run

Rowe's Revenge

Trail Legend

● ～～～ Easiest

■ ～～＼ More Difficult

◆ ⋅⋅＼⋅＼ Most Difficult

slow cross country skiing is, don't waste your time arguing — you're at Gunstock — where the variety of skiing opportunities rivals those of any other ski area in the East. Where else can you learn Alpine, cross country, ski jumping, snowboarding, and telemarking at a single ski area? If the children want to head over to the Alpine area, wait in lift lines, endure biting winds, and eat lunch against the backdrop of piped-in lodge music, so be it. One parent can ski with them, while the other one scoots up the road to enjoy a relaxing afternoon on skinny skis.

Several exciting loops lie curled around Cobble Mountain, awaiting your arrival. These trails were built the old-fashioned way: sinuous, bumpy, and narrow. Unlike many other New Hampshire cross country trails, they haven't all been bulldozed into offshoots of the interstate highway system.

Local Nordic legend T. Gary Allen designed and cut Gunstock's trails in the 1950s and 1960s. It had been several decades since Roosevelt's Civilian Conservation Corps sent laborers to Gilford to carve Alpine ski trails out of Gunstock Mountain; Mr. Allen felt that several decades was far too long for locals to suffer without the salubrious benefits of cross country skiing. Luckily for us, Mr. Allen is a perfectionist. You will find few flaws in his Cobble Mountain masterpiece.

The Trails

If you feel comfortable on skis, give the **Cobble Mountain Trail** a whirl. Don't start looking around for the "mountain." Cobble Mountain doesn't stand much taller than Bunker *Hill*. A steady climb along **Poor Farm Brook** and past the Alpine area's snowmaking pond is followed by several short but steep descents on the way back to the warming hut. Cobble's backbone is fairly straight and wide; don't miss the dips, turns, and surprises of the additional appendaged loops.

After about four kilometers of the **Cobble Mountain Trail**, skiers can either glide back toward the warming hut or they can branch off on a beautiful little loop that starts out on the **Birch Trail** and returns on the **Maple Trail**. The **Birch Trail** leads through a deciduous forest (yep, plenty of birches) and crosses a small field before passing the baton to **Maple**. **Maple** climbs to a fantastic forested traverse, then drops down a steep, twisting downhill that beginners may prefer to walk down.

If the downhills on **Maple** and **Cobble** don't satisfy your need for speed, try some of the shorter loops within the **Cobble Mountain Trail**. **Compound** offers both a scenic vista (don't expect uncharted wilderness; the Alpine area is what you'll see) and a steep downhill with an uncontrollable hairpin. **Target** climbs even higher, to a fantastic view of the frozen Lake Winnipesaukee and its many islands. During snowy winters, the **Ridge Trail** is worth a try: pay a nominal lift fee and take the Tiger Chair to the top of a high saddle. Follow a spectacular, exposed ridge for a few kilometers, then telemark down a challenging old Alpine trail. Experts only!

If you prefer more gentle terrain, stay on the south side of the road. **Brook Run** offers a fantastic, made-for-the-novice two kilometer loop that chases a winding brook through a mature stand of pines. At the far end of **Brook Run**, steal a peek at Gunstock's world class ski jumping complex (the largest of these jumps regularly sees flights over 200 feet long!)

Near **Brook Run** are the **Lanes**, a series of flat, parallel roads which provide space for camping during the summer months. In case you can't wait for warmer weather, several lanes are reserved for winter camping. You can pitch your tent or park your RV here for a modest fee. We don't envy you. Many of the upper lanes are groomed for beginners.

Finding your way: Take I-93 to Exit 20 and Route 3 north. After four or five miles on Route 3, bear right onto the Laconia Bypass (Route 11, just after a mall on your left) toward the Gunstock Recreation Area. The ski area is about ten minutes from the Bypass exit, on your right.

Great Glen Trails

Box 300
Gorham, New Hampshire 03581
(603)466-2333

Trail System: 15 km (15 km classical, 15 km skate, 35 km backcountry), 1 km snowmaking
Our Estimate: A bit longer than you'd think, since everything can be skied in two directions; plenty of beginner terrain.
Grooming: Excellent
Scenic Beauty: 4
Touring Center: An enormous lodge with rentals, lessons, a restaurant and lounge, waxing room, full retail, locker room, and a daycare center.
Favorite Trail: Great Grumpy Grade, which winds its way up to a trailside yurt.
Payment: All major credit cards
Lodging: Nestlenook Farm-Jackson (603-383-8071, $$$$, cross country on-site); The Lodge at Jackson Village-Jackson (603-383-0999, $$-$$$); A 250-room hotel is planned for Great Glen
Local's Tip: Take a snowcat ride 1,000 vertical feet up the Mount Washington Auto Road and hotdog it back down to the lodge.

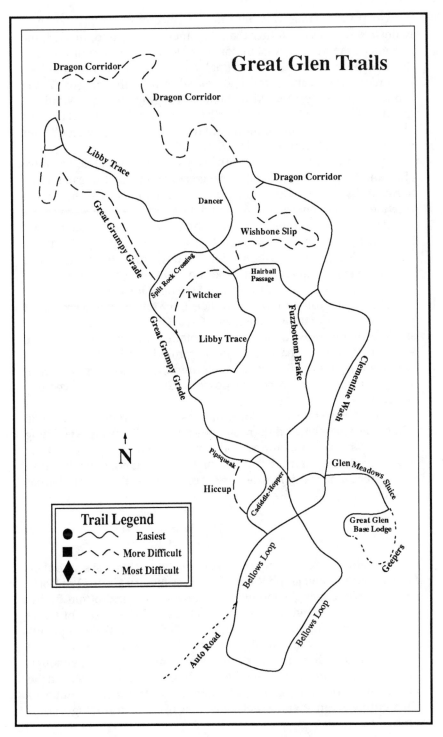

Great Glen Trails

Great Glen Trails was built to introduce cross county skiing to mainstream America, rather than the other way around. In 1994, the owners of the Mount Washington Auto Road began a multi-million dollar experiment to test New Englanders' enthusiasm for outdoor recreation. They carved trails so smooth out of the rugged, White Mountain wilderness that New Hampshire highway officials would be green with envy, and then constructed a lodge that looks like it belongs at the bottom of a small Alpine mountain. These planners weren't your run-of-the-mill, penny-pinching Yankees!

The result is a hybrid mixture of a cross country ski area, a country club, and Disney World. While most cross country centers cater to the hardy individualist, Great Glen intends to pamper. Trailside yurts provide complimentary hot cocoa and the finger-thawing warmth of a wood stove. The trails themselves are so smooth and wide that it would be no surprise to find fifteen kilometers of astroturf hiding beneath the snow. The lodge provides the services of a daycare center, a full-service restaurant and lounge, a waxing room, a retail shop, and a rental shop with employees that carry the skis out the door for you!

The gentle, rolling trails with their fairy-tale names seem out of place at the edge of the immense, wild Great Gulf wilderness, and in the shadow of the most dangerous mountain range in the Northeast. Wandering wild animals occasionally remind tourists that it is they who are trespassing. Bobcats, coyotes, mink, and raccoons have been spotted; a moose even chased down a Great Glen employee one summer!

Great Glen Trails is not for thrill seekers. Experienced skiers will admire the smooth trail design, but they may find themselves yearning for the sharp corners, bumps, and surprises that give personality to most other trail systems. Beginners, on the other hand, will fall in love with the ease and comfort of the cross country skiing that Great Glen has to offer.

The Trails

For glimpses of recent beaver construction activities, start out on **Glen Meadows** and climb **Rabbit Ears Pass** toward **Coffee Pot Rock**. Or for a different angle, follow the relatively flat **Fuzzbottom Brake**, which squeezes between an enormous field and the forests of **Great Dipper Swamp**. Return to the lodge via **Clementine Wash**, a picturesque trail which winds along a riverbank in the shade of scattered hardwoods. **Fuzzbottom Brake** and **Clementine Wash** provide enough open space for the ominous shoulders of the Carters (to the east) and the Presidentials (to the west) to rise into view. The lower section of **Clementine Wash** offers a spectacular view of the surrounding wilderness.

The Great Glen area can be lashed by brutal winds and bitter cold, so you may opt for the more protected skiing in the woods. Tuck your chin into your jacket and scurry across the fields toward the outer trails. Not only do they provide protection from the wind, but they are far more interesting than the flat field loops. **Great Grumpy Grade** offers a rewarding climb to **Great Angel Station** — a knoll top yurt with hot chocolate and a fulltime staffperson. Stop in and chat. Add your name to the guest book and warm yourself by the marvelously refurbished Glenwood stove.

Dragon Corridor provides an exciting descent from the yurt. Beginners need not fear unwieldy speed and dizzying turns; like the entire trail system, **Dragon Corridor** will treat you with gentle respect. Relax your legs and coast downhill. Every turn provides a new perspective of the Carter Range and Wildcat's Alpine trails.

Although the Great Glen trail system is relatively small, it promises to more than double over the next few years. In addition, all trails have sufficient width to be skied both ways. If you become bored, try a few trails backwards.

Finding your way: Route 16 north three miles past Pinkham Notch and two miles past Wildcat on the left. Great Glen is 22 miles from North Conway.

Mount Washington Valley
Ski Touring Association

P.O. Box 646
Intervale, New Hampshire 03845
(800) 282-5220 (Number rotates among the trailside inns), (603) 356-9920

Trail System: *60 km (60 km classical, 30 km skate, 5 km backcountry)*
Our Estimate: *A fabulous, ten kilometer out-and-back through the Saco River Valley, a few shorter wooded loops, and plenty of extra kilometers in Whitaker Woods.*
Grooming: *Good*
Scenic Beauty: *3*
Touring Center: *A tiny annex to a ski shop with rentals, lessons, hot drinks, and outhouses. You're better off buying a ticket at one of the trailside inns.*
Favorite Trail: *Intervale, which provides spectacular views of the valley and surrounding mountain.*
Payment: *No credit cards accepted.*
Lodging: *The 1785 Inn-Trailside (800-421-1785. $$$); Riverside Inn-Intervale (603-356-9060, $$-$$$); Telephone 800-282-5220 for information on other trailside inns.*
Local's Tip: *Every touring center has a run-of-the-mill moonlight tour. MWVSTA instead sends you on a gut-wrenching inn-to-inn chocolate moonlight tour, with several hundred calories waiting at every stop!*

In 1990, the Mount Washington Valley Ski Touring Association (MWVSTA) stitched together a trail system out of scattered patches of ski trails strewn through the valley. Local merchants and innkeepers joined forces to create a European-style network — a network where tourists and shoppers could step out of the inns and outlets of North Conway and directly onto their cross country skis. A first-rate, wide-open, western-style valley trail succeeds in luring skiers back year-after-year. Unfortunately, however, with Route 16 and a slew of back roads slicing through the trails, the network lacks a unified feeling, and there is very little isolated terrain for skiers with a penchant for escapism.

Although a few hundred kilometers of skiing lie just up the road at more extensive touring centers, most skiers are completely satisfied (*and* completely exhausted) with a solid 10 or 15 kilometers of touring. This is how MWVSTA stays alive with a single superstar trail and several other second-rate players. The wide, flat hayfields of the Saco River Valley cradle the meandering Intervale Trail and offer some of the most beautiful skiing in New England. With cliffs rearing out of the valley to the west and the snowcapped Presidentials to the north, you

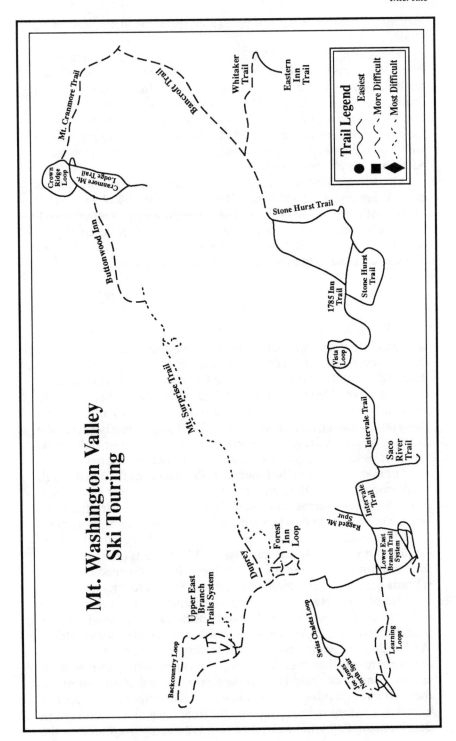

Mt. Washington Valley
Ski Touring

may find yourself looking over your shoulder for the rocky peaks of the Grand Tetons.

The touring center is at Joe Jones North, four miles out of town on Route 16. Unless you need to rent skis or chat with the manager, there's really no point to the drive. The center has only a single couch, a few hot drinks, and a port-a-potty. Start your tour closer to town, at the 1785 Inn. You can purchase your ticket there and step immediately onto one of the most scenic sections of the Intervale Trail. Beginners may want to walk down the steep hill to the floodplain before putting on their skis. After that, it's clear cruising.

Overall, neophytes have it easy at Intervale. The scenic valley trails can be conquered by the most timid tourist. Even hotshot skiers will fall in love with the Saco floodplain. The major drawback is that the midtown sections of the trail system have so many road crossings that by the end of the day, you will have perfected the roadway hop and learned that you don't have to take off both skis to cross a road!

The Trails

Except for a few small hills near the touring center, all of the trails west of Route 16 are fairly flat and easily managed. They provide good rhythm and great tanning on sunny days, but some of the fields can be downright brutal in the wind. **The Saco River Trail** is a worthwhile side trip to the river. (The steeper banks of the Saco are always on the outside of the meanders. The water flowing around the outside of the curve flows faster, tearing away at the soils and creating a steep bank. On the inside of the curve, the water is slower; it not only can't tear at the bank, but it drops sand and gravel onto a slowly-growing sand bar.)

The maze of loops in the **Lower East Branch** system winds through hardwoods near the confluence of the Saco and the Lower East Branch rivers. Trails jump across pinched-off meanders, dip into dry channels, and swing alongside the riverbank. Aimless wandering is the norm.

If the floodplains haven't sapped your strength, try either the **New England Inn Trail, Mount Surprise,** or **Whitaker Woods.** The **New England Inn Trail** is the easier of the three. After a few road crossings, it heads gradually up the valley of the East Branch River.

Mount Surprise was designed to expand into an extended day loop, cruising across a wooded mountainside, skirting the edge of the Cranmore parking lot, then dropping back into the valley via **Whitaker Woods.** But condominiums and road crossings and intermittent logging are more trouble than they're worth at the southern end; it's best skied as an out-and-back. Quickly climb the side of **Lower Bartlett Mountain,** then roll through mixed forests along a hillside terrace for a couple of kilometers, before running out onto the front lawn of a condominium development. Enjoy the view, then turn tail and try your luck on the twisting uphill you just climbed. Although challenging, there are just enough speed-checking turns to make the descent manageable. Don't expect much of the lookout on the **Mount Surprise Loop**. The only surprises are the trees obscuring the view.

Whitaker Woods has loads of challenging terrain in an evergreen forest set aside by the town of Conway for recreation and conservation. Although not part of the official network, the trails here are very popular and well-groomed. If you simply remember where you are in relation to the power lines and railroad tracks, you'll be able to find your way out. The all-new **Mount Cranmore Trail** follows an auto road slowly down the back side of Mount Cranmore. After beginning in evergreens, it descends through hardwood forests of birch, maple, and beech. Buy a one-ride lift ticket for a few dollars, then sit back and enjoy the ride!

Finding your way: Take I-95 to the Spaulding Turnpike, which eventually turns into Route 16. Continue on Route 16 north through Conway and North Conway. About 4 1/2 miles from Eastern Mountain Sports on the north side of North Conway, the touring center can be seen on the left side of Route 16, hiding behind Joe Jones North.

Jackson Ski Touring Foundation
P.O. Box 216
Jackson, New Hampshire 03846
(800) XC-SNOWS, (603) 383-9355

Trail System: *90 km (90 km classical, 60 km skate, 75 km backcountry)*
Our Estimate: *Infinite length, infinite variety.*
Grooming: *Excellent — but check at the touring center before skiing the far out loops*
Scenic Beauty: *5*
Touring Center: *Lessons, rentals, several restaurants across the street, wax room, full retail, and a good wall map of trail system. The touring center has very little lounging space!*
Favorite Trail: *Ellis River Trail*
Payment: *MC and VISA*
Lodging: *Eagle Mountain Resort-Trailside (800-777-1700, $$$); Carter Notch Inn-Jackson (603-383-9630, $)*
Local's Tip: *For a shortcut around the frustrating traffic of North Conway on the way home, take a right at the lights just before EMS. Turn left onto West Side Drive after about 1/2 mile. West Side Drive will bring you straight into Conway.*

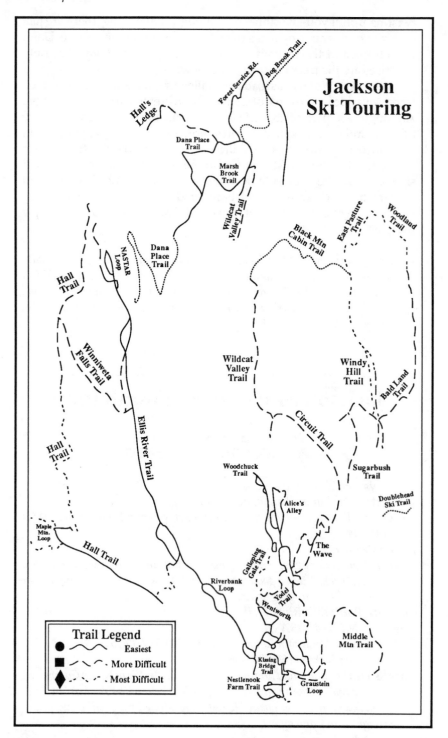

The way ski area managers sing Jackson's praises, they sound eerily starstruck: they're impressed, they're jealous, and they're nervous — and with good reason! The Jackson Ski Touring Foundation siphons upwards of 60,000 ardent admirers per year from lesser areas further south. With each subsequent winter, there emerges an even more finely tuned cross country ski area, created by flawless grooming, an extensive trail system, and a storybook mountain setting.

The tiny town of Jackson is so pretty and quaint — so disgustingly perfect for cross country skiing — that it is hard to believe it was designed by anyone other than a publicity agent given free reign. Imagine, for a moment, what the perfect cross country ski town would look like. Is it set in a narrow river valley, high in the mountains of northern New England? Does an old, wooden covered bridge lead to a quiet main street lined with inns and restaurants? Do the rolling greens of two golf courses stretch through the valley, joined by a magnificent set of cascading falls? If not, a visit to Jackson will help to stretch your imagination.

Your entire skiing career was no more than a prelude to a visit to Jackson. The skiing is intoxicating and seemingly limitless, with trails tangling the various backroads of Jackson like the relentless tendrils of a crazed vine. Wherever Jackson goes, trails follow in close pursuit. They chase the town up river valleys, across hillside meadows, and over ridges. Then they strike out on their own into miles and miles of lonely wilderness. If you have ever struggled with the concept of infinity, a few days at Jackson will clear things up. You could easily ski for a week here without a hint of boredom.

Jackson Ski Touring Foundation, founded in 1972 to consolidate several loosely-organized trail systems in town, has quickly blossomed into a world-class skiing center. The center currently commands three powerful pisten bulleys, publishes a monthly newsletter, and regularly hosts national and international ski races. All it needs now is a large, comfortable lodge. The little building behind the Jack Frost Ski Shop looks like it was designed for a 1972-sized crowd. A few picnic tables, a wood stove, and warm drinks — the bare minimum requirements for a welcoming touring center — are conspicuously absent from this Spartan little annex.

The Trails

The network is set up in several different sections, with many loops beginning and ending far from the touring center. The artful use of an automobile might enhance your skiing by eliminating road crossings and bringing you more quickly to your favorite trails.

For those with casual intentions, simply leave your car in the touring center parking lot. The adjacent **Wentworth Resort Course** provides plenty of fun, flat, sunny skiing, with more adventurous loops reaching into the woods on all sides. A natural snow bridge crosses the Wildcat River, and a small covered bridge built especially for skiers crosses the Ellis River.

The **Ellis River Trail**, one of the most popular and populated in New England, carries skiers gently five kilometers (one-way) upriver through park-like national forests. The trail quickly enters the woods and winds slowly uphill along the icy waters of the Ellis River toward the Dana Place Inn. (For a small fee, you can take a shuttle up to the inn and enjoy five kilometers of easy, downhill gliding.) A cabin a few kilometers along the trail provides an ideal destination for those unwilling to make a ten kilometer out-and-back commitment. Be sure to arrive early on weekends; over 1,000 skiers have skied this trail on busy Saturdays! A veteran patroller calls the **Ellis River Trail** hills "Yugo" hills, because courteous skiers stand at either end and shout "You go" at one another.

On clear, sunny days, park your car next to the Eagle Mountain Resort and explore the nearby fields. (You can ski there on the **Yodel Trail**, but be prepared for a moderately difficult descent on the way home at the end of the day.) A stately, nineteenth century hotel stands guard while you ski over the open hills of its golf course and across the narrow strip of farmlands of the Wildcat River Valley. Skiers looking for a surprise should try **The Wave**. After sneaking out of the valley and through an overgrown, hillside meadow (with terrific views of the golf course below), **The Wave** squeezes between boulders and ducks into an evergreen forest. The final descent to the golf course will toss you over a few crazy bumps which, if taken fast enough, become a pair of small ski jumps! Some of the best views at Jackson look out from the top of the **Betty Whitney Trail**, which climbs relentlessly from the top of **The Wave** toward Black Mountain. Ski up to Whitney's Inn for a good, hearty lunch!

Early season skiing can be found on the 13 kilometer **East Pasture Loop** — a short drive from the Black Mountain Alpine area. Don't come expecting gentle meadows: **East Pasture** is a blatant misnomer for an expert trail that begins by climbing straight up several kilometers (1,000 vertical feet) of mountainside and sees only a few hundred meters of pasture along its length. After the climb, it doodles along the east side of Black Mountain before dropping through wild S-turns and into a long, pole-dragging, open-mouthed coast. Intermediate skiers eager to ski **East Pasture's** early snow should make a counter-clockwise attempt of the first few kilometers.

For expert backcountry artists, the legendary **Wildcat Valley Trail** drops precipitously down the backside of the Wildcat's Alpine mountain.

Try it only after a generous snowstorm and a consultation with the JSTF patrollers. The western-style glade skiing, the fabulous view from **Hall's Ledge**, and the wild speed make this a favorite powder trail for locals.

Finding your way: Take either the Everett Turnpike or Route 93 and the Kancamagus to Route 16 north. Follow Route 16 through and beyond North Conway (see Local's Tip for an alternate route). A few miles after North Conway, Route 302 splits off to the left. Stay right on Route 16. 2.2 miles later, take a right onto Route 16A, cross the covered bridge, and the ski center is 1/ 2 mile ahead on the left (behind the Jack Frost Ski Shop).

Loon Mountain Cross Country Area

Route 112
Lincoln, New Hampshire   03251
(603) 745-8111 Extension: 5568

Trail System: *35 km groomed (35 km classical, 35 km skate)*
Our Personal Estimate: *Depending on snowcover, 35 km of skatable terrain may shrink to 25 km of classical trails.*
Grooming: *Excellent*
Scenic Beauty: *3*
Touring Center: *Rentals, lessons, candy bars and hot drinks, some retail*
Favorite Trail: *Serendipity, a beautiful lowland trail by the side of the Pemigewassett River*
Payment: *All major credit cards*
Lodging: *The Mountain Club at Loon-Lincoln (800-229-STAY, $$$-$$$$); Red Doors Motel-Lincoln (603-745-2267, $-$$)*
Local's Tip: *The Kancamagus Pass is one of the more dramatic notch es in the White Mountains with spectacular views. To get there, drive six miles up Route 12 East.*

If you don't mind being a second-class citizen, there is plenty of good skiing at Loon Mountain Cross Country. The area boasts top-of-the-line grooming, mountainside trails for all abilities, and woodlands of extraordinary beauty. But Nordic skiers, be prepared. This is no quaint ski touring center in the back of beyond. Loon Mountain may have the only ski trail in the world where you can catch a glimpse of the Golden Arches. Condominiums, euphemistically known as 'mountain

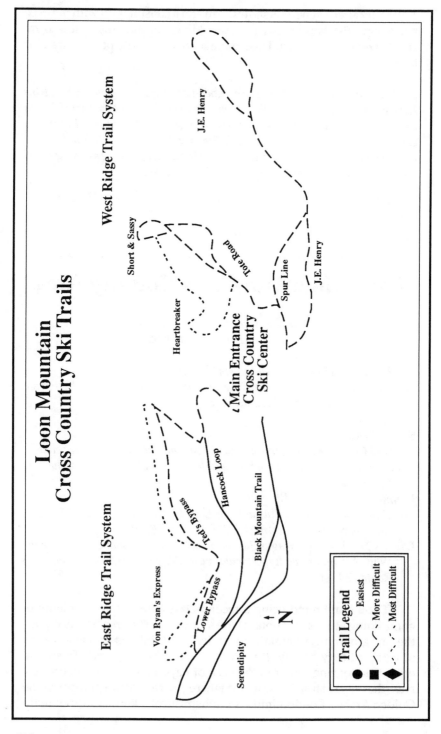

Loon Mountain
Cross Country Ski Trails

West Ridge Trail System

J.E. Henry

Short & Sassy

Tote Road

Heartbreaker

Spur Line

J.E. Henry

Main Entrance
Cross Country
Ski Center

East Ridge Trail System

Von Ryan's Express

Ted's Bypass

Hancock Loop

Black Mountain Trail

Lower Bypass

Serendipity

N

Trail Legend

● Easiest

■ More Difficult

◆ Most Difficult

villages', sprawl out indecorously, pushing the cross country trails onto the far reaches of the mountain. Many cross country customers are one-day refugees from the downhill slopes. Because of this, and because many trails follow old logging roads, the area appeals primarily to beginner and intermediate skiers.

There is no question that everything at Loon revolves around the Alpine area. The parking attendants will wave you into the Alpine parking lots if you let them. But Loon Cross Country has made a virtue of necessity and the area provides a happy host of amenities: free ice skating, snowshoe rentals, child care (if you call ahead), and all the pleasures that normally accompany an Alpine resort. The area has a particularly good telemarking program, thanks to its location on the mountain. Called *1-2-3 Learn to Ski,* you get equipment rental, a 90-minute lesson, and a novice lift ticket for $35.

The Nordic trails are split into two sections, East Ridge and West Ridge, which begin where the Alpine sprawl leaves off. This is about a mile to each side from the cross country center; you can drive and park there, or take the resort shuttle which comes about every fifteen minutes. Both systems have trails cut into the mountainside that look across to the surrounding peaks and down to the steeply dropping river valley below; they also both have pretty, mild river runs. Both are set up so that from the highest point on the highest trail, you can ski downhill all the way back to the parking lot with the help of only gravity and a few double poles.

The staff will steer you toward the easier terrain of the East Ridge, where former forest roads traverse the mountainside; the West Ridge has generally more exciting trails, but these need greater snow depth in order to be skiable. Nordic Director Ted Gartner is renowned for his grooming, which keeps the snow as long as possible. This can go to extremes. He has been known to "save" trails by not grooming them at all. Often only 25 of the 35 kilometers are open, and this may be groomed for classical skiing only. Call ahead to be sure.

Most of Loon's trails, particularly on the East Ridge, are take-overs of erstwhile logging roads. Forestry has been a critical force in Lincoln, ever since logger J.E. Henry came over the mountains in 1892 and saw the vast stands of timber. It was Henry's logging company and his railroad companies that carted timber down to the big sawmills which supported the Lincoln economy. The area was rife with logging camps in the 1930s, and although you can't detect them now, you will be able to tell that the Black Mountain trail was an old railroad bed. Loon has adopted the lumber/railroad connection as a leitmotif: an old engine stands by the area's entrance; Nordic trails are named "J.E. Henry" and "The Spur Line"; and a whistle-blowing choo-choo transports Alpine skiers from one side of the mountain to the other.

The Trails

Loon has some excellent beginner trails on the **East Ridge** trail system. **Black Mountain** is a lovely, lilting trail that feels very far away from condo-land. The peaceful railroad bed traverses the mountainside amongst yellow birches, while the Pemigewasset River Valley drops off below. Hancock has the same character, but the grade is steeper and the birches are white instead of yellow. **Serendipity** is a pretty, lowland trail along the river under large-trunked evergreens. It has more variety than the others, following the whimsical ups and downs of the riverbank. You'll see more people on this trail alone than on the rest of the system.

Intermediates should ski **J.E. Henry**, the more difficult counterpart to **Serendipity** on the **West Ridge** system. After a couple of short and sweet downhills, the trail makes a pretty trek amidst slim young trees along the river. The far loop climbs a couple ridges and drops down between unused power lines. The skiing is great, but this is not the place to go searching for unspoiled wilderness. You pass condominiums, parallel the road, and cross the overflow Alpine parking lot.

Tote Road is a better choice for natural beauty, or to access the rest of the **West Ridge** system. The wide access road makes some large S-curves at the base and then winds up the mountainside in a steady, pleasant climb. Since fewer humans venture up here, animals abound.

There are two trails for advanced skiers at Loon Mountain, one going predominantly up and one going predominantly down. **Heartbreaker** appeals to the few, the proud, and the strong of leg. The trail climbs high to the sky on a lovely scenic ridge before twisting into a pair of steep and wrenching uphills that only a masochist could enjoy. At the top, a welcoming sign congratulates you, "Yes!! You have reached the height of the land, take a short break, then enjoy some easy gliding downhills." **Heartbreaker** may not be groomed if the snow is not deep enough.

Von Ryan's Express begins with a half-kilometer herringbone. It climbs diagonally up the bouldery hillside before turning blessedly across the mountain. The upper part is a gratifying traverse that should be called Skyline Drive. You look down at the river valley far below, impressed with how high you have climbed. The bulk of the trail is a thrilling downhill that will make you feel like a log being sent on a river drive. On powder it is a silky ride; on ice, an experiment in terror.

Finding your way: Take I-93 to Exit 32 in Lincoln and follow the signs to Loon Mountain Resort. The mountain is 2.5 miles out of town on Route 112 East.

Windblown Ski Touring

Route 124
New Ipswich, New Hampshire 03071
(603) 878-2869

Trail System: *40 km (20 km skate, 25 km classical, 5 km groomed)*
Our Personal Estimate: *Good easy and intermediate skiing, with a couple*
ungroomed dare-devil trails. Not much for skaters.
Grooming: *Adequate*
Scenic Beauty: *3*
Touring Center: *Rentals — skis, snowshoes, pulk, lessons, wood stove,*
waxing room, homemade food
Favorite Trail: *Broken Dam Trail*
Payment: *MC and VISA*
Lodging: *Birchwood Inn-Temple (603-878-3711, $$$); The Ram in the*
Thicket-Wilton (603-654-6440, $$); Youth Hostel-Peterborough ($)
Local's Tip: *Check out the amazing ski-through outhouse at the intersection*
of Valley Trail and Pond Loop. If the snow is high enough you can ski in
and ski out the other side. It's a little harder for women, but can be done.

The peaceful, Windblown touring center lies just across the Massachusetts border in New Ipswich, New Hampshire. Forty kilometers of trails range over highlands, through valleys, and along the top of Barrett Mountain. The center was started in 1971. Although its trail system has substantially expanded, the atmosphere of the center is pretty much the same as in its earlier days. Wool pants and gaiters abound. The ski-in, ski-out warming hut sleeps eight and can be rented for big Epicurean parties; the scent of homecooked food issues from the upstairs restaurant; and friendly local skiers kick their feet up over the wood stove in the touring center and joke with owners Al and Irene Jenks. Windblown has a unique half-day rate for morning-only skiers. Pay the day rate and get money back on your trail fee if you're finished by 12:30.

Owner Al Jenks first knew he wanted to run a ski center in his early teens. When he got his driver's license at age 16, he drove around the back roads of New Hampshire and Vermont looking for the perfect spot. He found Windblown, and at the ripe old age of 17, purchased the property with money borrowed from his grandfather. After forestry college and a tour in Vietnam, Al came back to the land. He did not want to get involved with the increasing complexities of Alpine mechanics, opting instead for the blood, sweat, and tears of cross country. He cut eight miles of trails and opened for business. In those days, grooming

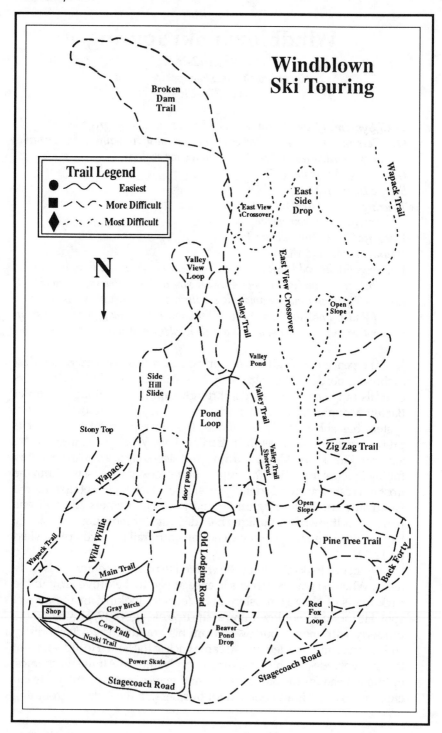

consisted of snowshoeing after a fresh snow, to pack the trail, and then skiing a set of tracks for tourers to follow.

Wood stoves crackle everywhere—in the ski center, the restaurant, the wax shed, and the warming hut. During Al's first winter, he ran out of his winter's supply of fuel in late February, and that March his first task in the morning was to cut down a tree and chop it up for the wood stove. Since then he's felled plenty of trees and hauled stone from the property to build the ski shop, trail shelters, and picnic shed. You buy your trail pass in the brick-floored, wood-walled ski shop. Rental and retail equipment hangs from the walls in neat rows, and couches and cushioned benches cluster by the wood stove. Upstairs, the bright sunny restaurant serves homemade soup, cookies, and muffins, all made on the premises by Irene. On busy weekends they serve hot dogs and hamburgers from the outdoor grill.

Windblown deserves its name, although Al will steer you to sheltered trails if you ask him. On days when the wind chill factor drops the temperature by tens, you'll feel it. Those are the days that the central warming hut on the trail system is at its most convivial: skiers build a fire in the wood stove and head out for the protected trails in the lowlands. Others help themselves to hot drinks on the honor system, sit in front of the stove, and chat. Grooming at Windblown is like Sisyphus doomed to roll his stone up the hill in Hades, only to have it roll back down: follow the trail system as well as you can, but you're still bound to get drifting. The area is best suited to classical touring, but there are 20 kilometers of packed trails for addicted skaters.

The Trails

The easy trails at Windblown are gatekeepers for the rest of the trail system. Right around the touring center are a series of short blink-and-you-miss-'em trails. **Gray Birch** is a wide teardrop of a trail leading up from the touring center through relatively open land. It takes you to the view fields below the Jenks' house where you can see long views north into the blue hills of New Hampshire. On a windy day, watch out. You'll be paragliding back where you came from, whether you want to or not.

The **Stagecoach Road** was once, naturally, the stagecoach road. The low-lying, sheltered trail is hemmed in by stone walls that mark where old pastures once met the road. **Stagecoach** becomes an intermediate trail at the intersection with **Old Logging Road**; just beyond, it crosses an old stone bridge built by the area's earliest settlers. This is easy to miss in the snow. The popular **Pond Loop** (not to be confused with **Pondside Loop**) was part of the original trail system. It takes off from the warming hut in a gentle evergreen climb and encloses **Wildlife Pond**. From the top of the loop you can ski through the outhouse and onto some of the intermediate level trails.

Intermediate level skiers will feel the terrain change on the **Valley View Loop**, which climbs the opposing molehill to Bartlett Mountain. The tail carves a curvey traverse of the wooded hillside while a ravine drops below. You'll ski past the pretty Valley View Shelter where the Jenks wanted to get married but the wedding guests threatened revolt at such a long walk. The mile-long **Broken Dam Trail** is a favorite with Windblown's regular curves and runouts. At the bottom you cross a tiny bridge and begin a series of hemlock-covered climbs to regain the lost elevation.

The most difficult trails at Windblown are groomed only by snowmobile, and climb over the top of Barrett Mountain. Even Evil Knievel wouldn't ski down them. The quick-climbing prelude to the **East View Trail** feels like a giant slalom course with trees; after another intensive uphill, the trail swiftly drops down the side of the mountain. Through the trees you can catch views of the eastern hills.

East Side Drop is a steeper version of the same terrain, with turns to cut your speed. Local skiers climb to the top of **East Side drop** and ski full bore to the bottom of **Broken Dam Trail**; the trail drops 550 feet and is downhill all the way. The really crazy skiers time themselves.

If you've climbed the mountain and the idea of skiing these trails makes your knees wobble, the **ZigZag** trail provide a humane way to get down. It swings out and back like a shuttle on a loose-warped loom, dropping 400 feet in elevation through thick evergreens.

You can take your dog on the ungroomed **Loop de Poop** (3-4 km) across the road. It is actually not a loop, but two prongs of the ungroomed **Wapack Trail**, which treks through the region. The left fork is a fairly level ski to a pond; the right is a rugged climb up Kidder Mountain. Then leave the beast in the car while you ski Windblown's regular trail system.

Finding your way: From Route 2 in Massachusetts, take the Leominster exit for Route 13 north. In Townsend, turn onto Route 119 west and follow it for two miles. You will see signs for New Ipswich and Windblown pointing right. Take that road for eleven miles. The touring center is three miles northwest of new Ipswich on N.H. Route 124. You can't miss the sign.

Norsk Cross Country

Box 2460 Route 11
New London, New Hampshire 03257
(800) 42-NORSK, (603) 526 4685

The Trails: *70 km (70 km classical, 20 km skate, no backcountry),*
2.5 km night skiing
Our Estimate: *A ten kilometer out-and-back to a warming hut, a large golf
course, and plenty of shorter loops to play around on for the rest of the day.*
Grooming: *Good*
Scenic Beauty: *2*
Touring Center: *A golfing clubhouse with rentals, lessons, small snacks and
hot drinks (plus a classy restaurant), full retail, and a bag lunch room.*
Favorite Trail: *Kearsarge Bound, with wide stone walls in a terrific hardwood
forest.*
Payment: *MC and VISA*
Lodging: *Fairway Motel at Lake Sunapee Country Club-Trailside (603-603-
526-6040, $$-$$$); Follansbee Inn-N.. Sutton (603-927-4221, $$-$$$)*
Local's Tip: *The New London police are usually quick to recognize a speeding
car. When you go through town, obey the speed limit — to the mph!*

The owners of Norsk don't exactly look like hippies. Then again,
they *did* abandon teaching careers in Boston to homestead in New
Hampshire with chickens and dogs and goats. They did live in a teepee
for a year with a dug pit as a fridge and tree limbs as clotheslines. They
do teach yoga on the side. Let's just call them "alternative."

But Norsk is far from an alternative sort of place. The heart of the
trail system is a stately golf course, and the cross country center borrows
the golfers' pro shop for the winter. The pro shop, the bathrooms, the
adjoining restaurant, and the "bag lunch room" all look as if they were
renovated, carpeted, and painted the day before yesterday. You almost
feel like taking off your boots when you come in from skiing. The trail
map is shiny and professional, and the trail signs look as if they were
manufactured in a tidy little shop in Switzerland. Even the trail-side
"hut" looks like it was sliced from the living room of a brand-new, rustic
chalet.

As the trails fan out from the golf course to explore the surrounding
pine forests and old sand pits, they tell a fascinating geologic story to
those willing to listen. Farmers throughout New England curse Ice Age
glaciers for scraping away their topsoil and sprinkling heavy boulders
in on their fields — but these same glaciers have been quite generous to
New London. Rather than unwieldy boulders, they left behind a thick,
rich deposit of sand and gravel called an esker. Eskers are the remains

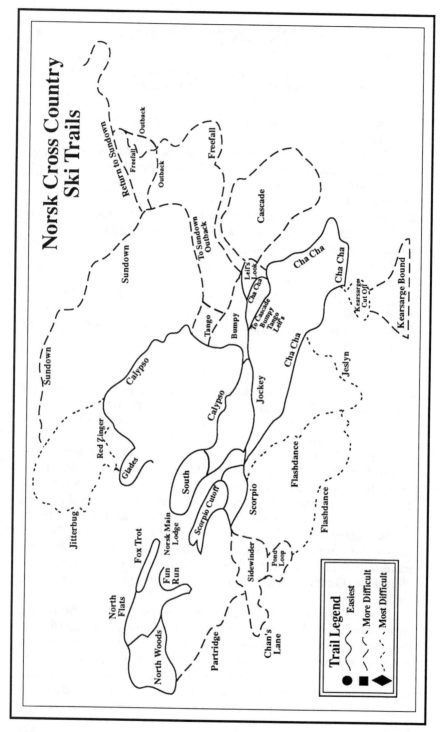

Norsk Cross Country Ski Trails

Trail Legend

● Easiest

■ More Difficult

◆ Most Difficult

of gravel-choked rivers that at one time meandered beneath glacier bellies. When the overlying ice melted away, the curving path of the rivers stayed behind as long, sinuous ridges of sand and gravel. Although "rich" might seem like a strange adjective for a bunch of sand and rocks, this stuff is often sold at a premium. You can thank New London's clean sand and gravel for the absence of frost-heaves on the high, well-drained I-89.

Norsk's trails are loathe to wander more than a few kilometers without running into these snow- and sapling-covered old sand pits. Some of the outer trails are also quite keen on wetlands. With their eerie, gray tree skeletons, the wetlands are remarkably pretty, and it is satisfying to glide smoothly and easily over what in the summer would be an inaccessible, mosquito-infested hell!

Overall, however, the fairways of the golf course enjoy a near-monopoly on Norsk's scenic beauty. With Kearsage Mountain's broad peak rising in the background and the handsome, posh clubhouse posing in the foreground, wandering the fields on a sunny day can be perfectly delightful. Trails further afield offer geologic edification and exercise.

The Trails

Goal-oriented skiers should strike out immediately for **Robb's Hut**, which beckons from a shady riverbank, five kilometers from the clubhouse. A round-trip ski out to the hut can easily fill a morning or afternoon — especially with a little leisurely lounging on the porch with a warm bowl of chile in your lap. The adventure begins with a quick, rolling glide across the golf course. **Mount Kearsarge** peaks out from behind the trees. After waddling across the road, follow **Calypso** down a short hill and through overgrown sand pits. **Outback** steers away from the pits and through an anemic little forest. You can almost see the pine trees smiling: the poor, sandy soil has killed off their deciduous competitors. After dropping across a frozen swamp, **Outback** settles into a winding, brookside downhill that finishes (quite abruptly) at **Robb's Hut**. Experienced skiers may opt for **Freefall**, a scenic and challenging alternative descent to the hut.

Some of the prettiest skiing at Norsk (besides the golf course) can be found on **Cascade** and **Kearsarge Bound**, two short loops that escape from the lowland areas and flirt with heartier forests. **Kearsage Bound** is a stately little wanderer (and owner Nancy Schlosser's favorite) that begins by climbing through pines and hemlocks. The second half breezes downhill past scattered stone walls that divvy up the woods like hedges in an English garden. **Cascade** starts with a long, flowing downhill then glides along the backbone of a low ridge. Thousands of small boulders lay strewn across a hillside of young birches and maples, where a well-placed picnic table provides terrific views of Kearsage. This overlook is much nicer than nearby **Leif's Look**; it is so pretty that it inspired a marriage proposal one winter!

Cascade and **Kearsarge Bound** are at the far edge of the trail system and are a bit difficult to reach. Closer to home, skiers can experiment with **The Glades**, which wriggles through an old stand of white pine. Beginners may want to try **Foxtrot, North Woods**, and **Partridge Run** — friendly, gentle trails which explore the northern reaches of the golf course. Although **Calypso** also provides beginners with an easy, five kilometer loop, it turns out to be little more than a full five kilometers of pitted esker. Interesting, but not all that inspiring.

Finding your way: Take Exit 11 off of I-89. Head east on Route 11 for two miles, then take a right onto Country Club Lane. The clubhouse is 1/2 mile up Country Club Lane.

Temple Mountain Cross Country

P.O. Box 368, Route 101
Peterborough, New Hampshire   03458
(603) 924-6949

Trail System: 25 km (25 km classical, 8 km skate, 15 km backcountry), 2.5 km snowmaking, 2.5 km night skiing
Our Estimate: A full afternoon of groomed skiing with limited beginner terrain.
Grooming: Fair
Scenic Beauty: 3
Touring Center: Rentals, lessons, wood stove, snacks and hot drinks (with cafeteria and bar in Alpine lodge), wax room, limited retail.
Favorite Trail: Wapack, a ridge-top backcountry descent from the top of the Alpine mountain that provides terrific views of the surrounding hills.
Payment: AE, MC, and VISA.
Lodging: Hannah Davis House-Fitzwilliam (603-585-3344, $$); Applegate B&B-Peterborough (603-924-6543, $$)
Local's Tip: The Eastern Mountain Store store in Peterborough has a back room called "Keith's Corner" which offers fantastic bargains on outdoor clothing.

According to manager Richard Block, the Alpine ski area at Temple is so close that "the smell of hamburgers sometimes drifts in this

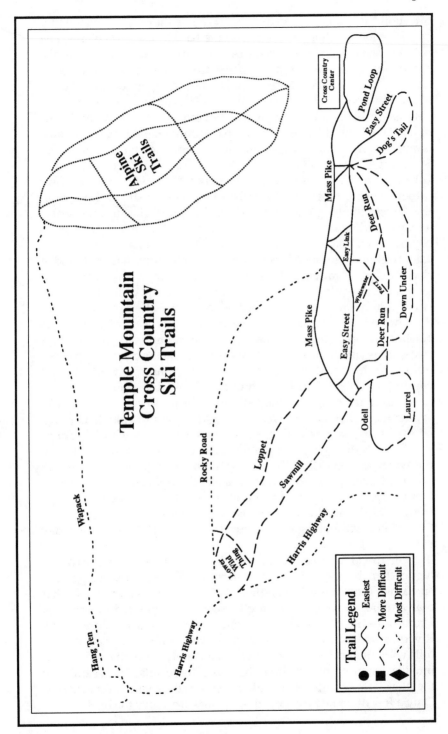

Temple Mountain
Cross Country
Ski Trails

direction." It's true. It's also true that reaching the cross country center by foot entails a short scurry across the base of the Alpine area, just behind the chairlift corral. But despite sharing a mountain with the Alpine folks, Temple Mountain Cross Country retains a quiet, comfortable, family atmosphere. It might be manager Richard Block's eagerness to chat, or the strength of the Bill Koch youth program, or the enthusiasm of the after-work crowd that comes out to ski laps under the lights. Whatever it is, visiting Temple Mountain gives you the same homey feeling you get when you watch a small-town baseball game.

Temple's cross country lodge has a surprisingly secluded atmosphere. Wide windows peer into the dark woods, while a wood stove in the corner breathes warmth into the room. Trails are strewn throughout the forest, climbing and descending the mountainside and nearly always heading *away* from the Alpine trails. With many of its trails etched into the side of a mountain, Temple unfortunately lacks good, easy beginner terrain. There is only a single, semi-flat trail, and it doesn't venture far enough from the Alpine area to give beginners a genuine taste of Nordic skiing. This concentration of difficult trails at a small, family-oriented ski area seems somewhat incongruous.

Located in southern New Hampshire only a short drive from Nashua, Temple Mountain is a terrific place to unwind after work. A two-and-a-half kilometer lighted loop gives you the chance to exercise outdoors when the short winter days are curtailing your workouts and causing fat cells to flourish. Families with divided interests have no need to suffer through long, expensive trips to resort towns like Waterville Valley and Stowe. Temple Mountain offers telemarking, cross country, snowboarding, and downhill in one tidy little package.

Temple Mountain isn't the place for a week's vacation, or even more than a couple days. There simply isn't enough playing room: 25 groomed kilometers won't remain unexplored for long. Even with a fabulous backcountry trail that slowly winds down the mountain ridge from the top of the Alpine slopes, the trail system isn't exactly extensive. Go farther north for longer stays, but come to Temple for the family day trip.

The top of Temple Mountain pokes its head a few hundred feet higher than the nearby hills of southern New Hampshire. Geologically speaking, Temple is a "monadnock," the remains of a mountain that many million years ago stood high above level plains in southern New Hampshire. As time passed, the entire region was slowly uplifted. Rivers carved their way into the plain, leaving behind a myriad of small hills with identical elevations. If you stand at the summit and look out into the distance, you'll see that the tops of these hills blend seamlessly together at the same level on the horizon—at the level of the old plains. Only a few other nearby monadnocks stick up above the hills.

The Trails

Beginners have it rough at Temple. With only a kilometer or two of generously labeled easy terrain, beginners need to dive into difficult trails before they've had a chance to test the waters. The **Mass Pike** (unfortunately named!), a rolling highway escorts skiers away from the Alpine action. Wide and smooth, the toll-free turnpike rides several large waves as it traverses the hillside hardwood forest. Although the descents have no frightening turns, the steepness of the inclines alone will intimidate many beginners. A return on **Easy Street** will bring you back the way you came — traversing the hillside, only a little lower.

If you're looking for a long loop and you like doing your climbing first thing, a trip up **Loppet** and back down on **Sawmill** is a fun, woodsy five kilometer tour. Start away from the lodge on **Mass Pike**. **Loppet** is the second exit on your right. It climbs in a series of steps through a recently-logged area to a wide, downhill road. Practice a few tele turns on the smooth, open downhills of **Harris Highway** before turning back into the woods on **Sawmill**. **Sawmill** begins with a curvy downhill stretch that was terraced into the side of a tiny hill. The slowly turning descent feels like a joyride down the threads of an enormous screw. It ends in a patch of evergreens, where laurel runs like weeds up a trailside ravine. A return to the lodge via **Deer Run** is a pleasant, forested, hillside traverse which guides you past stone walls and mountain laurels.

The adventurous should unquestionably take advantage of Temple's one-free-chairlift-ride offer to the top of the mountain. From there, you can either try telemarking down the Alpine slopes or, if you start early, you can head out on **Wapack**. A beautiful, ridgetop backcountry trail, **Wapack** provides remarkable views of the soft hills of southern New Hampshire and northern Massachusetts. Curling through a spruce-fir forest, you'll feel like you're in the wild and dangerous Presidential range, but you'll have the security of knowing that groomed trails await you at the end of a long, satisfying descent.

Finding your way: From Nashua, Take Route 101A west. After eight miles, turn left onto route 101 west. Temple Mountain is about 16 miles down the road on your left at the top of a hill.

Sunset Hill House Nordic Center

Sunset Hill Road
Sugar Hill, New Hampshire   03585
(800) SUN-HILL, (603) 823-5522

Trail System: *30 km groomed (30 km classical, 7 km skate)*
Our Personal Estimate: *A developing system with magnificent views.*
Grooming: *Casual*
Scenic Beauty: *5*
Touring Center: *Rentals available four miles away in Franconia, lessons by arrangement, soup available on weekends*
Payment: *All major credit cards*
Lodging: *Sunset Hill Inn-Sugar Hill (800-SUN-HILL, $$); Hilltop Inn-Sugar Hill (603-823-5695, $$)*
Favorite Trail: *Stewart's Sugar Run, a medley of woods and pastureland that leads to a sugaring operation in March.*
Local's Tip: *Wait until late afternoon to ski the Sunset Trail, and watch the sun melt spectacularly into the Green Mountains. In the morning, head over to the 50-year-old Polly's Pancake Parlor (near the top of Sugar Hill) for a fabulous pancake breakfast and amazing mountain views.*

The small mountain township of Sugar Hill, New Hampshire is one of the most beautiful places in New England. To the east rise endless ranges of blue and white mountains — the Presidentials, Cannon Mountain, and Lafayette — while in the west the Green Mountains slumber peacefully under their snowy cover. Sugar maples rim the wide, hilltop fields. There is no better way to appreciate the scenery than to ski at the Sunset Hill Inn Touring Center.

Sunset Hill's earlier incarnation as a touring center fell on hard times. After a hiatus and a change in ownership, the inn is reclaiming ski trails from the forest. The single-tracked, classical trails are primarily intended for guests at the inn, although everyone is welcome. (You can even bring well-behaved dogs.) Sedate trails loop around the bald pate of Sugar Hill, while more excitable ones dive into the variable terrain of the forest. You'll be thankful for the cover. With nothing to stop the wind between the Green Mountains and the Whites, it can be ferocious. There are days when it whips snowdrifts like egg whites and sends skiers scurrying for protection.

Offshoots from the main trail system lead to several 'Yankee amenities' in keeping with the area's subtle, pleasant tourism. The pretty little town boasts the requisite white church, old-fashioned houses, and American flag. Harman's Cheese Shop is an old-style creamery store selling gumdrops, maple candies, and smokily deli-

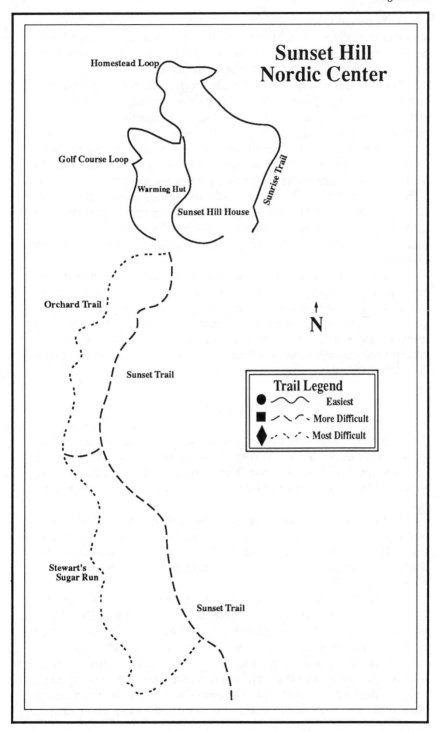

cious cheese samples. In the other direction, Stewart's Sugar House is a popular destination in March. During the sugaring season Charlie Stewart invites skiers in; you can see maple syrup being boiled off, breathe in the sweet scent, and take some home.

Tourism is not new to Sugar Hill. In the decades before and after the turn of the century, one of New Hampshire's grand old hotels stood firmly atop the ridge. Wealthy Easterners traveled to the train depot, where they were met by carriages and transported upward for genteel summer recreation. Although the hotel was torn down, a hundred hints to its existence remain. The imposing homes along the entrance roads were guest cottages, while the current inn housed the gentry's staff and servants. The former clubhouse walls are graced with intricate geometrical woodwork; since this is now the touring center, you can get a good look at it. Out on the Orchard trails you'll see the old apple trees and the Pig Pen, a big flat area where the hogs were fattened for slaughter.

You'll also find evidence of the iron industry. An iron vein running through the hilltop town was the richest known to man before iron ore was discovered out west. The trails pass by and over the old mines. You can thank the iron industry for the beautiful, wide-open hilltop. They converted all the trees to charcoal to fuel their smelter. The Iron Furnace Interpretive Center, located in Franconia, displays a scale model of the Iron Works for those who are interested.

The Trails

Sugar Hill Inn's new owners are working to expand their modest system: they open up more and more terrain every year. The trails are well-tended for their purpose, but narrow and not commercially groomed. You come to Sunset Hill for the views and the touring, not the workout.

The Golf Course compensates for the lack of perfectly flat trails. Several shortish loops — the **Sunrise Trail**, the **Homestead Loop**, and the **Golf Course Loop** — dance around the edge of the pastureland and duck into open woods. They embrace mild downhills and panoramic views.

The longer, wooded trails feel very different. The intermediate **Orchard Trail** carves a long, low parabola across the side of Ore Hill. It passes above the old hotel orchard, where deer come to munch winter apples, and through areas dense with young saplings. The more difficult **Stewart's Sugar Run** drops down an unforgettable spruce tunnel; it wends its merry way through pastures and stands of sugar maples.

The birch-lined **Sunset Trail** traverses Ore Hill at a slow and steady pace. It passes near two old iron mines: one looks like a giant gash in the earth, the other like a secret cavern with hand-dipped candles for icicles. Sunset Hill is working to reforge the **Inn Connection Trail**, which allows access to Franconia Inn's system. The trail drops 1200 feet and makes a leisurely five mile trip. Skiers should have strong intermediate skills and good control of the snowplow if they want to attempt this one.

Finding your way: Take I-93 north to the second Franconia exit (Exit 38). Follow Route 117 west for three miles almost to the town of Sugar Hill. At the top of the hill, follow the sign to Sunset Hill Inn and take a left on Sunset Hill Road.

Waterville Valley Cross Country
Waterville Valley, New Hampshire 03215
(603) 236-4666

Trail System: 70 km (70 km classical, 70 km skate, 35 km backcountry), 1/2 km snowmaking
Our Estimate: It feels like two completely different, large ski areas: one in the village and one just outside the village with more of a wilderness feel.
Grooming: Excellent
Scenic Beauty: 4 — only a few panoramas, but the trailside scenery is first-rate.
Touring Center: Rentals, lessons, restaurants nearby, some retail, and a terrific map of the trail system with separate profiles of every trail. Neighboring shops provide more services than you could ever need.
Favorite Trail: White Mountain Criterion, one of the best expert trails in the Northeast.
Payment: All major credit cards accepted.
Lodging: The Golden Eagle Lodge-Trailside (603-236-4551, $$$-$$$$); Mountain Fare Inn-Campton (603-726-4283, $$)
Local's Tip: The Common Man (exit 24 in Ashland) is a romantic little fine-dining favorite for New Hampshire folks.

If you like skiing for skiing's sake and could care less about wood stoves and quaint old farmhouses, we urge you to visit Waterville. One of the most exciting and diverse trail systems in New England lies only two hours of eager, reckless driving from Boston. Masterfully designed, exquisitely groomed trails splay through the village and sink deep into the forests of the White Mountains. No matter who you are, no matter what your ability level, you are certain to find a personal favorite at this popular valley resort.

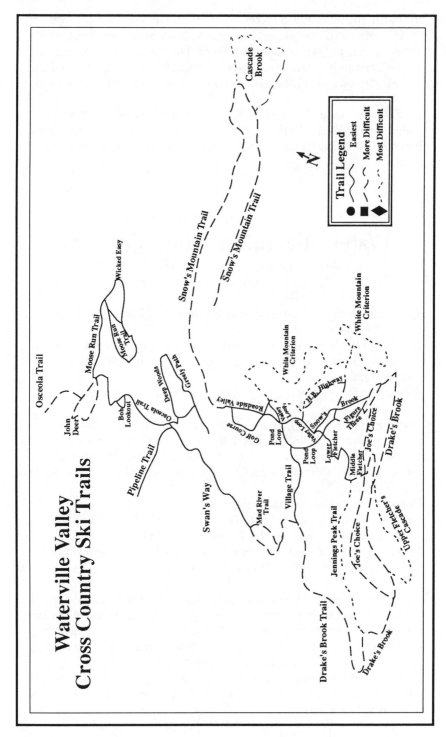

Waterville Valley
Cross Country Ski Trails

Racers' eyes sparkle when you mention Waterville Valley. They become restless and jittery. They eagerly blurt out incoherent, jumbled stories about terrific wipe-outs or close saves on high-speed downhills. It's no wonder they have trouble controlling their enthusiasm. With trails ingeniously designed by an ambitious ex-racer, Waterville has become a mecca for serious athletes. This is the only trail system east of Lake Placid that feels like it could easily accommodate the Nordic events at the next Winter Olympics.

The road to Waterville Valley leads along a winding river, through an ocean of secluded forest. After several miles of wilderness, the road rounds a final bend, and a condo-clogged island of busy development pops into view. Welcome to Waterville Valley. The town is settled in the far end of a valley cul-de-sac, pushing up against steep mountainsides. The touring center, unfortunately, shares an outdoor mall with a pizza joint, lounge, and gift shop.

The trail system itself is divided into two sections — the North End and the South End — and about a half-mile of driving separates the two. The entire North End is on loan from the U.S. Forest Service. Two long, gradual climbs ease their way up forest service roads and slowly work their way into the White Mountains, offering fine views of the valley along the way. The South End could be renamed "The Village," since many of its trails weave their way in and around the town of Waterville. Giant culverts beneath roadways provide excellent skier drainage.

Wildlife hounds will be in hog heaven at Waterville, thanks mostly to a recent blow-down. In 1980, a powerful storm lashed the valley with 80 to 90-mile per hour winds, flattening extensive tracts of forests. The dense thicket that thrives in the wind-ravaged areas is a popular foraging area for deer, rabbits, and coyotes.

The Trails

Novices can stick close to civilization on the trails in and around the village in the South End. The **Pond Loop**, **Village Trail**, and **Lower Fletcher's Cascade** are good for starters. They'll allow you to get used to your skis without venturing far from the warmth of the touring center and the security of the valley.

Stronger skiers who continue up **Lower Fletcher's Cascade** toward **Joe's Choice** will be rewarded by fabulous, secluded skiing along a low ridge. This is a great getaway on busy weekends. The **Hairpin Corner** at the end of **Drake's Brook** can be easily managed by experts and intermediates with plenty of chutzpah; beginners may want to hoof it. **H.B. Highway** climbs through the heart of the blowdown area and offers a good chance to see rabbit, deer, and coyote tracks.

The **White Mountain Criterion** trail has tempted, teased, and threatened expert skiers for several years. Only Lake Placid's Olympic

Women's five km can compare in design to this challenging heart-throb. **The Criterion's** one-two combination is a relentlessly grueling climb out of the valley followed by a long, fast, winding downhill. Forget about spectacular views and gurgling brooks. Take this one for what it is: fabulous, thrilling skiing.

If you're still itching for more terrain, stop in at the touring center for directions and hop in your car for a quick ride to the North End.

The North End offers two options. **Livermore Road** follows Avalanche Brook several miles up a gentle valley. If you're the type that likes to open their presents on Christmas Eve, this trail is not for you. It's a long, slow, monotonous climb. The return is ample payback: bring an extra jacket for the relaxing, sweeping, 20-minute downhill. Telemark skiers will swallow hard, bruit the monotony, and enjoy carving their way down the Alpine area's **Snow's Mountain** on the other side of the hill.

The second, more interesting option is the **Osceola Trail**. Although **Osceola** also begins with a smooth, steady climb, it soon offers greater variety. **Bob's Lookout** is a brief diversion that offers a terrific view of the mountain ring surrounding the valley. **Moose Run** and **Wicked Easy** — a few kilometers up **Osceola Trail** — wrap rhythmically through a hardwood forest with a yellow birch motif. Sunlight and glimpses of nearby mountains drift easily down to the trail. The upper section of **Osceola** curls toward a high cul-de-sac.

Finding your way: Take exit 28 off of I-93. Take a right onto Route 49 east. After 11 miles, turn left into Town Square (don't take earlier left toward the Alpine area). After parking, walk into Town Square. The cross country center will be on the right at the far end.

Maine

Carter's X-C Ski Area

Middle Intervale Road
Bethel, Maine 04217
(207) 539-4848

Trail System: *40 km groomed (40 km classical, 40 km skate) and 20 km backcountry*
Our Personal Estimate: *Mostly intermediate trails with a couple of the steepest hills on the planet.*
Grooming: *Casual. Don't expect to do interval training.*
Scenic Beauty: *3*
Touring Center: *Rentals, snack counter, couches, tables, and small shop*
Favorite Trail: *Scenic Outlook, with a fantastic view of the surrounding mountains*
Payment: *AE, DSC, MC, and VISA*
Lodging: *Telemark Inn-Bethel (207-836-2703, $$$, has own cross country ski trails); Chapman Inn (207-824-2657, $$$); Yurts and lodges available along the trail system*
Local's Tip: *From the top of the trail system, ski backcountry to the knife-edge along the top of Farwell Mountain. On a clear day you can see over into the Presidential Range in New Hampshire.*

If you can predict a person's fortune by examining his/her palms, then surely you can decipher their character by skiing their trail system. The 60 kilometers of trails at Carter's romp adventurously over reclaimed farmland and wooded mountainside. Unexpected curves repeatedly catch you off guard. Mountain cabins and a Mongolian yurt give you a place to kick up your feet and warm your toes. And trails careen down impossibly steep slopes, daring you to try them. Welcome to Dave Carter's fun-loving ski center at Bethel.

Carter's is dominated by the expansive, jovial personality of Dave Carter. In his sophomore year of high school, Dave played basketball until one fateful day before practice when he walked by the ski team doing loops around the school field. "That's what I want to do," he said to himself. He walked into the gym, quit basketball, and went out to join the skiers. At that moment, he decided he was going to put the world on skis. He harangued friends into going with him, and he even bought ski equipment for his girlfriends — which he took back when the relationships went sour. Later he alternated summers working on the railroad with winters skiing. Now Dave and his wife Anne run two touring centers — one in Bethel and one in Oxford — and are living out his dream.

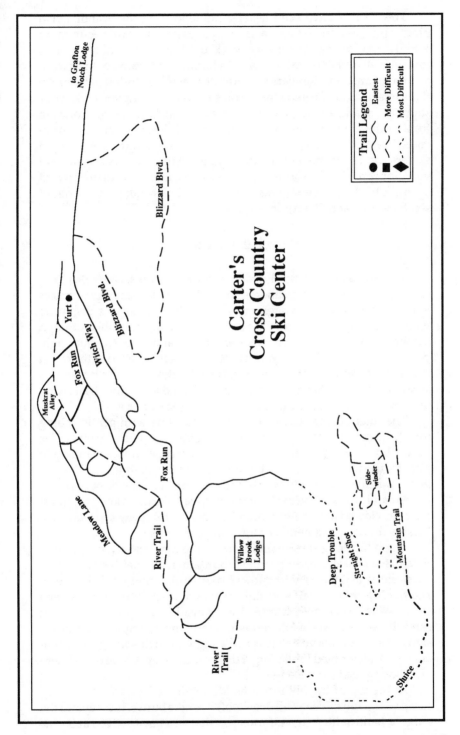

Carter's
Cross Country
Ski Center

to Grafton
Notch Lodge

Blizzard Blvd.

Blizzard Blvd.

Yurt ●

Muskrat
Alley

Fox Run

Witch Way

Fox Run

Meadow Lark

River Trail

Willow
Brook
Lodge

River
Trail

Deep Trouble

Straight Shot

Side-
winder

Mountain Trail

Shuice

Trail Legend

—— Easiest

⌐⌐⌐ More Difficult

- - - Most Difficult

● ■ ◆

The Carters have been heavily influenced by the Scandinavian philosophy of sport. Skiing is a natural part of life, not a calorie-burning activity you squeeze in between work and dinner. You don't have to fuss with all the details of equipment, clothing, and training. Just go out and have fun! Over the years he has built a small hut-to-hut network on the system. You can rent these trailside accommodations, ski your supplies in, and spend an evening playing cards or telling stories in front of the wood stove. This out-the-door philosophy has also influenced his ski trails, and the whole area has a backcountry feel. Intrepid skaters can cover most of the trail system, but be prepared for wild variation: broad trails shrink to five feet across and then splay outward again. A bird's-eye view looks like a snake that swallowed a series of small rodents at half hour intervals.

The Trails

The best easy skiing lies down along the river banks. The **Fields Trail** justifies its name, and meanders through Carter's only open spaces with views of the Androscoggin and surrounding mountains. Beginners who like a little variety can try the **River Trail**, which scrambles through the woods with unexpected twists and turns, and takes the skier right past the Mongolian Yurt. If you are intent on skating, head to the broad **Witch Way** and beyond it to **Blizzard Boulevard**, which plows a snowcovered swath over 100 acres in a 2.5 mile loop. Both trails were once roadways and provide the best skating at Carter's.

The intermediate **Lower Lodge Trail** begins with gentle rolling forest, but curves into an unexpected dive and a couple sharp turns. The Lower Lodge itself is a rebuilt 200 year old carriage house standing in a bristly field on acreage Dave bought while still in high school. You can go in, warm up, and help yourself to hot drinks on the honor system. Listen carefully and you can hear the highway. Further along, the forest has been cleared of underbrush, and the delightful **Anne's Moondance** flickers through a cathedral of towering evergreens.

If you like long steady uphills, cross the road and try the popular **Swan Hill Passage** leading to the **Mountain Trail**. Neither is prohibitively steep, and you can get into a pleasant uphill rhythm. Thirty years ago the **Mountain Trail** was still a working road. You'll ski between stone walls which once hemmed in roadside pastures; if you look carefully you can see a fallen down house and a couple cellar holes, signs of the community that was. Skiing this backward gives you a nearly uninterrupted (don't forget the road crossing!) three mile downhill glide to the Lower Lodge.

At the top of the hill lurks the Mountain Lodge, an old hunting camp with a full kitchen and deer hoofs over the bunks. Just beyond the lodge, a handwritten sign informs you that you have arrived at Scenic

Overview. You can see Sunday River, Mount Will, and Mount Ellingworth through a dozen evergreen columns, but don't 'ooh' and 'ahh' here — the better views are higher up.

Straight Shot traverses the mountain and provides an honorable way to ski down for those who don't embrace the thought of death. **The Sluice** and **Deep Trouble** are contradictorily marked "Don't Ski Down" and "For Triple Diamond Experts Only." The truth is that you can ski them, but only if you're a hotshot. These trails shoot straight down the mountainside in a series of unrepenting drops and will set even the stoutest heart aflutter. They are steep!

The **Scenic Lookout** trail is a broad king's highway running the length of the mountain plateau. It teases you with hints of a view through the trees but doesn't deliver until you climb through the trees and curve around the side of the hill. The trees fall away below, with vistas revealing a spectacular layering of mountains: Sunday River, the Carter Mariahs, the Meehoosuks, and the caps of the Presidential Range. From here, the trails are all backcountry.

Finding your way: Take I-95 to Route 26 north, and drive almost into Bethel. Just south of town you'll see signs for Carter's. Take a right on Middle Intervale Road and drive 3.5 miles to the center.

Sunday River Cross Country Center

RFD #2, Box 1688
Bethel, Maine 04217
(207) 824-2410

Trail System: 40 km (40 km classical, 40 km skate, no backcountry)
Our Estimate: Lots of short, flat easy trails in a tight evergreen forest, with a few longer loops that climb a hillside.
Grooming: Good
Scenic Beauty: 3
Touring Center: A cozy annex to the inn with rentals, lessons, snacks and hot drinks, full retail, and a beautiful, sunny room with windows that look out toward the trails.
Favorite Trail: Cruiser, a bumpy, winding, hillside traverse
Payment: All major credit cards accepted.
Lodging: Sunday River Inn-Sunday River (207-824-2410, $$-$$$); Douglass Place-Bethel (207-824-2229, $$)
Local's Tip: Guided candlelight skiing every Friday night to a bonfire in the woods.

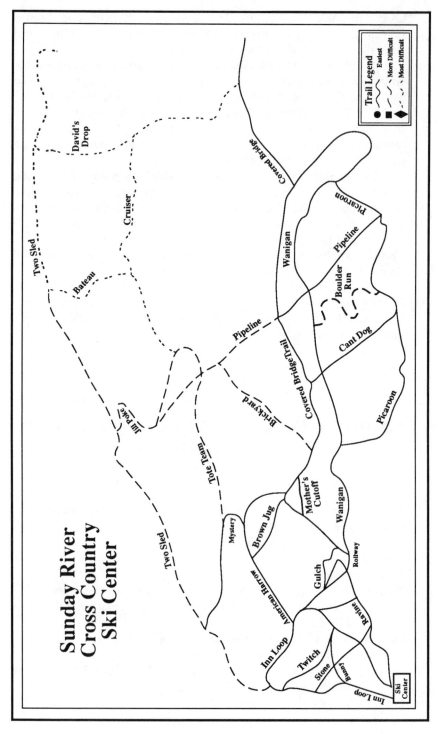

Despite sharing a name with its Alpine cousin up the road, the Sunday River Inn and Cross Country Center is far from an amenity for bored Alpine skiers. *Au contraire.* Watching the footloose weekend activities from the sunny front deck of the inn, you'll begin thinking that Alpine skiers are second-class citizens in the area. That wouldn't be far off the mark. Nordic skiing at Sunday River stands on its own.

The atmosphere at Sunday River is friendly and fun — not unlike a Labor Day party or a festive family gathering. A long, wooden deck curves around the side of the inn like an extended running board. Porch potatoes watch skiers testing their strides on the practice field before they disappear beneath the dark evergreens on the far side. Fun, games, and action prevail: an Elderhostel visitor tests telemark turns on a bulldozed blob they call the telemark "hill," an instructor videotapes beginners' strides, and kids rush eagerly into the forest on cross country scavenger hunts.

If you're just getting started with skiing, if you have young children tagging along, or if you prefer the social aspects of sport, Sunday River is an ideal destination. Enjoy the well-marked and well-groomed trails. Take advantage of the fire ring storytelling and the lantern-lined ski loop on Friday nights. Design a costume and return in April to compete in the annual Pole, Paddle, and Paw competition/celebration: ski to the covered bridge, paddle down the Sunday River, and snowshoe toward the finish line back at the inn. Then, as innkeeper Steve Wight says, "drink beer and fall down until springtime!"

More serious skiers — those that ski too fast to appreciate picnic tables and bird feeders and the bench swings scattered throughout the forest — may be less enthused by Sunday River's offerings. A large part of the trail system lies in a relatively flat, somber evergreen forest. You may find yourself yearning for more light and variety.

The Trails

There is only a fuzzy divide between the inn and the trail system: step right off the front porch and onto your skis. The field in front of the center is terrific for a quick warm-up, and, however small the Telemark Hill may appear from the porch, you will certainly be tempted to test a few snowplows or telemark turns on it. Be forewarned, however, your crashes will be embarrassingly public!

A twisted net of beginner trails reaches into the forest from the fields. Stick a trail map in your back pocket and wander aimlessly beneath the evergreens. The trails are so short and their interconnections so complex, that following your progress on the trail map can be exceedingly tedious. Not to worry, though, with every intersection numbered and with signs pointing the way back to the inn, you'll have no trouble finding your way home. The trails closer to the river receive a bit more natural light. **Wanigan** and **Picaroon** offer gently rolling terrain without any intimidating climbs or descents. **Wanigan** eventually joins the **Covered Bridge Trail**, a Sunday River favorite.

The **Covered Bridge Trail** is a flat, out-and-back path with a goal: the Artists' Covered Bridge, a splendid wooden structure which at one time helped horses, cars, pedestrians, and skiers get across the Sunday River. Today, it provides a brainteaser for photographers, who struggle to frame snapshots without the concrete replacement looming in the background. Painters have it easy.

Skiers anxious to escape the beginner net should wind their way up **Two Sled**, then drop down to **Cruiser** via **Jill Poke**. **Two Sled** follows a curvy brook up a subtle valley, while **Cruiser** offers an exciting bumpy, winding hillside traverse through evergreens. Alternatively, skip **Cruiser** and continue up **Two Sled** out of the evergreens (finally!) toward **Overlook**. **Overlook** lives up to its name, providing a fine view of the river valley and Alpine area. A bench sits conveniently at the top of a small cliff — a terrific spot for lunch.

Masochists should head for **David's Drop**, a precipitous 300-foot descent that could easily pass for an Olympic bobsled run. Don't take this hill lightly! After the downhill, the trail passes by a beaver pond, coming within a pole's length of their lodge.

Finding your way: Follow the Maine Turnpike (I-95) to Exit 11 in Gray. Take Route 26 north to Bethel. In Bethel, Route 26 joins with Route 2. Follow Routes 2/26 east out of town. About three miles out of town, take a left onto Sunday River Road (by the Sunday River Brewing Company). After about two miles, turn left onto the Sunday River Access Road (heading toward the Alpine mountain). The cross country center and inn will be on your right.

Harris Farm Cross Country Ski Center

252 Buzzell Road
Dayton, Maine 04005
(207) 499-2678

Trail System: 40 km (40 km classical, 30 km skate, no backcountry)
Our Estimate: Rolling field after field after field with a few
woodsy connections.
Grooming: Good
Scenic Beauty: 3
Touring Center: A small, comfortable lodge with rentals, lessons, wood stove,
homemade snacks and hot drinks, wax bench, and some retail.
Favorite Trail: Bobcat Loop, a 3 km spin with a nice balance of meadows and
forests.
Payment: DSC
Lodging: Captain Lord Mansion-Kennebunkport (800-522-3141, $$$); Green
Heron Inn-Kennebunkport (207-967-3315, $$)
Local's Tip: Get off-season rates in nearby Kennebunkport or Ogunquit's
oceanside inns. Stroll Kennebunkport's beaches or Ogunquit's cliff walk
in the morning, then ski in the afternoon.

Dairy farms in Dayton aren't exactly thriving. At one time numbering
over 20, only two working farms survive in the town today. With such
an inauspicious business climate, one would have expected Bill and
Dixie Harris's half dozen seedlings to grow up on the farm, then scatter
in a half dozen different directions. Yet all six kids have settled within
ten miles of the roost, and three currently work alongside their parents
on the farm. The Harris' began grooming ski trails in 1988, partly to
supplement the income from the dairy and vegetable farm, and partly
to give this boomerang generation something to keep them busy on the
farm!

The magnet which kept the kids within close range also works its
magic on skiers: a welcoming, familial atmosphere. As Bill puts it, "the
people are friendly...even the dog's friendly." It's true. A visit to the ski
touring center is a thinly disguised trip to the neighbors. Several of the
boys will likely be lounging in the warming hut, while their mother zips
back and forth from the kitchen with warm trays of muffins and
cookies. They'll all appear completely relaxed and at home. They
should; this *was* their home for ten years — before their father threw
together a new house across the street.

Hibernating, snow-covered pastures are the heart of the trail system at Harris Farm. Mixed woods surround and interrupt ocean-like

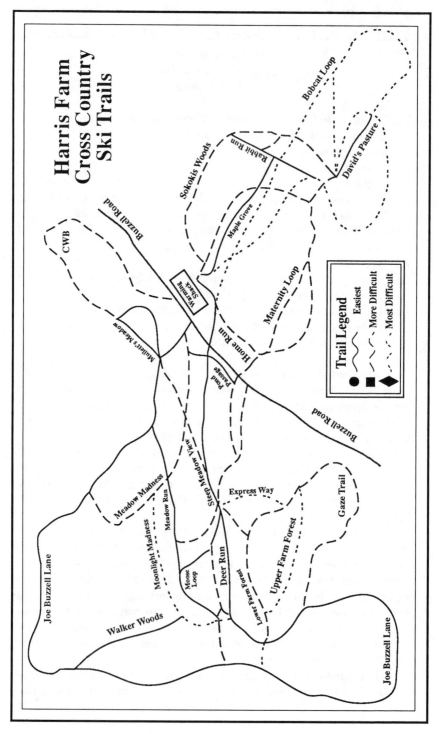

swells of pasture. The passageways through the woods developed out of a combination of driveways, hand-cut trails, and "tote roads." All of the wooded areas have been logged at one time or another, and tote roads were the winding ascents cut into hillsides to allow horses to drag the logs uphill. Most of these tote roads were quite overgrown by 1988, but Bill searched them out: "If you have sharp enough eyes and know the woods at all, you can see the roads."

The skiing at Harris Farm is decidedly tame. Ninety-five percent of the trail system could be easily negotiated by a novice. The careful grooming and easy terrain make this a great place to relax and work comfortably on your stride. Bright, sunny afternoons are ideal. Stay away on cold, windy days — drifting snow and frostbite take charge!

The Trails

If you can say "rolling meadow with gradual uphills and easy downhills," then you've gone a long way toward describing most of the Harris Farm trail network. Although the pastures are beautiful on sunny days, we would have to recommend the wooded loops for a little more fun and variety.

After crossing the pasture by the ice skating rink, **Joe Buzzell Lane** burrows around in mixed forests for a few kilometers, then shoots back into daylight for a long trek back to the farm across the pastures. The initial wooded section is flat as a board. There's an old cellar hole just past the **Walker Woods Trail** on your left, and if you use the hilly **Gaze Trail** as an extension, you'll coast past the rusted carcass of a 1930s truck. **Joe Buzzell Lane** allows for as many short-cuts and extensions as you please. **Express Way** is a fun little downhill — possibly the steepest on the entire farm.

Back on the other side of Buzzell Road are several more rolling pasture options. The **Bobcat Loop's** dips and turns challenge hotshots with a few curve balls. On **Bobcat's** first wooded climb, you'll see sap lines linking sugar maples on your right. After creeping around the birched hillcrest, **Bobcat** lunges over a quick hill, then runs over pastures back to the farmhouse. The spruces and firs of a nearby Christmas tree farm will poke over the horizon on your right. **Sokokis Woods** provides for a pretty, short trek through evergreens, then spits you back into the middle of two enormous swells of white pasture.

Finding your way: Take exit 3 off of the Maine Turnpike. Follow Route 35 north 11 miles, through Goodwin's Mills, then take a right onto Gould Road. Take the first right onto Buzzell Road. Follow Buzzell road 3/4 mile, and Harris Farm will be on your left.

Troll Valley Ski Touring Center
RFD #4, Box 5215
Farmington, Maine 04938
(207) 778-3656

Trail System: 40 km (40 km classical, 35 km skate, limitless backcountry)
Our Estimate: A full day of skiing, with trails for all abilities, plus an
   additional 15 kilometer challenge at Titcomb Mountain.
Grooming: Excellent
Scenic Beauty: 3
Touring Center: A house with rentals, lessons, wood stove, homey cafeteria,
   some retail, a locker room with showers, and a comfy couch.
Favorite Trail: Tom's Challenge is the hands down winner. A testy, three km
   scenic wonder. You'll feel like you've been beamed to the Rockies.
Payment: No credit cards accepted.
Lodging: The Herbert-Kingfield (800-THE-HERB, $$-$$$); Colonial Valley
   Motel-Farmington (207-778-3391, $$)
Local's Tip: For an extra $5, you can roast in the sauna then simmer in the
   whirlpool after a taxing ski.

Many touring center managers let cross country skiing dominate
their lives, but Galen Sayward didn't stop there. He let the sport invade
his home, seduce his family, and take over his spare time. A visit to Troll
Valley differs little from a personal invite to the Sayward residence. The
skiers' lounge is just below the family bedrooms, and cross country ski
trails fan out in all directions from their backyard. Galen can stand on
his front steps and point skiers toward over 30 kilometers of meticulously
groomed trails through woods, fields, and beaver bogs.

In the early 1980s, Galen had just finished creating a 15 kilometer
racing network on the side of Farmington's Titcomb Mountain. Real-
izing that the rugged terrain at Titcomb would never quite suit beginners,
he purchased a solid, 130-acre chunk of old farmland in a gentle valley
on the other side of the mountain and began mixing from scratch the
ingredients for an entirely new touring center. Today, the two ski areas
are joined at the hip by a low ridge, but they offer completely different
skiing: Titcomb has hilly, forested terrain with steep climbs and fast
downhills, while Troll Valley offers gentler trails and more open
meadow skiing. Both are blessed with the generous early snow that is
typical of northern Maine.

Personal attention is central to the Troll Valley experience. Do you
need a quick lesson? Let Galen, the former director of the U.S. Ski
Team's Ski Coaches Association, teach you the basics of the diagonal
stride! Are you a bit sore? End the day in the soothing relaxation of the

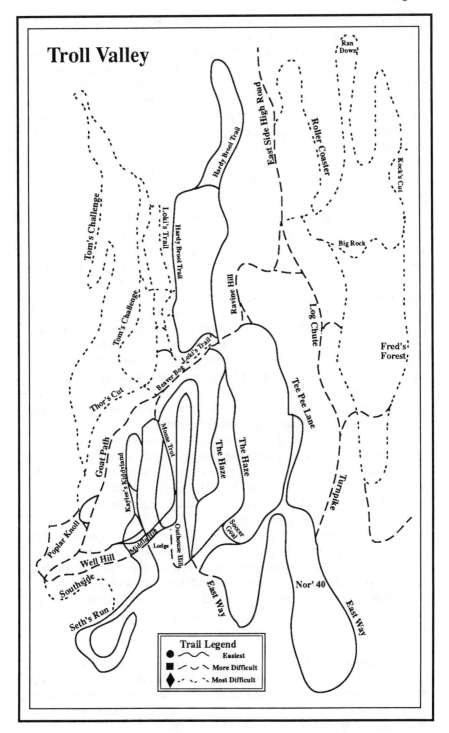

Troll Valley

Trail Legend

● ～～ Easiest
■ ～～ More Difficult
◆ ～．～ Most Difficult

hot tub! At Troll Valley, you will be treated well — pampered in a relaxed, down-home sort of way.

Despite advertising unlimited backcountry and despite connections to the trails at Titcomb Mountain, the Troll Valley trail system itself is not unmanageably large. A trip around the perimeter of the entire area might involve about 15 kilometers of skiing at the most. Quality triumphs over quantity in this case, you will certainly relish the masterful trail design and impeccable grooming, but you may hanker after a few longer, more out-of-the-way loops.

The Trails

If you're confident on your skis, waste no time and head straight for **Tom's Challenge**. It is an exquisitely designed masterpiece, providing everything you could ever want in a trail packed into a three kilometer loop: a challenging climb, spectacular views of the Longfellow Mountains, and a 180 degree whiplash corner. Ski it fast or take the good-life approach: pack cheese and crackers, ski up to one of the picnic tables, and enjoy a relaxing break at the top of the world.

Neophytes shouldn't miss the chance to ski with the former director of the U.S. Ski Team's Ski Coaches Association; fork over the few extra dollars for a private lesson. Then, setting out on your own with your newly developed skiing aplomb, lose yourself on the appropriately named **Maze** loop, or try **Easy Way**. Both are a little difficult to follow. They will probably spit you out onto **Nor 40**, which loops loosely around the field in front of a beautiful white farmhouse.

The South Side, Troll Valley's annex across the road, provides approximately five kilometers of solid intermediate skiing through dense, protected forest — a smart choice (along with the **Hardy Brook Trail**) on a windy day. You'll ski by "Ralph's House" at the far end of the South Side trails. Don't be surprised if either Ralph or his wife steps outside to greet you as you ski over their front lawn.

Experts craving more challenging kilometers should explore the racing trails at Titcomb Mountain. Once you cross the ridge by **Ravine Hill** and breach the stone wall, you stand on Titcomb territory. Titcomb's trails wrap like a string of sausages around the side of a small Alpine ski mountain. The Alpine area is short and steep, which makes it a great place to telemark ski. Grooming on this side of the ridge is a little more casual.

Finding your way: Take Exit 12 off of I-495 in Maine and head north on Route 4. You'll stay on Route 4 for nearly an hour. Route 4 runs into Route 2 east, and the two head toward Farmington together. About four miles after this merge, take a left onto Red Schoolhouse Road (just before Pizza Hut). Troll Valley will be on your right about a mile up the road.

Sugarloaf Ski Touring Center

(formerly Carrabassett Valley)
RR 1 Box 5000
Kingfield, Maine 04947
(207) 237-2000, (207) 237-6830

Trail System: *85 km groomed (85 km classical, 70 km skate)*
Our Personal Estimate: *One of the most extensive areas in the East, with lots of trails for every kind of skier.*
Grooming: *Excellent, particularly near the center; less-traveled trails are also less-groomed*
Scenic Beauty: *4*
Touring Center: *Extensive Nordic lodge with rentals, lessons, hot food, full retail shop*
Favorite Trail: *Matagwesue, which slips along a secret hillside and then cascades down over the resort golf course*
Payment: *AE, MC, and VISA*
Lodging: *Sugarloaf Mountain Hotel-Carrabassett Valley (800-237-2222, $$$); Lumberjack Lodge-Carrabassett Valley (207-237-2141, $)*
Local's Tip: *Sugarbush has great glade skiing in March. Selective cutting on Geesoos and Neeburbun has opened up the forest so there is room to ski between the trees. With five or six feet of snow burying boulders and stumps, you can strike out where ever you want through the woods.*

In a world where advertising slogans outshout each other with impossible claims, Sugarloaf Ski Touring Center's motto is decidedly modest: "Sugarloaf Nordic. It's closer than you think!" Maybe it is and maybe it isn't, but the area would be worth a trip from Florida. Sugarloaf is gunning for Nordic superstardom and is getting there fast. The beauty of the Carrabassett Valley, the quality and quantity of the trails, and the area's attention to detail contribute to a first-rate Nordic center.

Mother Nature does her part. Sugarloaf Ski Touring Center lies just inside a ring of mountains in Western Maine. Snow-bearing clouds come over the pass at the headwaters of the Carrabassett River and loose their load on the valley below. The area reaps the snowy benefit of its high, northern location; even in dry years, their careful attention to summer trail maintenance means that they can have 40 kilometers of good skiing with only four to six inches of snow.

Reminders of western Maine's two economic strongholds — logging and tourism — dominate the trail network. The eastern lands consist mostly of low-elevation evergreen forests and boggy flatlands. Many of the trails cover old logging roads, and forests of slim young

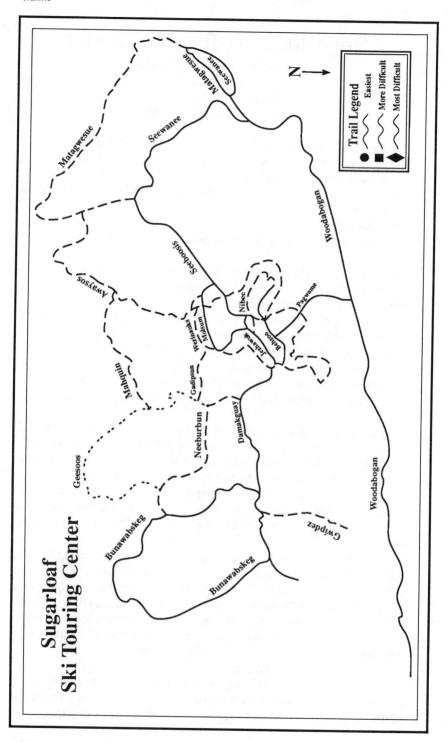

Sugarloaf
Ski Touring Center

trees attest to recent logging. The western lands extend to Sugarloaf's Alpine area, passing by condominiums, over downhill trails, and along the backbone of a resort golf course.

You can also feel the influence of the Penobscot nation. Trails are named and marked in their native language — Seeboosis, Damakguay, and Gwipdiz — and obligingly translated on the map (Small River, Beaver, and Colored Leaf). This recognition of the area's original inhabitants is a judicious, respectful gesture, but for practical getting-around purposes most skiers fall back on the numbers. It can be hard to distinguish Gwipdiz from Gadipsun at the end of a long day.

Unlike many Nordic centers that find themselves shackled to an Alpine area, Sugarloaf allows plenty of pure Nordic escape. The two areas are several miles apart. Sugarloaf mountain need only be a striking visual backdrop to your wilderness ski experience; you can ski for days on the remote and forested trails. Alternatively, bridge the gap. Brazen your way onto the chairlift and shake your skinny skis at the downhillers below. Alpine tickets buy Nordic access — unfortunately this doesn't work the other way around.

A few years ago, Sugarloaf was called "the best kept secret in Maine." Today, they are intent on getting the word out. With remarkable cooperation between town and mountain, Sugarloaf is giving itself a make-over and aims to be the top touring center in the East. Their expansive solar-heated touring center feels like an Alpine lodge. The Klister Kitchen concocts wholesome gourmet fare from scratch. On the trails, you'll repeatedly encounter friendly, red-jacketed ski patrol volunteers trained to haul you out of emergency situations. If you're going to break a leg, this is the place to do it! Future plans include a hut-to-hut system, snowmaking, night skiing, and 200 kilometers of trails: a network linking Sugarloaf to its neighbors Burnt Mountain and Crocker Mountain, and extending across the valley to the Bigelow Preserve.

The Trails

Sugarbush's trails cover an exciting variety of terrain, and the land encompasses four distinct environments. The trails clustered around the touring center and to the east meander through dense spruce and fir forests, past bogs, and over gently rolling terrain. Pilliated woodpeckers drill at dead trees in machine-gun staccato. The **Jezhawuk** (Mosquito) trail, named for the scourge of Maine summers, is a winding private flicker of a trail, crowded on both sides by evergreens. The **Damakguay** trail, leading to the **Bunawabseg** trail, provides wooded, lowland skiing across land belonging to the Penobscot nation. The narrow, low terrain of these trails is best for classical skiing. The competition loop is appropriately named **Wezinauks**, which translates to "Go Fast." It weaves and bobs through more difficult variations, and has more than one fast downhill with a sharp turn at the bottom. **Pretty Bog** is an unexpected clearing with a mountain vista and a picnic bench to enjoy it from.

The second environment is the mature hardwood forest, higher up on the mountain. Open and airy, the hillside affords only scenic glimpses: go elsewhere for the panorama. Coyote and bobcat leave signs for skiers to identify; and we know of one patroller who would have preferred a few more of these signs as he rounded a downhill corner in this section, and nearly crashed into a moose. The upwardly mobile **Neeburban** rises in a series of plateaus, while saplings overhead form a deciduous arch. Skiing down it, you can put your skis in the tracks and take a nap: with only one blip the trail slopes downward for nearly two kilometers. **Maquin** traverses Burnt Mountain, winding up and down through challenging terrain. Sugarloaf's most difficult trail, **Geesoos** (meaning 'Power of the Sun') treks 600 feet up from the lodge in steady climb, and points back downward in a rushing descent.

The third environment encompasses the Alpine terrain and golf course. Leaving the center, **Seeboosis** feels a little like a highway. It is wider than most roads in Maine, and you'll see more people on this one trail than on the rest of them combined. **Seeboosis** is the Alpine link. You will run into a barely graded Alpine slope and all of a sudden your trail disappears. Don't be confused. Defying gravity and good sense, the trail goes up the slope while Alpine skiers come down. Have you ever watched a salmon struggling upstream, dodging pieces of river flotsam and jetsam? After skiing this trail, you will empathize.

The trail signs are hard to spot near the Alpine mountain's Base Lodge. The **X-C** trail turns right and cuts beneath a series of chairlifts. Ask the operators where to duck into the woods. The **Matagwesue** trail is a secret, lesser-groomed trail which dallies across the mountain; later, it crosses the road and heads down through a scenic series of fields and fairways, rimmed by birches and affording spectacular views of the mountains.

The fourth environment is a one-trail footnote to the area, but a popular one. The out-and-back **Woodabogan** trail follows the Carrabassett River on the old Narrow Gauge railroad bed. Scenic and flat, it cruises past a beaver pond, a beaver dam, and several bogs on its five mile length.

Finding your way: Take I-95 north to Augusta; from there follow Route 27 north through Farmington and Kingfield. Sugarloaf is 15 miles north of Kingfield on Route 27. Watch for the touring center sign on the left side of the road.

The Birches Ski Touring Center
Rockwood, Maine 04478
(800) 825-WILD, (207) 534-7305

Trail System: 40 km (40 km classical, 15 km skate, limitless backcountry on snowmobile trails)

Our Estimate: This is one of the few ski areas that seems to underestimate its trail system. With the frozen lake and nearby snowmobile trails, you almost feel like you could ski forever.

Favorite Trail: Moosehead Lake (after it freezes!)

Grooming: Good, but geared more toward classical.

Scenic Beauty: 3; far better on or near the lakes than in the woods.

Touring Center: A small lodge with rentals, lessons by reservation, hot food and drinks; hot tub!

Payment: All major credit cards.

Lodging: The Birches-Trailside (207-534-7305, $$); The Lodge at Moosehead Lake-Greenville (207-695-4400, $$$).

Local's Tip: Skate across the lake to Mount Kineo. By removing your skis and climbing for about 45 minutes, you can reach the fire tower at the top of the mountain and enjoy amazing views of Moosehead Lake.

Most happy homeowners in northern New England have an acre or two of land. A few boast more, maybe 20 or 30 acres —plenty to spread their wings a little and get away from the neighbors. John Willard's fiefdom covers 10,500 acres. That's about 16 square miles of forests and hills and lakefront. John could set out with his kids, Joel and Jamie, and walk straight into the woods for well over an hour without ever leaving his own property! He could lay a button over The Birches on a map of Maine, and some of his land would still slip out immodestly at the edges.

With a small town's worth of land on the edge of one of Maine's longest lakes, John has the raw ingredients for a premier wilderness resort. Trail designers in other areas of New England bend over backwards to throw in the feeling of isolation that John takes for granted. Driving north from Greenville on the way to The Birches, you'll see no signs of civilization for a good ten miles. The outer fringes of the trail network are clearly visited more often by moose and deer than by people: some of the more popular spots have been trampled into snowy replicas of the cratered, lunar surface.

The fifteen lakefront log cabins that flank the touring center at The Birches were put together by loggers lacking gainful employment during the Great Depression. The owner, Oz Fayey, gave the men room and board for their efforts, while he slowly created a do-it-yourself type

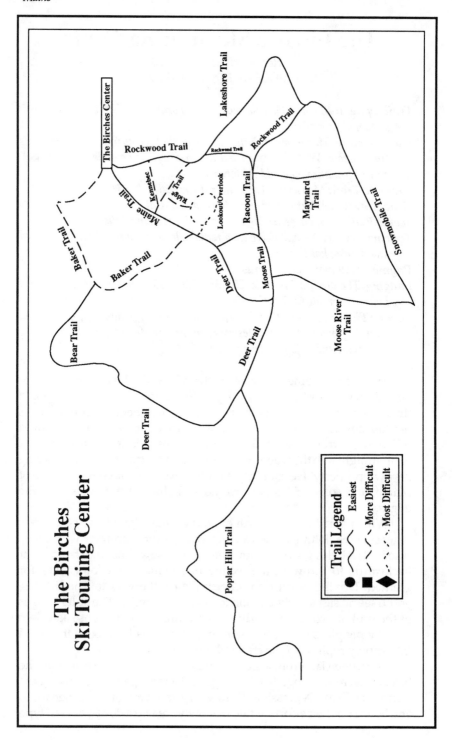

of summer resort for wealthy businessmen who didn't need to be coddled by superfluous conveniences like running water. John Willard's father took over in 1969 and with a Henry Mancini album at his side, he named the fifteen cabins with painted pieces of driftwood: "Hello Dolly," "In the Mood," and "Never on Sunday." Guests call in advance to make a reservation with their favorite Mancini tune.

When John returned to The Birches from his forestry studies at the University of Maine, he eschewed paper company employment to start an outdoor recreation-centered resort. (One wonders whether the word "resort" can legitimately describe log cabin living, but The Birches uses the term quite freely.) For several winters he lived in one of the cabins, trekking to town for showers, and fishing his drinking water out of a hole in the ice on Moosehead Lake.

The endless forests that stretched behind the cabins were then paper company dominion, and they had been logged intermittently for hundreds of years. John discovered that the winding paths and logging roads that loggers left in their wake were well-suited for cross country skiing. He began as no more than a sharecropper, cultivating a few trails at a time on paper company land, never entirely certain when or where renewed logging would occur. In 1993, he anchored his vision with the purchase of a huge tract of land. Although some of the scars of recent clear-cuts remain, the forest is rapidly gaining ground, and it will only get more beautiful as the years pass.

The Trails

Let's face it, this is logging territory. Ten years ago, the paper company looked at these woods the same way you might look at your stock portfolio: a diversified collection of wood lots which should be harvested and sold after a period of steady, long term growth. You won't travel far at The Birches without skiing by, through, or near an area that has been thinned within the last thirty or forty years. However, intense logging stopped over a decade ago, and most areas are either mature second growth or well on their way there.

Close to the cabins, wonderfully narrow, tunnel-like classical trails spin through dense second-growth forests. The latter part of **Rockwood** is a terrifically twisting classical trail whose high-frequency undulations through mixed forest require loose knees and supple ankles. Be ready to dance your way through this one! **Moose River, Maynard,** and the final stretch of **Baker** have similarly fun, narrow, curvy terrain.

A favorite destination of ours at The Birches is a one-mile climb via **Main** and **Lookout** to a friendly, knoll-top yurt. Yurts are fast becoming a fad at cross country centers all over the Northeast. These canvas cousins of Mongolian dwellings are easy to drag to the far corners of any trail system. Ski out with wine and cheese, start a fire in the tiny wood stove, and rest your bones on a comfy couch. Strong skiers can test their endurance on a ten-kilometer (one-way!) trek to the second yurt on **Brassau Lake**. A beautiful final stretch beneath ancient hemlocks and yellow birches is just reward for several straight kilometers on a 100-foot-wide logging corridor. Ski out in the afternoon with sleeping bags for an overnight sojourn.

Although not officially part of the trail system, a well-packed snowmobile highway that sails across the frozen lake to **Mount Kineo** is one of the most spectacular trails at The Birches. Native Americans used to travel from hundreds of miles away to chip arrow-heads out of the shale cliffs at the base of the mountain. The flat, hard-packed trail is a terrific place to cruise. Intrepid speedsters can try to cajole snowmobilers into allowing them to skitch a ride across the lake, but don't come crying to us with treadmarks on your face. When the frozen lake lacks the requisite snow, try skating with ice-skates!

On windy days and early in the winter before the lake freezes solid, stick to the safety of the woods. Solid, intermediate 5 to 10 kilometer loops like the **Deer**, **Bear**, and **Baker** trails lie waiting. All are accessed by a wide, easy climb up **Main**. **Deer** takes you across open fields, while **Bear** is a short, winding climb and descent through hardwoods and evergreens. Both are very pretty trails. **Baker** starts by twisting into a small ravine, then climbing out toward a straight, downhill road, before finishing on a fun slalom through evergreens. **Baker** and **Bear** may be a bit tricky for the novice, but they are delightfully manageable on slow snow.

Finding Your Way: Take I-95 north to Exit 39 in Newport. Take Route 7 into Dexter. Follow Route 23 out of Dexter toward Sangerville, then stick to Routes 6/15 through Monson and Greenville. In Rockwood, just over 20 miles from the blinking light in the center of Greenville, turn right and cross a river (just after the Moose River Store); here there will be a sign for The Birches. For the final two miles, simply follow the signs and fight to keep your car out of the ditch.

Black Mountain of Maine

Isthmus Road
Rumford, Maine 04276
(207) 364-8977

Trail System: 15 km groomed (15 km classical, 15 km skate)
Our Personal Estimate: This area is less a touring center than a well-groomed set of inter-connected racing trails
Grooming: Excellent
Scenic Beauty: 2
Touring Center: Alpine lodge with rentals, lessons, cafeteria, some retail
Favorite Trail: Ladies 5 km loop, with enough twists, turns, and steep to keep everyone, including the ladies, challenged.
Payment: MC and VISA
Lodging: The Madison Motor Inn-Rumford (207-364-7973, $$$); Blue Iris-Rumford (207-364-4495, $)
Local's Tip: Local ski legend Chummy Broomhall is often at the mountain; talk to him if you can. Mr. Broomhall was a two-time Olympian who designed the trail systems at Squaw Valley and Lake Placid as well as Rumford. He is a very human, very entertaining, walking encyclopedia of skiing in New England.

If there's snow anywhere in New England, you're likely to find it in Rumford at the Black Mountain of Maine ski area. Black Mountain and its neighbor Whiteface poke up out of the Longfellow Range of Western Maine, and siphon off whatever snowflakes are available. The area is a tight, impeccably groomed set of four race loops that spin off a medium sized family-style Alpine operation. National championship races are regularly held here, and the area is known as one of the East's best race courses. It is not a traditional touring center with an extended web of trails and the prospect of getting pleasantly lost and found again.

Racing is the focus at Black Mountain. Kilometer signs are posted and color-coded throughout the woods. Gray timing shacks dot the trails. On weekends, a host of determined racers will push by — from pink-parkaed "Lollipops" to national caliber competitors. It can be quite a thrill for an old racehorse to power into the open Broomhall 'stadium' with both arms raised to an imaginary crowd. Just make sure no one is watching.

Rumford itself is a mill town. For nearly a century it has been dominated by the sight and sound of the Boise Cascade paper mill, an impressive citadel of steam and motion. In the early 1900s, many Norwegians migrated to Rumford to work at the mill, and they built an incomparable tradition of skis and snow sports in Rumford. The list of

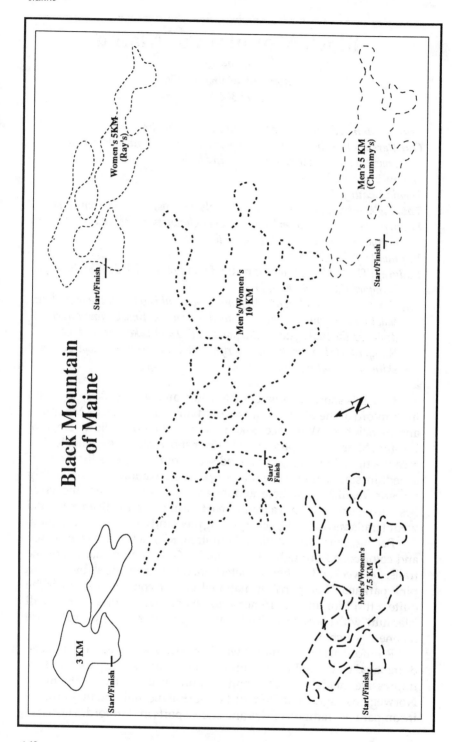

Rumford residents reads like the list of Who's Who in skiing. These Scandinavians built the biggest ski jump east of the Mississippi and competed in winter races crazily compiled out of a smorgasbord of events: dashes on skis and snowshoes, ski jumping, speed skating, a ski relay, and endurance runs on both snowshoes and skis.

After WWII, Rumford citizens founded the Chisholm Ski Club, and in 1961 they built Black Mountain of Maine on an old dairy farm that was selling cheap. Building the mountain was like making stone soup: businesses put up supplies and financial support, contractors donated their services, and the yeomanry contributed time and elbow grease. It is a fierce point of pride that not a nickel came from taxes until recently when the town decided to help with the cost of snowmaking. Community spirit still reigns: whole armies of local volunteers officiate weekend races.

Family spirit pervades the main floor of the lodge, mostly in the form of bundled-up children learning to walk in Alpine boots. You'll hear the accent of Western Maine throughout. Clusters of parents hover at the big picture window which looks out onto the single t-bar and the Alpine slopes. The managers walk around picking up lost hats, carrying race bibs, and doling out french fries, cheeseburgers, and buffalo wings from the cafeteria. Downstairs a shop sells extra mittens and gloves, and rents Alpine equipment and a sparse selection of cross country skis. Upstairs, the Last Run Lounge is a more peaceful version of downstairs. Old-fashioned skis and poles are nailed to the ceiling, and the walls document the ski area's beginnings.

The Trails

The area's 15 kilometers of trails feel as if they've been groomed with a toothbrush. A continuous band of trail curls around the base of Black Mountain. By mixing cutoffs and appendages, trail planners have come up with five separate race loops: the **3 km Relay Track**, the **Ladies 5 km** (a.k.a. Ray's), the **Men's 5 km** (a.k.a. Chummy's), the **7.5 km** and the **10 km**. You aren't given a trail map because you don't need one: the markings are patently obvious.

The **3 km Relay Track** is a good warm up loop, and gives you a chance to stretch your legs. After a brief flirtation with the road and some subtle descents that gather surprising speed under your skis, the trail turns upward for a gentle climb through hardwood forests. By craning your neck you can catch glimpses of Black Mountain and nearby Whiteface.

The **Ladies 5 km** loop splits off the relay loop for a quick dip to the lowest part of the trail system. Immediately the trail turns abusive and slaps you with an uphill resembling the walls of Jericho. After a long steady climb, the trail twists back on itself and at four km it turns momentarily into terrain worthy of an Alpine slope — wide and steep, but with plenty of room to maneuver. The last kilometer levels off as it climbs around the pool and coasts back to the stadium.

The **Men's 5 km** loop shares a basic structure with the **7.5 km** and **10 km** loops. After splitting off from the **Ladies 5 km** it launches into a long, steady climb lasting nearly two kilometers, and reattaches itself with a steep drop. The longer trails — the **7.5 km** and the **10 km** — transport skiers high onto the neighboring ridge where the terrain levels off. The **10 km** loop adds a kilometer of cakewalk which gradually extends up and down Black Mountain; it returns to the main loop with a brief, challenging downhill and fills out its full distance by crisscrossing the Alpine trails. Without the authority of a race behind you, it is probably better to cede those last two km to the downhill skiers.

Finding your way: Take I-95 north to Route 495 north; take 495 into Lewiston and drive on Route 4 north to Wilton. Follow Route 2 west into Rumford. You will come to Puiaa's Home Furnishings and Food Trend; at this point turn right onto Swain Road. At the top of the hill bear to the right on Isthmus Road. The area is approximately five miles from town, and marked by a small highway sign that tells you to turn left.

Massachusetts

Great Brook Farm Ski Touring Center
P.O. Box 720
Carlisle, Massachusetts 01741-0720
(508) 369-7486

Trail System: 15 km (15 km classical, 15 km skate, 15 km backcountry),
  1.5 km night skiing
Our Estimate: Many little loops and fields. One longer, more isolated loop.
Grooming: Good, despite the difficulties of drifting snow in the fields
Scenic Beauty: 3
Touring Center: A converted barn with rentals, lessons, wood stove, snacks
  and hot drinks, limited retail, and outhouses.
Favorite Trail: Chicken, which wobbles happily over a bunch of fun little hills.
Payment: No credit cards accepted.
Lodging: Hawthorne Inn-Concord (508-369-5610, $$$);
  Longfellow's Wayside Inn-Sudbury (508-443-8846, $$$)
Local's Tip: Return with your kids during the summer to explore the
  interpretive dairy farm and indulge in their homemade ice cream.

The town of Carlisle has miraculously managed to dodge the ugly waves of suburbia rolling relentlessly westward from Boston. While development crawled over the top of nearby cities, the well-to-do, historic little town held its ground. Great Brook Farm State Park defends the northern edge of this rural enclave with 1,000 acres of sunny cow pastures and quiet forests. A visit to Great Brook, with the sweet smell of manure, stubbly corn stalks, and old farm buildings, is more reminiscent of the peaceful, rolling hills of southern Vermont.

No other cross country touring center lies so near to Boston. Sure, the Weston Ski Track may be just ten miles away by turnpike, but can you really call a place where the after-work crowd spins in circles under floodlights on *ersatz* snow a "touring center?" I think not. Weston is for technique development and exercise. Great Brook is for cross country skiing the old fashioned way: in a beautiful setting and on natural snow.

Unfortunately, natural snow comes and goes wildly in Carlisle; some ski seasons peter out after just a few days, and even the longest winters rarely last more than a few weeks. Despite extended snowless frustrations, the management patiently awaits the Bostonian gold mine that accompanies every storm. On busy weekends, more than 1,000 skiers will abandon the long drive and higher prices up north for a local tour of a working dairy farm replete with cows, corn, and Canada geese.

Men may choose to leave their wives behind, lest they lose the loyalty of their loved-ones to the chiseled, Nordic faces of the Johnstone brothers, the current custodians of Great Brook. One brother raced for the United States in the Calgary Olympics. Another wrote a guide to

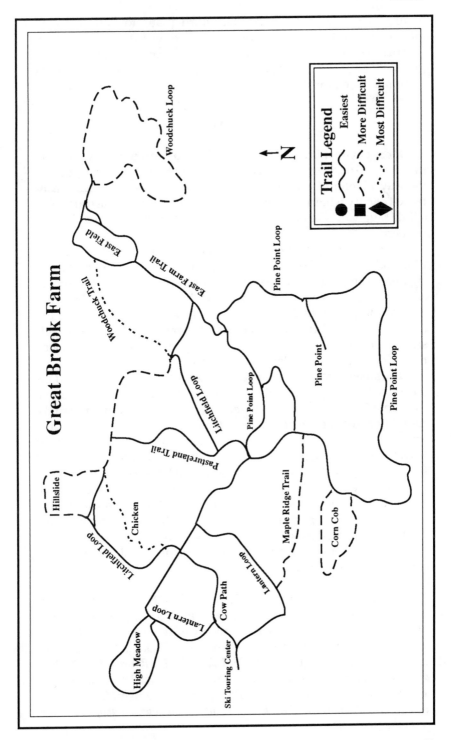

mountain biking in Concord. The third plans to open his own microbrewery. All three lead the type of free-wheeling, outdoor lives that many cross country skiers dream about. Don't hesitate to ask the Johnstones about trail conditions at Great Brook or the best places to mountain bike nearby.

The Trails

Most of Great Brook's trails are a bit too short to follow for more than 30 or 40 minutes, so don't count on disappearing on a long, out-of-the-way adventure. Your best bet is to stick the trail map in your back pocket and try whichever trails strike your fancy. When you start to feel a little fatigued, take the map out and use it to work your way back to the barn.

On cold, windy days however, it is worth your while to search out **Pine Point Loop**, the only trail that lingers in the woods for any significant amount of time. The **Pine Point Loop** is also a great spot to search for signs of wildlife. After twisting through a stand of white pine, the trail drops gently down toward a far finger of Meadow Pond. It crosses the pond's spillway and melts into a pine forest on the opposite side, where a level, easy-going forest and a few frozen swamps provide time for reflection and a lengthened, steady stride.

The adventuresome will invariably work their way out toward the far end of the trail system and the **Woodchuck Loop**. The initial descent from **East Field** might land you into a chilly brook on an icy day, so take care. After crossing the bridge, **Woodchuck** follows a tiny stream to its source pond, climbing through a rigid army of white pine along the way. From the pond, the trail drops back though the pines toward **East Field**. Don't miss the old cellar hole on your left just before the descent.

The **Woodchuck Trail** (not to be confused with the **Woodchuck Loop**) leads experts back toward the barn from **East Field** via a rough, testy little hill. Be sure to finish on **Chicken**, which wobbles cheerfully home over huge, breaking waves of forest floor. **Chicken** lets you practice carrying your momentum from the downhills through each trough and up over the top of the following wave.

Finding your way: From I-95: Take Exit 31B off of I-95. Follow Route 4 north for nearly three miles, where Route 225 branches off to the left. After four miles on Route 225 west, take a right onto Lowell Road (at the rotary in the center of Carlisle, follow the sign for Chelmsford). Great Brook is two miles down Lowell Road on your right. From I-495: Take Exit 34 to Route 110 west. After about a mile, turn onto Route 4 south. After one more mile, the road will fork, and you should follow the Concord Road prong on the right. Concord Road becomes Lowell Street, and the touring center is on your left about two miles from the fork.

Swift River Inn

151 South Street
Cummington, Massachusetts 01026
(413) 634-0263

Trail System: 13 km groomed (13 km classical, 13 km skate, and 10 km backcountry), 2.5 km snowmaking and 5 km night skiing
Our Personal Estimate: Not many kilometers, but the many short connector trails allow you to ski different combinations without getting bored.
Grooming: Good. The trails are skied often, however, and you'll feel the effects of so much traffic by late afternoon.
Scenic Beauty: 3
Touring Center: A massive Nordic lodge with rentals, lessons, cafeteria, waxing room, extensive retail, locker rooms, and a bar
Favorite Trail: Beaver Pond Loop, a pleasant wooded tour of beaver ponds over rolling terrain
Payment: AE, DSC, MC, and VISA
Lodging: Swift River Inn-Trailside (413-634-0263, $$$); Cumworth Farm-Cummington (413-634-5529, $-$$); Windfields Farm-Cummington (413-684-3786, cross country trails on site, $$)
Local's Tip: Fun-style ski races on Wednesday nights draw a high-spirited crowd of 40 some-odd skiers, from beginners to experts. Race fee — $8.

The popular Swift River Inn in Cummington is pleasantly, mildly schizophrenic. The touring center offers high-tech snowmaking and night skiing on half of its trails, but leaves half its trails ungroomed. It appeals to spandex-suited racers, but also to furry-pelted, real-life beavers. It is a timeless, elegant inn, yet its owner created the pop culture icons Teenage Mutant Ninja Turtles. The Swift River Inn can't seem to fix on one identity. That's fine. They have something for everyone, as long as you don't mind company.

The touring center used to be located in the lobby of the inn, but so many skiers came tromping in and out that they sent overnight guests running for shelter. Now a large and lovely lodge stands a quarter mile down the road, allowing the inn plenty of elbow room. High schoolers and Bill Koch League racers can run wild without disturbing any highbrow guests. And when it comes to skiing, Swift River has more than meets the eye. Although the official tally comes to only 23 kilometers, an explosion of short, connector trails produces an infinite number of permutations and combinations. Plus, with snowmaking letting skiers come early and night skiing letting them stay late, Swift River's 23 kilometers get plenty of use.

Beavers also love Swift River. While most touring centers have a Beaver Pond trail which, predictably, circles a beaver pond, at Swift

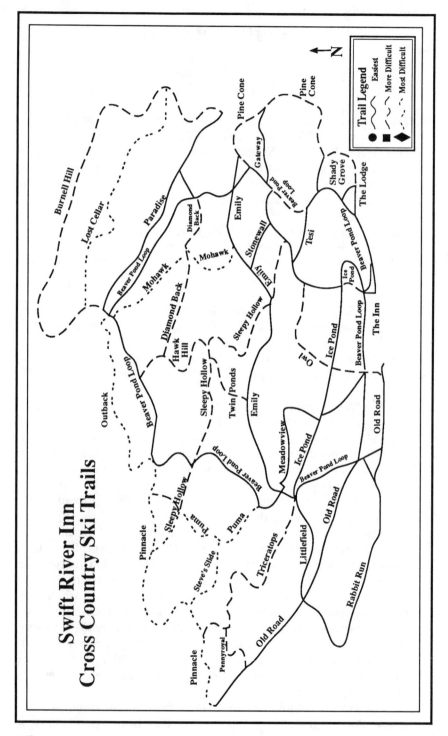

Massachusetts

168

River you can't get away from the furry critters. They thrive in the river, and the ski area's central loop takes you on a beavery tour passing at least three ponds. See if you can see signs of them. You should be able to spot their distinctive tree-felling tooth marks. You can also look at the beaver lodge itself. If beavers are sleeping inside, their escaping body heat will melt the snow off the top. Oddly enough, the animals have helped Swift River's snowmaking operation. When the area built a pond to draw water from, the beavers cheerfully pitched in by building a massive dam. You can see it off the Pine Cone trail.

A few decades ago, these same trails, under different management, sparked a skiing craze in the area. In 1973, a couple named the Dawsons built a rustic, family-style Nordic center that was an overnight success. Cars parked along the road for a mile in both directions. Skiers by the hundreds ate their peanut butter and jelly sandwiches in the barn (now reincarnated as the inn's Hayloft Ballroom). But even fresh air and cross country skiing couldn't save Mr. Dawson. His unhealthy habits proved his undoing in the end — he had been the Marlboro Man, gruff and handsome, but lung cancer eventually overcame him. Fortunately, though, the Dawson's knew a good thing when they saw it, and today their skiing legacy lives on.

The Trails

The lovely, sedate **Old Road** travels an avenue of tall trees, paralleling the current South Street. **Old Road** was part of a gentleman's farm. While working out there one summer, the trail crew discovered a cellar hole set in among a glade of huge sugar maples: stone steps led down to a foundation brimming with day lilies. Look closely — it is easy to miss. **Meadowview** skirts the top of the meadow and ducks behind a thicket of pine scrub. Skiing the length of the downward-sloping field you get a short-range view of the hills and pastures opposite: this is one of the few vistas on the groomed trails. Swift River's most beautiful terrain is in the woods. **Emily** intersects the middle of the trail system, following the contours of the rolling forested hillside from hardwoods into evergreens. She's not technically difficult, but she's not dead either.

The popular **Beaver Pond Loop** was one of the original trails at the Dawson's ski center. This jaunty trail passes over a ridge between a marshy old beaver pond holding the ghosts of tall trees, and its tiny, pool-sized sidekick. Returning along the Swift River, it passes under giant, shadowy hemlocks where only crevices let the sky peek through. On windy days you can hear the trees tossing overhead, but the air underneath is still. **Sleepy Hollow** is one of the more difficult of the groomed trails. It leads from high ground near Pinnacle Hill to the valley in the middle of the trail system. Skiing it can be tricky. The trail takes a sharp turn and then a little dip, while rocks loom on the right.

Ungroomed trails are far less traveled at Swift River and its a good idea to bring sturdy touring equipment if you want to ski them. Pine trees line the bumpy **Hawk Hill** trail, which leads over a series of hillocks that will make your teeth chatter. The trail passes a towering boulder, once a favorite practice spot for local rock climbers until they were banned by hotel management. Now a full-grown hemlock grows firmly ensconced in its ledgey heights.

Burnell Hill climbs through a beautiful, desolate forest for nearly a kilometer before reaching an old road, where it runs easily downhill between two stone walls. It's a good place to get away from the crowd. **Pinnacle** is an older trail that climbs up from **Triceratops** and dips between two conifer-covered hills into a wind funnel. The trail drifts in and out of hardwoods, comes to a long-looking scenic vista over reclaimed farmlands, and drops quickly back to the groomed system.

Finding your way: Take the Northampton exit (Exit 18 from the south; Exit 19 from the north) off I-89. Proceed west along Route 9 to Cummington and follow the signs.

Brodie Ski Touring Center
Route 7
Lanesboro, Massachusetts 01237
(413) 443-4752 (Alpine phone number)

Trail System: 25 km (25 km skate, about 40 km of backcountry in the adjacent Mount Greylock Reservation)

Our Estimate: A day trip's worth of hilly terrain, consistently rolled for skating and inconsistently tracked for classical.

Grooming: Good for skating, inconsistent for classical

Scenic Beauty: 4

Touring Center: A tiny shack with rentals, lessons, wood stove, and a cafeteria in the Alpine lodge. Call ahead to be sure that the touring center is open!

Favorite Trail: Becky's Brim, a feisty little loop that lulls with easy terrain, then practically threatens to scale a cliff.

Payment: All major credit cards.

Lodging: Field Farm Guest House-Williamstown (413-458-3135, $$); Jericho Valley Inn-Williamstown (800-JERICHO, $$-$$$)

Local's Tip: Keep an eye out for what manager Matt Kelley calls the "Fountain of Youth," a gurgling natural spring to the right off of Abbey's Climb. A long drink will add years to your life.

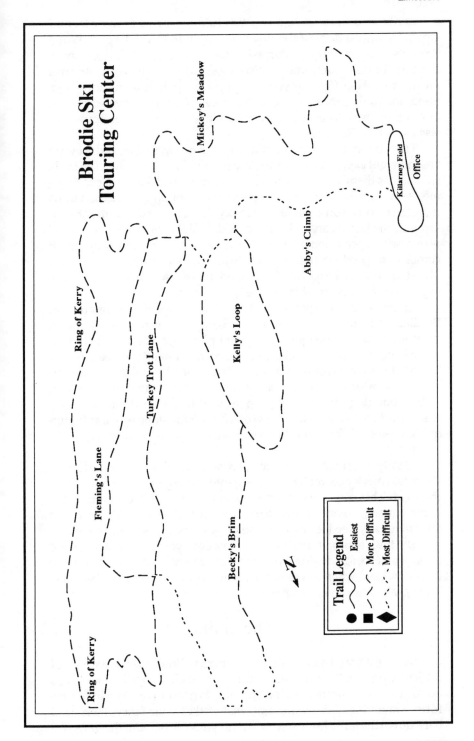

Brodie Ski Touring Center

Mickey's Meadow

Ring of Kerry

Turkey Trot Lane

Fleming's Lane

Kelly's Loop

Abby's Climb

Killarney Field

Office

Becky's Brim

Ring of Kerry

N

Trail Legend

Easiest ●

More Difficult ■

Most Difficult ♦

Arrive on a weekday and you may find a deserted parking lot and a padlock on the door of the tiny warming hut. Don't despair! While Brodie's cross country center asks that you forego a few common creature comforts, supremely satisfying skiing more than compensates for the loss. After fighting your way up a steep, hillside meadow to a pond, the trails dance between limestone ledges and forested ridges, offering uniquely rugged, rocky terrain that you won't see anywhere else east of the Rockies.

The trails at Brodie were designed by an ex-Olympian, and they are anything but easy. The meadows are truly *hillside* meadows. The trails spin across them at a cant, and you sometimes feel like a cat chasing a mouse around on a slippery, steep tin roof. A couple of the expert trails threaten to force you straight up a rocky cliff, before reluctantly shying away at the last second. The steepest downhills will make your eyes water with speed and fear. Still, the open terrain and hilly climb combine to produce fantastic westward views of the Taconics, the oldest mountain range in the United States. Anyone with a little experience on skis should give these trails a try.

An amateur geologist would be a dangerous skiing companion at Brodie. With platey, gray boulders oozing out of the hillside in all directions like a buried jumble of giant playing cards, rock jocks will leave Brodie with sore necks and heavy, specimen-laden backpacks. This sedimentary layer stretches in a narrow, north-south band through most of western Massachusetts and Vermont, providing excellent, slabby building stones along the way. (Limestone dissolves fairly easily, and you'll notice that a few of the trailside stone walls, although quickly erected from the blocky boulders, have already begun to crumble.)

Clearly, the center of attention at Brodie Mountain is Alpine skiing; the cross country center has been sent into a lonely exile 1/2 mile down the road. This suits cross country skiers just fine. Unfortunately, the Alpine management seems to believe that a nearby Alpine lodge eliminates any need to upgrade the pitiful little cross country shack.

The trails at Brodie are fantastic. However, you may want to call the Alpine area before making the trip. Ask them if their cross country center is open, when it was last groomed, and if tracks have been set. Then grab your camera and go.

The Trails

Despite a brand-new map, newcomers to Brodie will have a bit of difficulty finding their way around any particular loop. The trail signs are sketchy, and the map itself is anything but intuitive. Try a little free-form wandering. Follow any trail that strikes your fancy, then head back down the hillside when you've had your fill. None of the trails will bring you further than a few kilometers from the warming hut, so venture forth without fear.

If you insist on fumbling your way around the marked loops, then you may want to try either **Mickey's Meadow** or **Becky's Brim**. **Mickey's Meadow** offers some of the best views across the valley toward the Taconics. Cross the brook at the southern end of the field, then loop slowly uphill along the edge of a long, steep meadow. Finish with a fun dive toward the frozen pond.

To reach **Becky's Brim** from the pond, follow the funneling field uphill past stranded limestone boulders and ancient oaks on **Kelley's Loop**. After a brief, steep climb, **Becky's Brim** branches off to the left and follows an easy ravine through a thicket of hardwoods. The trail seems to promise an equally mellow return, when it suddenly bears sharply to the left and climbs laboriously uphill, just below a birch-covered, rocky ridge. By finishing at **Rainbow Corner**, the trail leaves you in a great starting point for the longer, more difficult loops that define the outer limits of Brodie's trails.

Finding your way: From Route 2, take Route 7 south out of Williamstown. After 10 miles, the Brodie Alpine area will be on your right. The cross country center is 1/2 mile further on your left. From I-90, get off Exit 2 (Lee) and take Route 20 north to Route 7 north. Brodie Mountain is roughly 10 miles north of Pittsfield on your right. The cross country center is 1/2 mile before the Alpine area on the right.

Northfield Mountain
Cross Country Ski Area

99 Millers Falls Road
Northfield, Massachusetts   01360
(800) 859-2960, (413) 659-3714

Trail System: *40 km groomed (40 km classical, 40 km skate)*
Our Personal Estimate: *An exciting, mountainous area; wide, well-groomed trails make it easily accessible to intermediate skiers.*
Grooming: *Excellent*
Scenic Beauty: *2*
Touring Center: *Rentals, lessons, vending machines, and some retail*
Payment: *No credit cards accepted*
Lodging: *Brandt House-Greenfield (800-235-3329, $$$);*
  Deerfield Inn-Deerfield (413-774-5587, $$-$$$)
Favorite Trail: *Sidewinder, a delightful romp across the mountainside.*
Local's Tip: *Eat breakfast at the local yokel hangout: Shady Glen Restaurant in Turner's Falls, ten miles away. Good homemade food, dirt cheap prices, and lively banter. The restaurant opens at 5 a.m.*

If you long for a crackling fire in a central woodstove, if you like to warm your fingers around a cup of homemade chili at day's end, if it thrills you to be greeted by a clear-eyed, idealistic family of ex-hippies — in other words, if you want romance in your Nordic center — turn the page. You will rarely find a touring center with less character than Northfield Mountain. It is a concrete cube of a room in a decidedly business-like building. It is owned and operated by the impersonal (and decidedly un-hip) Northeast Utilities power company.

That said, Northfield Mountain Cross Country Ski Area is well worth a two-hour drive from Boston. The friendly, no-frills touring center on the side of forested Northfield Mountain has pleasant, wide trails and exquisite grooming. Besides the knot of flatter trails on fields by the lodge, skiers face a choice: they can chug straight up the mountain or make a series of passes across it. Coming down is fun, no matter which route you choose. Even the steepest trails are wide and well-groomed with few abrupt turns. This cuts down exponentially on the fear factor. A strong set of legs and a love of hills will serve you well at Northfield.

As we mentioned, the ski touring center is run, oddly enough, by the Northeast Utilities power company. The power company operates a pumped-storage hydroelectric station on the land. At night, when energy use is low, they pump water up to the reservoir at the top of

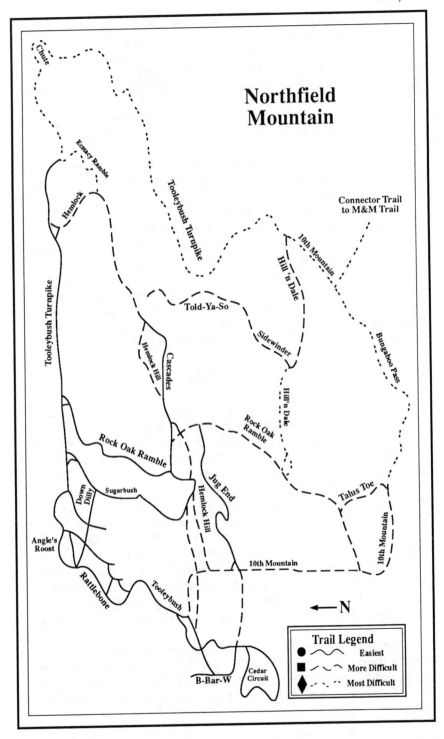

Chute

Ecstacy Ramble

Hemlock

Tooleybush Turnpike

Northfield
Mountain

Connector Trail
to M&M Trail

10th Mountain

Hill 'n Dale

Told-Ya-So

Sidewinder

Tooleybush Turnpike

Hemlock Hill

Cascades

Hill'n Dale

Bungaboo Pass

Rock Oak
Ramble

Rock Oak Ramble

Jug End

Down
Dilly

Sugarbush

Hemlock Hill

Talus Toe

Angle's
Roost

10th Mountain

10th Mountain

Rattlebone

Tooleybush

← **N**

B-Bar-W

Cedar
Circuit

```
Trail Legend
●  ∿∿  Easiest
■  ⌒⌒  More Difficult
◆  ∙∙∙  Most Difficult
```

Northfield Mountain. That stored energy is released during the day, when the water flows back down to the Connecticut River and generates electricity during peak power times. In the summer, you can visit the station itself, which lies a half mile inside Northfield Mountain. In the winter, ski trails climb right to the top of the property, where you can picnic and look out at nearly six billion gallons of stored water.

This combination of hydroplant and recreation center is not unusual, although it is more common in the West than the Northeast. Before granting a license, the Federal Energy Regulatory Commission requires utilities to come up with a recreation plan for the local area, the idea being that since utilities profit from the people's water they should provide something in return.

In the case of Northfield, this arrangement works very well. Aside from the skiing, the Recreation and Environmental Center runs mountain biking and hiking programs seasonally, has a permanent exhibit, and hosts a barrage of natural history programs. The top shelf of the library upstairs is loaded with a stuffed Great Horned Owl and a flock of other fierce-looking birds; the staff naturalist uses these to give talks to school children and local people. If you want to learn something about the area's geology, natural history, and human history, buy the *Northfield Mountain Interpreter* ($3), a fascinating 150-page book.

The Trails

Since Northfield is built on a mountain, beginner terrain is generally confined to the lower region near the touring center, known as **Fuller's Pasture**. The pretty, exposed **Rattlebone** glides gently over fields below the road and into the woods. The bump at the trail head is a huge rock pile from the excavation of the reservoir at the top of the mountain; while trying to give it a smooth grade, the bulldozer operator claimed he could feel his bones rattle. **Angel's Roost** is a pretty comma of a trail with rolling terrain; it curves off **Rattlebone** through a tall pine forest.

For a satisfying elevation change, take the **Reservoir Road** to the top of the mountain. A road in summertime, this trail is the wide, popular, interstate of skiing at Northfield. The oh-so-gradual three-mile climb seems interminable without any of the imaginative dips and curves of a good ski trail, but arriving at the top is well worth it. The reservoir looks like a crater on the moon. From here there is nowhere to go but down!

The **Chocolate Pot** is a three-sided shelter in a sunny mid-mountain spot at the meeting of many trails. On weekends, the staff lights a fire there and serves hot chocolate, lemonade, and Snickers bars. Sheltered from the wind, picnic tables and benches encourage skiers to stop for a bite.

Most of the intermediate trails crisscross the mountain. Going up them, the crisscrossing mitigates the climb; going down them, you'll have a blast. **Hill and Dale** meanders flatly on a surprising plateau at the top of the mountain, then gathers speed through an intermediate section and hurtles down the mountain into expert terrain.

Sidewinder traverses the mountain through an open hillside forest; through the trees you can see out into the blue hills beyond for some of the best views at Northfield. The trail dips into **Told-Ya-So Pass** and down into the evergreens, where the grades get steeper and the corners more thrilling. The exciting **Jug End** dives down a narrow tunnel of dark trees; in the middle section, woods and clearings alternate like stripes on a zebra, and the final segment levels out into a sedate jog.

Expert skiers are going to have fun here. The **10th Mountain** descends from a hardwood ramble over **Bugaboo Pass**, down the full height of the mountain, and over exciting terrain. One section resembles a runaway truck ramp: just let your skis go! The fast and curvy **Ecstasy Ramble** feels like a waterslide with good speed and smooth turns — a great trail for venturesome intermediates.

Skiing up **Tooleybush Turnpike** is like watching a trail grow up. The not-very-scenic broad, flat lower section obediently follows the power lines; then, suddenly enlightened, the trail ducks into the woods for some pretty twists and turns. After the junction with **Hemlock Hill**, **Tooleybush Turnpike** turns into a match for the most dedicated climber with a kilometer of shifting grade changes, where the only constant factor is up. Daredevils can ski it downward, through the famous **Chute**.

Finding your way: Take I-91 to Exit 28 in Bernardston. Follow Route 10 east for five miles to where it hits Route 63 just south of Northfield. Take Route 63 south for five miles. The ski area will be on your left.

Bucksteep Manor
Cross Country Ski Center

Washington Mountain Road
Washington, Massachusetts 01223
(800) 645-BUCK, (413) 623-5535

Trail System: 25 km (25 km classical, 8 km skate, no backcountry)
Our Estimate: If you stay at the inn, you'll find plenty of variety for a weekend
   of classical skiing.
Grooming: Good on weekends; caters to classical skiers
Scenic Beauty: 3
Touring Center: A converted barn with rentals, lessons, wood stove,
   restaurant in the manor, wax tables, and some retail.
Favorite Trail: Upper Deer Run slides along the underside of a rocky ledge.
Payment: All major credit cards
Lodging: Manor Inn-Trailside (413-623-5535, $$$);
   Walker House-Lenox (800-235-3098, $$$)
Local's Tip: The modest, friendly area of Canterbury X-C offers good skiing
   in nearby Becket. You'll find it at the intersection of Route 8 and
   McNerney Road (about 4 miles from Bucksteep).

We fully expected to be greeted by a well-dressed baron at the gate.
Perhaps he'd gallop toward us on a horse with a pair of servants
shuffling obsequiously a few yards back. Any knave would expect such
a welcome from a place that sits on top of a stately hill and calls itself the
"Bucksteep Manor." We were pleased to discover that we could slip out
of our Prince Alberts and pull on our ski jackets; the manor was far less
regal than we had imagined, and the skiing turned out to be fabulous.

A hundred years ago, the scene would have been far different.
Through the latter part of the nineteenth century the manor served as
the Berkshire cottage for a well-to-do porcelain family from England.
At the time, it was quite fashionable for the English gentry to maintain
country cottages in western Massachusetts — cottages they might only
visit a few weeks out of the year. With wide open pastures dropping
away in all directions, their estates often commanded wonderful,
unobstructed views of the surrounding hills and valleys.

The Bucksteep Manor Cross Country Ski Center opened in the late
1970s with a few kilometers of converted logging roads and bridal
paths. Except for the mowed fields close to the manor, Bucksteep no
longer has an open, estate-like feel. The 25 kilometers of trails thread
through young hardwood forests and only rarely pop into an ancestral
meadow. However, they do occasionally pass by skeletons of the
manor's past lives — a well, a collapsed cabin, several stone walls, and

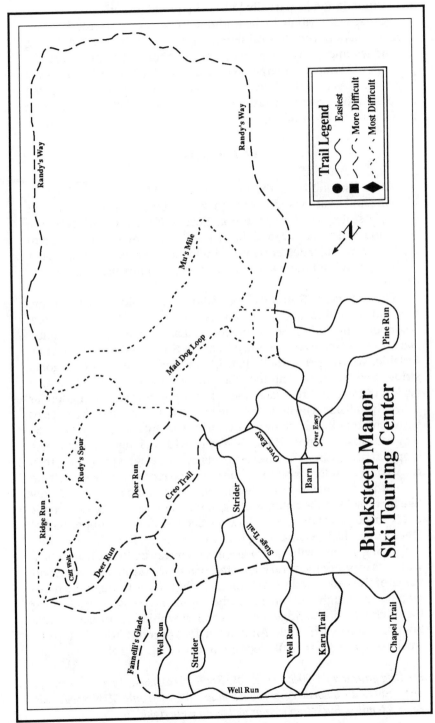

Bucksteep Manor
Ski Touring Center

an old foundation lie partially hidden by recent growth.

Perhaps as a tribute to the tradition in Bucksteep's past, the management has allowed classical skiing to brush aside the upstart skating techniques and remain the center of attention. Classical skiers are pampered! While most larger ski areas force classical tracks to shyly hug the edges of trails, Bucksteep's tracks brazenly barge down the middle, cutting corners whenever they choose and closely following the fall-line on downhill curves.

The Trails

After chatting with the baron and the hired hands, choose a kickwax and visit the old barn to pick up a trail map. This map isn't properly scaled, so don't take it as gospel. (One trail wanders in a suspiciously tidy loop around the map's title and key.) Writing "downhill" on every major descent is an addition that a practiced cartographer probably wouldn't think to include, but these comments help tremendously.

Except for **Pine Run** and a few trails that hug fields close to the inn, the trail system is decidedly woodsy. Few frostbite worries here. Beginners can shuffle their way around a short loop near the manor: start down **Over Easy**, then head out on **Strider** — a smooth, comfortable, winding trail that's perfect for working on your diagonal stride. **Strider** passes through the young hardwoods that are now typical of the 400-acre estate. It also keeps you from dropping too far down the hillside. Finish the loop on the **Chapel Trail**, which squeezes between a brook and a stone wall, then brushes by a stone chapel on the way back to the manor. **Randy's Way** provides a longer, intermediate loop that passes underneath evergreens, cuts through a stone wall, then coasts downhill for a visit to an enormous beaver pond. Trees with no fault other than having sprouted in a low area of the forest stand now like toothpicks in the pond, waiting to rot and topple. If beaver ponds don't strike your fancy, try following **Creo Trail** to the upper half of **Deer Run**, which sneaks along beneath the curled lips of a rock face.

Stronger skiers will want to shimmy their way up **Ridge Run**, which works its way along several kilometers of the far side of a low ridge. Soft views of the valley and surrounding low hills filter through the hardwoods. The rough and tumble **Rudy's Spur** carries skiers back along the other side of the ridge, with several downhill bloodrushes and a brief detour on **Cliff Walk**. Although it does peer out from the top of a small rock face, **Cliff Walk** does not live up to its name!

Finding your way: I-90 to Exit 2. Take Route 20 east about 12 miles, then take a left onto Route 8 north. After about 5 miles, take a left onto McNerney Road. After 3.6 miles, Bucksteep Manor will be on your right.

Weston Ski Track

Box 426 Park Road
Weston, Massachusetts   02193
(617) 891-6575

Trail System: 14 km (14 km classical, 14 km skate, no backcountry), 2 km
   snowmaking, 3 km night skiing
Our Estimate: A 1 1/2 km track on man-made snow open most of the winter.
   After big storms there are gentle, open trails on the golf course.
Grooming: Good, but not quite as good as the grooming equipment.
Scenic Beauty: 2
Touring Center: A golf clubhouse with rentals, lessons, snacks and hot drinks,
   some retail, and a locker room with showers.
Favorite Trail: Fox Track, with a good view of the Charles and away-from-the-
   crowd skiing.
Payment: DSC, MC, and VISA
Lodging: This is a local spot for Bostonians and suburban skiers — there are
   plenty of places to stay in the area for those who might be visiting from out
   of town.
Local's Tip: Call ahead to see if (1) a high school race is planned for the
   afternoon or (2) the noisy snow-guns will be operating.

Wait a minute! How did the Weston Ski Track slip into a guide to
the best cross country ski areas in the Northeast? Is this the same Weston
with the 1 1/2 kilometer artificial snow loop, where hundreds of snow-
starved athletes try in vain to re-create the feeling of north country
Nordic skiing? Is this the same place where even after one of Boston's
twice-a-year snowstorms, only another 10 to 15 kilometers of golf
course terrain opens up? Is this a cruel joke?

Well, not exactly. Although Weston is a far cry from gourmet
Nordic, it does provide Boston area residents with accessible and
dependable skiing December through March. A few hours at Weston
during the week emboldens skiers for challenging weekend excursions
in the mountains of New Hampshire and Vermont. It lets them unwind
in the crisp evening air after being glued to an office chair all day.

There's no sense beating around the bush: Weston's trails are laid
out on a golf course. While most golf course touring centers include at
least a few wooded sections, all of Weston's trails are out in the open.
It would be a safe bet that none of the trails were cut or even improved
for the sake of cross country skiing. Skiing on golf courses can be fun,
especially with Weston's high-quality, Pisten Bulley grooming machine
laying down a hard-packed path. It's easy to get into a rhythm on a well-
groomed two or three kilometer loop and forget that the hectic rush of
Boston's busy interstates lie less than a mile away.

181

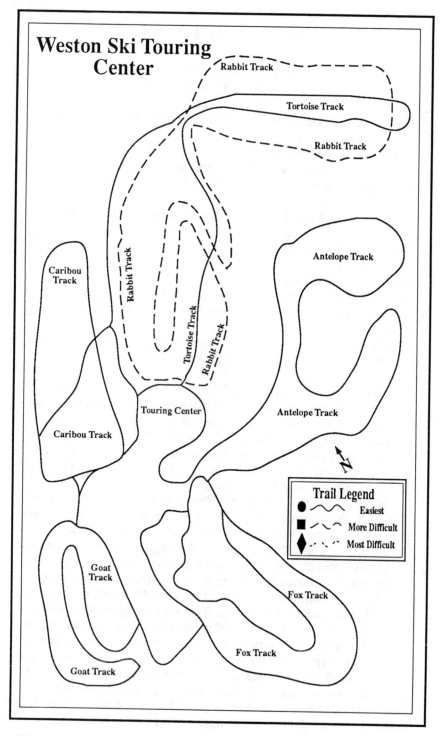

Weston Ski Touring Center

Rabbit Track

Tortoise Track

Rabbit Track

Rabbit Track

Tortoise Track

Rabbit Track

Caribou Track

Antelope Track

Caribou Track

Touring Center

Antelope Track

N

Trail Legend
● ‿‿‿ Easiest
■ ⌇⌇ More Difficult
◆ ⌇⌇ Most Difficult

Goat Track

Fox Track

Goat Track

Fox Track

It's no accident that they call it the "Weston Ski Track." Ninety percent of the time, the center of the action is the 1 1/2 kilometer snowmaking loop, where skiers spin dizzily around and around until boredom or fatigue overwhelms them. High school teams, local racers, and the after-work crowd give Weston the flavor of a popular track or fitness center. The clubhouse even has a locker room and showers. Ability levels range from the traffic-stopping neophyte to the traffic-dodging experts on the Harvard Ski Team. Tuesday night races and Thursday night training sessions only enhance the "ski track" atmosphere.

With a few inches of natural snow, Weston metamorphoses from mini-golf to eighteen holes. Then again, with sufficient snowfall, Weston loses its man-made snow advantage, and Great Brook in Carlisle becomes a very persuasive alternative!

The Trails

During snowless weeks, Weston's 1 1/2 kilometer loop of man-made snow is your only option. Several convoluted mini-loops squeeze into an open, hilly field. Although a narrow strip of pines bisects the field, you'll still be able to see every other skier at all times and from every spot on the trail. On busy weekday afternoons, the mass of skiers can resemble a confused, milling herd of buffalo; call ahead to be sure that high school ski team practices aren't planned.

With a bit of natural snow, the rest of the golf course opens up. The **Antelope Track** offers a 2.5 kilometer loop with several fun little hills. On the opposite side of Concord Street, the **Fox Track** can combine with the **Goat Track** to provide the longest continuous loop — and the least crowded skiing. Between the **Fox Track** and **Goat Track** is a pretty, narrow crossing of the Charles River. Bostonians will have a hard time recognizing this gurgling little unpolluted gem — a far cry from the sluggish, murky, waterway they have come to know and love farther downstream.

Finding your way: From Boston, get off I-90 at Exit 15. Stay left at the toll booth and follow signs for Route 30. At the end of the ramp, turn left. The Ski Track is 1/4 mile on your left. From the West, get off I-90 at Exit 14. Follow signs for Route 128 north and Route 30. Turn left onto Route 30. At the second set of lights, turn left onto Park Road. The Ski Track is 3/4 mile on your left. From the North, get off Route 128 at Exit 24. At the end of the ramp, turn left onto Route 30. At the next set of lights, turn left, and the Ski Track is 3/4 mile on your left. From the South, get off Route 128 at exit 21. Turn left at the end of the ramp and follow Route 16 west for 1/2 mile. At the second set of lights, turn right onto Concord Street. The Ski Track is 3/4 mile on your right.

Hickory Hill Touring Center

Buffington Hill Road
Worthington, Massachusetts 01098
(413) 238-5813

Trail System: 25 km groomed (25 km classical, 25 km skate)
Our Personal Estimate: Well-planned trails make the system seem bigger than 25 km.
Grooming: Excellent
Scenic Beauty: 4
Touring Center: Rentals, lessons, food, wax bench, some retail (good deals on used equipment), fully stocked bar.
Favorite Trail: Jackrabbit, a thrilling, twisting downhill run; skiing it is like trying to hang on to a snake with the shivers.
Payment: No credit cards
Lodging: Worthington Inn-Worthington (413-238-4441, $$); Remington Lodge, dorm-style-West Cummington (413-634-5493 or 634-5388, $)
Local's Tip: Hickory Hill is closed Tuesdays and Wednesdays, except during holiday weeks.

At the Hickory Hill Center in Worthington, Tim Sena will tell you about his racing days back in the heady adolescence of Nordic skiing. He'd get all decked out in a full tux, add a cowboy hat for good measure, and head over to the rollicking Bread Race in Cummington. No stopwatch, no lycra, no medals. You started when they yelled "GO!" and scrambled head over tail for the finish line. The first one across won a loaf of bread.

Just like the days that inspired it, skiing at Hickory Hill is a lot of fun. It's a friendly, family-run area where they appreciate good food, good times, and good skiing. This is where the ski shop owners ski on their days off; it's the kind of place where you stop and talk to people you meet on the trails. It's an area for people who appreciate top quality skiing far from the madding crowd. Initiates guard the secret jealously. One skier heard about *Tracks and Trails* with the dismay of a California prospector in 1848. "Don't tell them about this place," he urged. "*Everyone* will come."

Hickory Hill occupies the hilltop site of the Sena family farm. This is part of Massachusetts' former potato kingdom, and thousands of potatoes used to grow in the moist, cool soil. No longer. In the summer the Senas run hot air balloon rides and preside at local auctions; in the winter, ski trails fan up and down over the three ridges. Tim and his brother Paul cut the trails themselves, custom designing every foot for enjoyable skiing. You'll appreciate their work. Natural runouts and

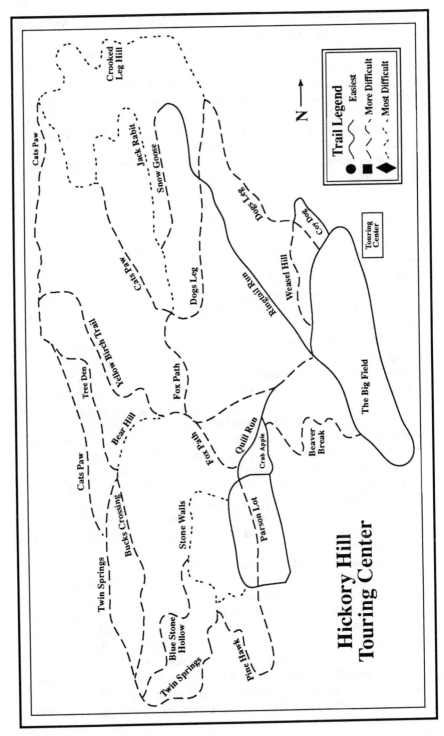

Hickory Hill
Touring Center

wide open turns allow you to ski corners fast and furious without actually endangering your life.

Don't pack a lunch. The Hickory Hill kitchen would be worth a visit even if you weren't going skiing. Delicious aromas issue from the food counter in the big, rehabilitated barn. Kathy and Judy Sena are the other half of the family operation, and their hearty, wholesome cooking is a welcome complement to the skiing. Their goal is to make food so good and cheap you can't help but buy it. It works. Their famous pretzels are as soft and doughy as a baby's bottom, and you can also get chili, muffins, cookies, and hot drinks. Around the corner, in an ell off the barn, a mounted boar's head presides over the sunny, well-stocked bar.

The Trails

The **Big Field** trails dally around the large sloping meadow above the touring center. Specific routes on the field may vary according to the inclination of the groomer, but all of them afford a broad, flat view of the hills just west of the Connecticut River Valley. Every summer the field teems with history nuts in period costume, busy reenacting scenes from the Civil War.

Take **Quill Run** for a pleasant, wood-lined climb across the trout bridge and up to **Parson Lot**. The slope is unwavering and constant in its grade. **Parson Lot** is a pretty, tree-lined meadow ringed by a double-tracked trail. Trails lead off in all directions like an elaborate children's game of Fox and Geese. Many people enjoy skiing laps around it.

Dog's Leg and **Cat's Paw** are two halves of the same trail, which wends its curvy way through beautiful hardwood forest. This route is the main artery to the northern, and prettier, section of the trail system. The trail swoops and climbs over a couple ridges; the last section dips momentarily into a hemlock gully and then rises to the height of the land. The protected **Yellow Birch Trail** sinks down through a forest of, predictably, yellow birch, and traces the bottom of the hill like a topographic line. It is pretty and isolated, and less skied than many of the other trails.

Pine Hawk cascades through scrubby forestland in a series of curving downhills; at the end the trail flattens and passes under a majestic stand of white pines. A number of years ago these pines were home to a red-tailed hawk, a species notorious for being dominant about territory. The hawk attacked a friend of the family who was helping with the trails. It clung to him, clawed him, pecked at him, and didn't give up until it chased him from its domain.

Experts will love these trails. **Bear Hill** is rated most difficult because of its initial hill. It departs from the higher ridge trails and curls into a beauty of a nose dive: let those skis fly! A straight, extended runout takes you all the way to **Fox Path**, without your having to lift a leg. The wily curves of **Jackrabbit** should be skied from **Cat's Paw** to **Dog's Leg** to appreciate their full glory. As soon as you're finished with one curve, the trail will throw you another: there's a long outrun and a big cleared area for unobstructed falling at the bottom. **Crooked Leg Hill** trail climbs steadily, curling around the hill that was named for a series of broken legs and ankles. The trail reaches a plateau in a hemlock forest and then plunges earthward with an extended shivering downhill.

Finding your way: Take I-89 to Exit 19 at Northampton and follow Route 9 west to Williamsburg. Take Route 143 west to Worthington. At the stoplight in town, go straight onto Buffington Hill Road. The center is one mile out of town.

Appendix

Cross Country Ski Areas — Northeast

Eastern New York State

Adirondack Park VIC
Saranac Lake 12983
(518) 327-3000
Trails: 17 km

Ausable Chasm/Cross Country
St. Huberts 12943
(518) 834-9990
Trails: 21 km

Bark Eater Inn/Cross Country
Keene 12942
(518) 576-2221
Trails: 20 km

Cascade Cross Country
Lake Placid 12946
(518) 523-9605
Trails: 20 km

Christmas Tree Cross Country
Caroga Lake 12032
(518) 835-9902
Trails: 25 km

Crandall Park
Glens Falls 12804
(518) 793-5676
Trails: 12 km

Cunningham's Ski Barn
Lake Placid 12946
(518) 523-4460
Trails: 25 km

Cunningham's Ski Barn
North Creek 12853
(518) 251-3215
Trails: 45 km

Dewey Mountain
Saranac Lake 12983
(518) 891-2697
Trails: 15 km

Friends Lake Inn
Chestertown 12817
(518) 494-4751
Trails: 32 km

Frost Valley YMCA
Claryville 12725
(914) 985-2291
Trails: 25 km

Gore Moutain
North Creek 12853
(800) 342-1234, (518) 251-2411
Trails: 10 km

Grafton Lakes State Park
Grafton 12082
(518) 279-1155
Trails: 16 km

Hiland Golf Club
Glens Falls 12801
(518) 761-4653
Trails: 15 km

Howe Caverns X-C
Howes Cave 12092
(518) 296-8900
Trails: 20 km

John Boyd Thatcher State Park
Voorheesville 12186
(518) 872-1237
Trails: 15 km

Minerva Hill Lodge
Minerva 12851
(518) 251-2710
Trails: 20 km

Moreau Lake State Park
Gansevoort 12831
(518) 793-0511
Trails: 15 km

Mountain Trails XC
Tannersville 12485
(518) 589-5361
Trails: 35 km

Oak Hill Farms
Esperance 12066
(518) 875-6700
Trails: 25 km

Rogers Rock Campground
Hague 12836
(518) 543-6161
Trails: 10 km

Saranac Lake/Lake Clear Area
Lake Clear 12945
(518) 891-2697
Trails: 18 km

Saratoga State Park
Saratoga 12866
(518) 587-3116
Trails: 25 km

Top of the World
Lake George 12845
(518) 587-3116
Trails: 25 km

Tree Haven Trails
Hagaman 12086
(518) 882-9455
Trails: 45 km

Warren County Trails
Warrensburg 12885
(518) 668-5032
Trails: 25 km

Whiteface Nordic Center
Lake Placid 12946
(518) 523-2551
Trails: 30 km

Williams Lake Resort
Rosendale 12472
(914) 658-3101
Trails: 20 km

Winter Clove Inn
Round Top 12473
(518) 622-3267
Trails: 15 km

Vermont

Amiski Ski Area
Moretown 05673
(802) 244-5677
Trails: 15 km

Blueberry Lake
East Warren 05674
(802) 496-6687
Trails: 23 km

Bolton Valley
Bolton 05477
(802) 434-2131
Trails: 20 km

Brattleboro Outing Club
Brattleboro 05301
(802) 254-4081
Trails: 25 km

Churchill House Inn
Brandon 05733
(802) 247-3300
Trails: 25 km

Edson Hill Manor
Stowe 05672
(802) 253-8954
Trails: 55 km

Fox Run XC Ski Center
Ludlow 05149
(802) 228-8871
Trails: 20 km

Grafton Ponds
Grafton 05146
(802) 843-2231
Trails: 30 km

Green Trails
Brookfield 05036
(802) 276-3412
Trails: 35 km

Heermansmith Farm Inn
Irasburg 05845
(802) 754-8866
Trails: 30 km

The Hermitage
Wilmington 05363
(802) 464-3511
Trails: 50 km

Highland Lodge
Greensboro 05841
(802) 533-2647
Trails: 64 km

Hildene Ski Touring
Manchester 05254
(802) 362-1788
Trails: 17 km

Jay Peak
Jay Peak 05858
(802) 988-2611
Trails: 20 km

Lake Morey Inn
Fairlee 05045
(802)333-4800
Trails: 12 km

Merck Forest
Rupert 05768
(802) 394-7836
Trails: 50 km

Mountain Meadows
Killington 05751
(802) 775-7077
Trails: 50 km

Nordic Inn
Landgrove 05148
(802) 824-6444
Trails: 26 km

Round Barn Farm
Waitsfield 05673
(802) 496-6111
Trails: 30 km

Sitzmark
Wilmington 05363
(802) 464-3384
Trails: 40 km

Smugglers' Notch
Jeffersonville 05464
(802) 644-8851
Trails: 23 km

Sterling Ridge Inn
Jeffersonville 05464
(802) 644-8265
Trails: 40 km

Stowe Mountain Resort
Stowe 05672
(802) 253-7311
Trails: 80 km

Stratton
Stratton Mt. 05155
(802) 297-2200
Trails: 20 km

Sugarbush Resort
Warren 05674
(802) 583-2605
Trails: 23 km

Sugarmill Farm
Barton 05822
(802) 525-3701
Trails: 14 km

Timber Creek XC
Wilmington 05363
(802) 464-0999
Trails: 16 km

Topnotch
Stowe 05672
(802) 253-8585
Trails: 25 km

Trail Head
Stockbridge 05772
(802) 746-8038
Trails: 60 km

West Mountain Inn
Arlington 05250
(802) 373-6516
Trails: 15 km

White House
Wilmington 05363
(802) 464-2135
Trails: 45 km

Wilderness Trails
Quechee 05059
(802) 295-7620
Trails: 18 km

**Green Mountain
National Forest**
No Telephone
Trails: Infinite

New Hampshire

AMC Pinkham Notch
Gorham 03581
(603) 466-2725
Trails: 40 km

Bear Notch
Bartlett 03812
(603) 374-2277
Trails: 60 km

Dartmouth Outing Club
Hanover 03755
(603) 646-2428
Trails: 25 km

Deer Cap
Ossipee 03814
(603) 539-6030
Trails: 20 km

Eastman
Grantham 03753
(603) 863-4500
Trails: 30 km

Franconia Notch State Park
Franconia 03580
No Telephone
Trails: 8 km

Inn at East Hill Farm
Troy 03465
(603) 242-6495
Trails: 22 km

King Pine
East Madison 03849
(800) FREE-SKI
Trails: 20 km

Nansen Ski Trail
Berlin 03570
(603) 752-1573
Trails: 32 km

Nestlenook Farm
Jackson 03846
(603) 383-0845
Trails: 4 km

Nordic Skier
Wolfeboro 03894
(603) 569-3151
Trails: 20 km

Rye Town Forest
Rye 03870
No Telephone
Trails: 5 km

Snowvillage Inn
Snowville 03849
(603) 447-2818
Trails: 10 km

Whittaker Woods
North Conway 03860
No Telephone
Trails: 15 km

Woodbound Inn
Jaffrey 03452
(603) 532-8341
Trails: 15 km

**White Mountain
National Forest**
No Telephone
Trails: Infinite

Maine

Acadia National Park
Bar Harbor 04609
(207) 288-3338
Trails: 110 km

Aroostook State Park
Presque Isle 04769
(207) 287-3821
Trails: 10 km

Baxter State Park
Millinocket 04462
(207) 723-5140
Trails: 72 km

Beech Ridge Farm X-C
Scarborough 04074
(207) 839-4098
Trails: 14 km

Bethel Inn Ski Center
Bethel 04217
(207) 824-2175
Trails: 40 km

Bowlin Camps
Patten 04765
(207) 528-2022
Trails: 32 km

Bradbury Mtn. State Park
Pownal 04069
(207) 688-4712
Trails: 5 km

Camden Hills State Park
Camden 04843
(207) 236-3109
Trails: 15 km

Christmas Tree Farm T.C.
Skowhegan 04976
(207) 474-2859
Trails: 18 km

Cobscook Bay State Park
Dennysvile 04628
(207) 726-4412
Trails: 10 km

Hermon Meadow Touring
Bangor 04401
(207) 848-3741
Trails: 6 km

Hilltop Homestead Ski Area
Seboeis 04448
(207) 723-3561
Trails: 15 km

Holbrook Island Sanctuary
Brookville 04617
(207) 326-4012
Trails: 7 km

Katahdin Camps
Millinocket 04462
(207) 723-4050
Trails: 40 km

Lake George State Park
Liberty 04949
(207) 589-4255
Trails: 15 km

Little Lyford Pond Camps
Greenville 04441
(207) 695-2821
Trails: 80 km

Little Lyford Pond Camps
Greenville 04441
(207) 695-2821
Trails: 80 km

Lonesome Pine Trails
Fort Kent 04743
(207) 834-5202
Trails: 10 km

Maine Audubon Society
Falmouth 04105
(207) 781-2330
Trails: 3.5 km

Maine Audubon Society
Freeport 04032
(207) 781-2330
Trails: 5 km

Moosehead Natl. Wildlife Ref.
Calais 04619
(207) 454-3521
Trails: 60 km

Moosehead Nordic
Greenville 04441
(207) 695-2870
Trails: 5 km

Mount Blue State Park
Weld 04285
(207) 585-2261
Trails: 22 km

Mount Chase Lodge
Greenville 04441
(207) 528-2183
Trails: 24 km

Natanis X-Country Trails
Augusta 04330
(207) 622-6533
Trails: 15 km

Nordic Lakers
Stockholm 04783
(207) 896-3067
Trails: 10 km

Orono Recreation Trails
Orono 04473
(207) 581-1081
Trails: 20 km

Rangeley Municipal Trails
Rangeley 04970
(207) 864-3326
Trails: 20 km

Saddleback
Rangeley 04970
(207) 864-5671
Trails: 40 km

Samoset Resort
Rockport 04856
(207) 594-2511
Trails: 10 km

Sebago Lake State Park
Naples 04055
(2070 693-6231
Trails: 8 km

Ski-a-Bit
West Buxton 04093
(207) 929-4824
Trails: 25 km

Spruce Mtn. X-C Center
Jay 04239
(207) 897-4090
Trails: 15 km

Tanglewood 4-H Camp XCTC
Linconville 04849
(2070 789-5868
Trails: 20 km

Telemark Inn
Bethel 04217
(207) 836-2703
Trails: 20 km

Titcomb Mountain
West Farmington 04992
(207) 778-9031
Trails: 25 km

Up Country Winter Sports
Fort Fairfield 04742
(207) 473-7265
Trails: 16 km

Vaughn Woods Historic Site
S. Berwick 03908
(207) 693-6231
Trails: 10 km

White Mountain
National Forest
No Telephone
Trails: Infinite

Massachusetts

Blue Hills Reservation
Milton   02186
(617) 698-1802
Trails: 50 km

Butternut Cross Country
Great Barrington 01230
(413) 528-0610
Trails: 8 km

Canterbury Farm
Becket 01223
(413) 623-8765
Trails: 14 km

Fox Hollow Resort
Lenox 01240
(413) 637-2000
Trails: 14 km

Kennedy Park
Lenox 01240
(413) 637-3010
Trails: 30 km

Lynn Woods
Lynn   01901
No telephone
Trail: 25 km

Maple Corner Farm
Granville 01034
(413) 357-8829
Trails: 15 km

Middlesex Fells
Stoneham
(617) 662-5230
Trails: 30 km

Mount Greylock
Lanesboro 01237
(413) 499-4262, 499-4263
Trails: 11 km

Notchview Reservation
Windsor 01270
(413) 684-0148
Trails: 15 km

Oak N' Spruce
South Lee 01260
(413) 243-3500
Trails: 10 km

Pittsfield State Forest
Pittsfield 01201
(413) 442-8992
Trails: 20 km

Pro-Motion Sports
Bedford 01730
(617) 275-1113
Trails: 20 km

Stow Acres XC
Stow 01775
(508) 568-9090
Trails: 10 km

Stump Sprouts
West Hawley 01339
(413) 339-4265
Trails: 18 km

Wachusett Mountain Ski Area
Princeton 01541
(508) 464-2788
Trails: 20 km

Connecticut

Cedar Brook Farms
West Suffield 06093
(203) 668-5026
Trails: 10 km

White Memorial Foundation
Litchfield 06759
(203) 567-0857
Trails: 21 km

Winding Trails Ski Touring
Farmington 06032
(203) 677-8458
Trails: 20 km

Index

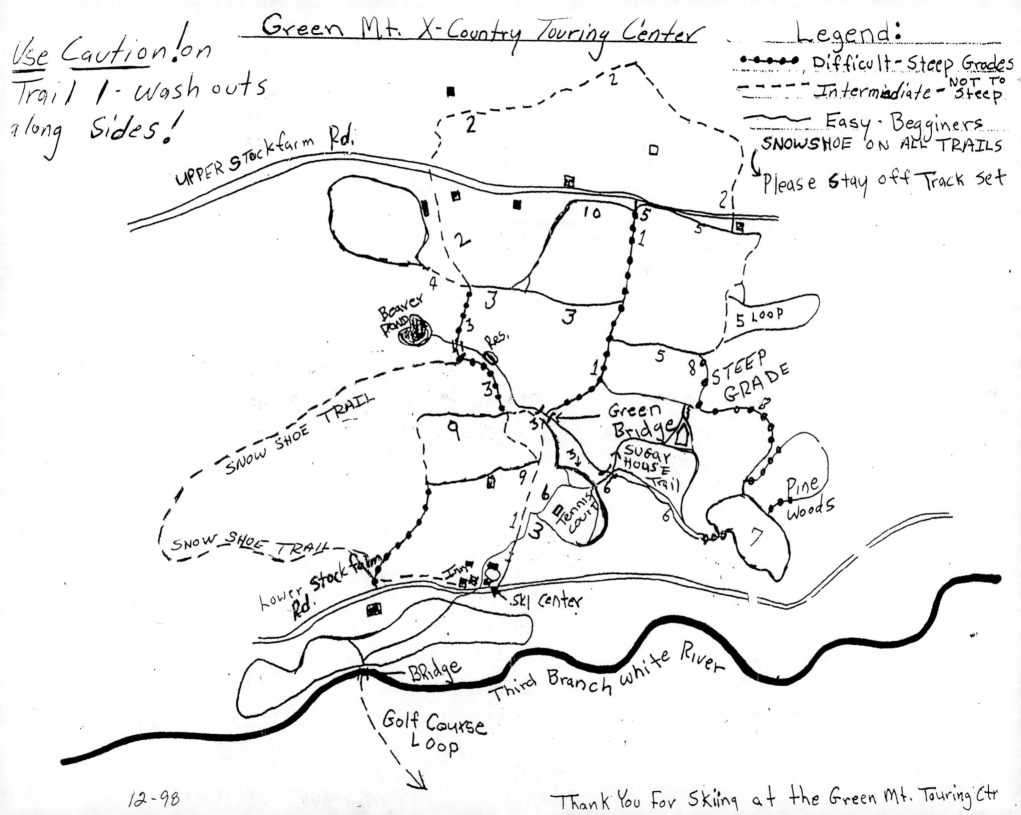

Tracks and Trails

An Insider's Guide to the Best
Cross Country Skiing in the Northeast

Tracks and Trails —*An Insider's Guide to the Best Cross Country Skiing in the Northeast* is available in book, recreational, and specialty stores. If you are unable to find this book and wish to purchase one or more copies, please contact the publisher:

Dawbert Press, Inc.
P.O. Box 2758
Duxbury, Mass 02331

Or if you prefer, you may order by telephone:

(800) 93-DAWBERT, (617) 934-7202, Fax (617) 934-7202

Dawbert Press Inc. specializes in travel and recreational books.

For more information or a catalogue describing the other titles published by Dawbert Press, please call or write to us at the aforementioned numbers.